CW01510101

Modernist and Avant-Garde Performance

Modernist and Avant-Garde Performance

An introduction

Claire Warden

EDINBURGH
University Press

© Claire Warden, 2015

Edinburgh University Press Ltd
The Tun – Holyrood Road, 12(2f)
Jackson's Entry
Edinburgh EH8 8PJ

www.euppublishing.com

Typeset in 11/13 Ehrhardt by
Servis Filmsetting Ltd, Stockport, Cheshire,
and printed and bound in Great Britain by
Printondemand-worldwide, Peterborough

A CIP record for this book is available from the British Library

ISBN 978 0 7486 8154 9 (hardback)
ISBN 978 0 7486 8156 3 (webready PDF)
ISBN 978 0 7486 8155 6 (paperback)
ISBN 978 0 7486 8157 0 (epub)

The right of Claire Warden to be identified as Author of this work has been asserted in accordance with the Copyright, Designs and Patents Act 1988, and the Copyright and Related Rights Regulations 2003 (SI No. 2498).

We thank the Scouloudi Foundation Grant for financial support for this book.

Contents

List of Figures	vi
Acknowledgements	vii
Manifesto for Modernist Performance	ix
Introduction: Modern/Modernism/Modernist, (the) Avant-garde and Performance	1
1. The Conventions of Modernist Performance	21
2. Performing Modernisms: Expressionism, Dada, Surrealism and Futurism	43
3. Politics and Performance	71
4. The Modernist Body	92
5. Total Theatre and Interdisciplinarity	116
Conclusion	139
Glossaries	149
Further Reading	152
Bibliography	154
Index	165

Figures

1   An image from W.B. Yeats's *Dreaming of the Bones*, 1916 © courtesy
    of the National Library of Ireland   30
2   Enrico Prampolini, set design for Filippo Tommaso Marinetti's play
    Cocktail, 1927 © Yale University Library, Beinecke Digital
    Collections   50
3   The backdrop for Vladimir Mayakovsky's *Vladimir Mayakovsky.
    A Tragedy*, 1913, painted in cubo-futurist style by Iosif Shkolnik
    and Pavel Filonov © Northwestern University   53
4   Poster by Oskar Kokoschka advertising the première of his play
    Murderer Hope of Womankind, 1907, image in the public domain   63
5   Zita Johann and Clark Gable in Sophie Treadwell's *Machinal*,
    1928 © courtesy Billy Rose Performing Arts Collection, New York
    Public Library   65
6   A photograph of masks from the end of *Power*, 1937 © New Deal
    Network   84
7   William Rousey and Oksana Petrova demonstrate biomechanics,
    Moscow © 2014 Performance Prompt   97
8   Martha Graham, *Lamentation*, 1935 (Oblique) © Library of
    Congress   101
9   Robot rebellion scene from Karel Čapek's *R.U.R. (Rossum's
    Universal Robots)*, 1928–29 © Billy Rose Theatre Division, The
    New York Public Library for the Performing Arts, Astor, Lenox
    and Tilden Foundations   106
10 Concrete poetry from Filippo Tommaso Marinetti, *Zang Tumb
    Tumb*, 1914 © 2013 Filippo Tommaso Marinetti / Artists Rights
    Society (ARS), New York / SIAE, Rome   122

Acknowledgements

Committing to make this book fit for purpose has been a wonderful collaborative effort and many, many friends, performers, scholars and students have contributed (knowingly or unknowingly) to its realisation. I acknowledge that although my name is on the cover, this book has many authors and is, in fact, to be authored afresh by all who pick it up.

Edinburgh University Press has been the most wonderful partner through the process. Thanks particularly to Jackie Jones, Dhara Patel, Rebecca Mackenzie, Jenny Daly and James Dale. I also appreciate the grant awarded by the Scouloudi Foundation in association with the Institute of Historical Research which enabled me to complete this book.

A debt of gratitude goes to Adrian Curtin who has been the most generous (and humorous) reader, and to all I have met at various conferences and events over the past three years who have been so positive and enthusiastic about the project.

I would like to extend my thanks to the School of Fine and Performing Arts at the University of Lincoln, particularly for generously granting me a term sabbatical. Special thanks go to various colleagues who have supported the project: Mark O'Thomas, Dominic Symonds, James Hudson, Jacqueline Bolton and Ann Gray. The students of LSFPA have made a significant contribution to this book, particularly all those who have tentatively made their way through the madness that is the Modern European Drama module, and the groups of students who performed *Uranium 235*, *The Adding Machine* and *R.U.R.* You made me realise that this material could connect with twenty-first-century performers ... and made me laugh a lot in the process! I reserve particular thanks for Tom Briggs, Andy Tinley, Phoebe Wall-Palmer, Jozey Wade, Sophie Bullivant, Casey Wells, Chris Greenhall and Chloe Doherty (and all involved in the *Modernist Trilogy* project) who read early drafts of the book or encouraged me to read the material in fresh ways. I also want to thank Darren Page and Martin Rousseau for technical support.

My thinking about this period and its aesthetics began during my time at the University of Edinburgh and the Institute for Advanced Studies in the Humanities. Olga Taxidou, Roger Savage and Robert Leach continue to influence my work in a range of ways and I thank them for the tremendous support they provided, particularly early in my career. I also thank Kevin Riordan whose insightful comments about a separate project influenced the writing of this book.

And finally thanks to my friends and family. As always David's support, intellectual challenge and willingness to drive me everywhere made this book possible. I reserve particular thanks for him.

Manifesto for Modernist Performance

We believe that the canon of modernist avant-garde performance contains some of the most **exciting, vibrant** and **stimulating** examples of interdisciplinary art. We challenge you to be **inspired** by the material you find here and to <u>create your own work</u> based on, responding to or rejecting the modernist avant-garde. As part of this project we want to encourage you to record your work as **YouTube** videos, informing Edinburgh University Press or the Author that you have done so. We hope to create a flexible, open-access body of work that visually and orally reacts to the modernist avant-garde.

Whether you are a designer, a musician, an actor, a director, a playwright, a performer, a dancer, a crafter, a scholar, an artist, a sculptor, a documentor, a poet, a filmmaker, a researcher, a technician, an audience member, a theatre company . . . you are invited to <u>get involved</u>.

This book is dedicated to all who, in seeking to create their own work (performances or scholarship), are inspired by the characters in this book. It's also dedicated to my grandparents whom I miss very much and who inspired me.

Introduction:
Modern / Modernism / Modernist,
(the) Avant-garde and Performance

MODERNISM: ART AND ITS CONTEXT

In this book we will explore a range of terms that have a number of different meanings or can be easily misunderstood. Two obvious examples are in the title – 'modernist' and 'avant-garde'. There are many misconceptions about these terms and in our contemporary media-led parlance they are often used in indistinct and inaccurate ways. 'Modernist' and 'avant-garde' have become increasingly difficult to pin down, denoting a multiplicity of meanings, influenced by geography, politics (governmental or identity), aesthetic techniques, language and critical reception. Such diversity of opinion does not, you might conclude, bode well for a book working with such troublesome terms!

However, as we begin our journey through 'modernism', 'the avant-garde' and 'performance' it may be a relief to know that, despite this plurality, these terms *do* refer to specific art created during a specific period. Turning to 'modernism' first: Peter Childs suggests that modernism can be regarded as either a 'time-bound or a genre-bound art form' (2000: 18), that is, as a way of designating a particular **period of history** or as a **way of describing artwork**. Often it becomes difficult to differentiate between these two interpretations: is a piece of art modernist because it was created during the early part of the twentieth century or is it modernist because it has particular stylistic attributes? As well as a method of historicising and describing art, artists can also be described as 'modernists': those writing, performing or creating during a certain period of time but also producing work with distinctive characteristics; 'modernism' is both a time and what is created in that time, context and the art coming out of that context.

It might initially appear odd to call a movement that began over a hundred years ago 'modern'. Forced to *look back* on the modern, we return to a particular historical period far outside our own experience. What one generation presumes is modern, the next generation regards as old hat: bell-bottom trousers, synth-based rock music and pre-CGI visual effects are three arbitrarily chosen cases in point. The 'modern', like time itself, is constantly on the move.

'Modernist' is, then, **inherently suggestive of change**, whether subtle, gradual alteration or dramatic, overnight transformation. The 'modern' stands in opposition to the 'past' or 'tradition' and pre-empts the 'future'. It refers to an ever-shifting cusp. Modernist artists seemed, therefore, to be consciously creating new styles and new methods, challenging established conventions. However, practitioners spanned a broad spectrum of approaches, from those who wanted to destroy all previous artistic methods to those whose work did not differ considerably from the art that had gone before. Many took a more balanced approach, rejecting much historical artwork as dull, artisti-cally unsuccessful, facile entertainment, while praising particular traditions as innovative or inspirational. To be modernist, therefore, artists had to address this tricky question of genealogy and constantly define themselves by what had previously been and what was about to arrive.

Clearly a term like 'modernism' suggests its etymologically related cousins: 'modernity' (the conditions of society, with the implications of technologi-cal advancement, secularisation and industrialisation) and 'modernisation' (the process of moving towards modernity). Recognising these definitions, 'modernist' describes an artistic work produced with the **characteristics of modernity as its backdrop**. This means that the rise of modernism is often associated with influential figures and movements of nineteenth- and twentieth-century history – Sigmund Freud, Charles Darwin, the suffragettes, Charles Baudelaire, Friedrich Nietzsche, Albert Einstein, the Chartists, the leaders of the Harlem Renaissance, Henri Bergson, Marie Curie, Karl Marx and many others. Broadly speaking, these figures and groups made people from all walks of life think differently about important issues, such as human identity, social structures and the organisation of the universe. Some promoted equality, some claimed science as the definitive method of understanding the world and others focused on changing forms of artistic expression.

The twentieth century was also dominated by important defining events and changes: the technological terrors of the two world wars (new explosives, gas, aeroplanes), the mechanisation of the workplace, the worldwide economic depressions of 1929, the rise of dictatorships in Europe, the more strident demands of minority voices (racial, class and gender-based) and a growing global perspective. The forces of modernity engendered and defined each; for example, war had always been part of human experience but was now domi-nated by machines, technology and science, rather than swords and cavalry. This meant that war spilled over the boundaries of the battlefield and directly impacted civilian populations across the world. However, focusing on events like this can give a false impression of an epoch; as Ástráður Eysteinsson suggests, most of us do not experience life in such a dramatically fragmented way, lurching from disaster to disaster. Rather our lives remain a constant flow of events and circumstances, some big, some small. Therefore he contends, it might be better to see modernist art as **interrupting modernity** rather than directly reflecting the structures of world history or the way we, as human beings, interpret them (Eysteinsson and Liska 2007: 6). That is, modernist art punctuated the unceasing flow of the everyday, providing remarkable, shocking, disconcerting and groundbreaking moments. Certainly, as we will see, much modernist art disrupts the way we see the world. Either way the connection between modernism and modernity remains central to our investigations.

The ways the art of the period engaged with this changing, tumultuous world differed considerably. Some decided to follow a route that maintained the autonomy of the artwork, thereby preventing it from being subsumed by profit-led capitalism. But this approach potentially disconnected art from the everyday experience of its recipients. Some, therefore, used their art to fully engage with the complex modern world, creating work that often directly and unequivocally challenged hegemonic systems, that is, those dominant structures in society.

The question of whether art should be **autonomous or engaged** has preoccupied many thinkers and makers across the cultural landscape and throughout the centuries. The Marxist Frankfurt School philosopher Theodor Adorno and the German playwright Bertolt Brecht held different views on this issue and their subsequent conversations help us to understand the intricacies of the problem. Adorno was convinced of the importance of creating wholly independent art, work that refused to directly discuss world issues such as power hierarchies or complex systems of hegemony and oppression. Only then, thought Adorno, could art totally reject the domination of the dictatorial ruling systems that sprang up throughout Europe during this period. He advocated 'autonomous rather than committed art' (Jameson 2007: 193), as political works of art, in his view, always rely on falsities, assumptions, caricaturing and a reduction of ideas into simple concepts. Brecht, by contrast, wanted to produce 'daring, unusual things for the proletariat . . . [that] deal with its real situation' (Jameson 2007: 84). His plays reflect his lifelong intention to address inequality, class division and economic unfairness. Examining these contrasting opinions, we are inevitably drawn to ask questions:

- Can art directly address modernity?
- Should art engage with modernity?
- Are there modern events/circumstances/incidents that should not be artistically engaged?

- Are there issues that are impossible to address in art?
- How can art escape from hegemonic capitalist-based systems?

Such questions will recur throughout our investigation of these performances and (be warned), by the end, definitive answers may still be elusive.

AVANT-GARDE: LEADING THE WAY

The term 'avant-garde' has different origins. Until the nineteenth century it was used in war to describe those soldiers who went first into battle. But French socialist Henri Saint-Simon used the term in a broader way. In 1803 he clearly detailed the progression of society:

> You, the scientists and artists, and those of you also who devote something of your energies and means to promoting enlightenment, are the section of humanity who possess the greatest intellectual force, and are best fitted to grasp a new idea. You are the most directly interested in the success of the subscription; it is for you to overcome the forces of inertia. Let the mathematicians, who are in the vanguard, begin!
>
> (Saint-Simon 1952: 2)

For Saint-Simon, intellectuals (both scientists and artists) represented a vanguard or 'avant-garde', leading society towards new ways of understanding the world. Originally a French term, by the early years of the twentieth century it described the art scenes in various countries. The *Oxford English Dictionary* suggests that it was first used in this artistic sense in English in 1910. The timely arrival of 'avant-garde' into the English lexicon does not seem arbitrary: this was the year of Bloomsbury Group member and art critic Roger Fry's influential exhibition *Manet and the Post-Impressionists*. The British public, only just coming to terms with the innovations of the Impressionists, were by and large perplexed by the effervescent, synthetic colours of Vincent Van Gogh and Paul Gauguin. With tongue-in-cheek humour, 1910 was also the year that fellow Bloomsbury Group member and novelist Virginia Woolf suggested that 'human character changed' (Scott 1990: 635).

In one of the most influential studies of the avant-garde, Renato Poggioli suggests that it is defined by '**antagonism**' (1968: 26), be that artistic antagonism (challenging the institutions of art, the way artworks are created or – in the case of Fry's exhibition – established techniques) or political antagonism (adopting a strong feminist position or advocating class warfare). Often it proves impossible to separate these two types of antagonism. This antagonism is active, looking beyond the artwork, hoping to engender some form of actual material change. As Boris Groys has it, one can 'define . . . [the avant-garde's] basic spirit in terms of the demand that art move from representing to transforming the world' (1992: 14).

'Avant-garde' also suggests the notion of leading, to use the military analogy, those who **march forward** while the rest follow. In war, of course, this means almost inevitable death but in the art world it can connote a sense of elitism. Certainly in Saint-Simon's proclamation above, there remains the strong impression of a section of more intelligent, creatively gifted and/or educated people who will inevitably lead the mass of humanity. In another important analysis of avant-gardism, *Five Faces of Modernity*, Matei Calinescu identifies the elite but concludes that this elite is actually committed to the eventual destruction of all elites (1987: 143). This seems like a worthwhile, democratising venture and one can discern a number of moments when artists did indeed attempt to destroy any sense of elitism.

MODERNISM AND THE AVANT-GARDE: NEW WAYS OF UNDERSTANDING THE TERMS

The terms 'modernism' and 'avant-garde' became more complicated in the later decades of the twentieth century when a number of critics tried to reassess them. The Marxist thinker Raymond Williams, for example, defines the terms like this:

> It is not easy to make simple distinctions between 'modernism' and the 'avant-garde', especially as many uses of these labels are retrospective. But it can be taken as a working hypothesis that Modernism can be said to begin with the second type of group – the alternative, radically innovating experimental artists and writers – while the avant-garde begins with groups of the third, fully oppositional type.
>
> (1989: 51)

For Williams, the modernists exhibited radicalism but the avant-gardists pushed this further, creating distinctly oppositional works, art that demolished aesthetic ideas and societal structures. One of the most important thinkers in avant-garde studies, Peter Bürger, made a similar distinction (although far more dismissive of the modernist project), comparing the passive stance of modernism to the more aggressive approach of the avant-garde (1984). This way of thinking has been developed in more recent studies. Jane Goldman, for example, suggests that modernism has been irredeemably tainted by the Holocaust which marked an end to the modernist project of enlightenment and rational thinking. She proclaims 'it is time to return to the term "avant-garde" as a way of overcoming "modernism's" semantic problems' (2004: 247).

What unites these diverse commentators is their differentiation between 'modernist' and 'avant-garde'. However, further reassessments of these terms obfuscate the boundaries between them. Marjorie Perloff recognises this implosion of terminology in contemporary reappraisals:

> It may be countered, of course, that I am blurring the well-known distinctions between the terms *modernist* and *avant-garde*. But if the past decade has taught us anything, it is that the opposition between the 'established', 'conservative' modernist artist and the 'radical' avant-gardist no longer has much meaning.
>
> (Bradshaw and Dettmar 2006: 577)

Perloff's analysis gives both a useful assessment of current readings of modernism and the avant-garde, and full licence to continue to question them as new scholars publish their research. Some scholars disregard any sense of antagonism between these terms, instead bringing them together to create a new term – the **'modernist avant-garde'** – which seems to combine both the important delineation of historical period and a sense of experimental aesthetics (time and ethos). In the current volume, I most regularly use 'modernist avant-garde' in order to signify period and aesthetics, although this should not gloss over tangible differences between practitioners and movements.

Further complicating matters, both terms have also been updated by their articulation in the plural, as in 'avant-gardes' and 'modernisms'. This plurality suggests that constructing a single, overarching definition is impossible – there are simply too many different experiments that can be read as modernist or avant-gardist. Indeed, using these well-worn monikers can actually lead to more confusion than clarification, and most certainly suggests a unity between artworks that seem to be almost oppositional in approach. Using them in the plural at least enables us to maintain a strong sense of diversity.

Another layer of complexity results from the recurrence of 'modernism' and 'avant-garde' in a variety of different artistic and scholarly fields. These complex terms are not specific to performance studies but have been used to describe a range of artistic genres from film to painting, literature to architecture. This makes the modernist avant-garde particularly interesting to study as this work is intrinsically **interdisciplinary**, that is, it brings the characteristics of different artistic disciplines together to create new work. This means that it is difficult to talk simply of 'drama' or 'theatre': hence the use of the broader term 'performance' in this book. This is not to reject the former terms entirely, of course. While contemporary performance studies often abandons terms such as 'drama' and 'theatre', this is not my intention here. 'Performance' simply enables us to embrace the interdisciplinary nature of this artwork and frees us from automatically thinking about playtexts, rehearsals or cast lists. This interdisciplinary feel was reflected in the behaviour of some of the most prominent modernist artists. Often performance practitioners accomplished highly original creative work in other disciplines; for example, a playwright might also have been a painter (Oskar Kokoschka or Wyndham Lewis); or a set designer, an artist (Lyubov Popova or John Piper); or a poet, a playwright (Gertrude Stein or Vladimir Mayakovsky). It also means that we can look to other artistic genres to help us in our discoveries of performance. Visual art gives a particularly useful, accessible way of understanding the movements and ideas we will be dealing with; nothing illustrates (or 'performs') the basic tenets of surrealism better than a picture by René Magritte and examining models of Vladimir Tatlin's Tower provides a helpful image of constructivism in Russia.

In fact discussions of modernism and the avant-garde often ignore performance altogether. As James Harding and John Rouse suggest, other artistic genres have been read through the lens of the avant-garde far more than performance. They claim an **'antiperformative bias'** (2006: 1), a contention confirmed by Mike Sell in *Avant-Garde Performance and Material Exchange* (2011: 6). Yet theatrical performance gives one of the most insightful and imaginative renderings of the modernist avant-garde because of the unique relationship between actor and audience. Much of the performance we will be thinking about was composed with reference to specific historical moments (a war, the rise of fascism, levels of unemployment) and some scripts were even altered overnight in response to changing circumstances. The immediacy and accessibility of performance meant it could reflect (and maybe even seek to change) real circumstances. In fact the very act of performance, as Sell suggests, is inextricably connected with the avant-garde, as *'to be avant-garde is to perform'* (2011: 6); the process of creating innovative, challenging work requires a spirit of performance – of bringing something into existence and presenting it before an audience.

'Modernism' and the 'avant-garde' have often been embroiled in fierce arguments, not least in debates about **high and low culture**. Low culture, as it is often described, can be read in two opposing ways: as simple (potentially mindless) entertainment for the masses or as a democratisation of art. High art, by contrast, supposedly defends artistic standards, rejecting the commodification of the culture and reasserting a cultural hierarchy of elitism. It is here that the differentiation between modernism and the avant-garde has been most acute. As you might have gathered from Raymond Williams's comments above, modernism has often been associated with high artistic values (so-called 'high modernism'), while the avant-garde cavorted with the techniques of low art. Actually this proves a problematic claim, with many examples that seem to contend with it, most noticeably the prevalence of the modern, popular variety theatre mode which appears in the plays of quintessential Anglo-American modernists T.S. Eliot, W.H. Auden and Christopher Isherwood, on the one hand, and in the experiments of futurist leader F.T. Marinetti and the work of the constructivist Vsevolod Meyerhold on the other. Suffice to say, in the modernist avant-garde we can often identify 'high' and 'low' techniques, images and ideas; more often than not they either amicably coexist or else jostle for pre-eminence in a single artwork.

Furthermore, and whether justified or not, modernist avant-garde art is often accused of being obscure. While critics like Daniel Tiffany (2009) critique this notion of **obscurity** as having a potentially democratising effect (if no one can understand it that makes the undergraduate and the professor equal!), it can sometimes feel as if the artistic elite merely maintained its own position by making its work utterly impenetrable to anyone outside of a very small circle of like-minded enthusiasts. Indeed, in *The Metaphysical Poets* (1921) American-British poet T.S. Eliot contended that, given the complexity of the modern world, 'poets in our civilization, as it exists at present, must be *difficult*' (Greenblatt and Abrams 2006: 2330). In reality, for all their difficulty or obscurity, these artworks are also punctuated by jokes, participatory roles for the audience and exciting images. In addition, often the key is not to discover what an artwork *means* but what it is *doing*. It is virtually impossible, for example, to say what dadaist Hugo Ball's performative sound poem *Karawane* (1916) means. It does not *mean* anything. But it does *do* something: it makes the audience question the solidity of language, draws spectators into a powerful shamanistic incantation and challenges ideas of logic, coherence and dialogue. While reading this book I would strongly suggest that you (on occasions) switch off that ever-present need to make sense of everything and simply feel, experience or viscerally respond to the artwork. We must certainly resist the temptation to immediately reject artworks simply because they do not appear straightforward.

If these are fairly vague definitions of the terms most central to this book, then they are intentionally vague (or perhaps 'open-ended' is a better word), for I am following the pattern of the most recent modernist scholarship. The aim of this book is not to solve the problems of terminology. In fact we are going to consciously resist the easy demarcation of artworks, preferring instead to focus very specifically on particular examples, whether playtexts, movements, performances or the proclamations of artists. Theatre history might initially appear to be a fairly stable body of knowledge, particularly when we compare it to the study of contemporary performance practice which can be difficult to analyse objectively, given that we are in the midst of it. Actually 'new modernist studies', as it is termed, is less about discovering a definitive way of understanding this art or applying overarching banners of meaning than it is about simply opening up the material and approaching it afresh. Douglas Mao and Rebecca L. Walkowitz suggest that new modernist studies is defined by '**expansion**': challenging delineations of time periods, the inclusion (or not) of particular figures or movements and established geographical specificity (Mao and Walkowitz 2008: 727). New modernist studies brings a new set of problems; at times it becomes almost impossible to define modernism at all. However, in order to bring some focus without negating the welcome expansion of the field, we will turn to scholar Susan Stanford Friedman who will help us on our way through our studies of modernist performance:

> I despair – especially for the new scholar just entering the field of dreams, a Tower of Babel with too many levels to climb; but also for the older scholar, trained in old modernist studies: vertigo out on a limb, whirled up into a vortex of the new. Yet I also rejoice. Change is what drew me to modernism in the beginning. Why should it ossify? Why should the fluid freeze over, the undecidable become decided?
>
> (2010: 473)

DATING THE MODERNIST AVANT-GARDE

For all Stanford Friedman's liberating view of new modernist studies, beginning with a defined focus is a useful start, particularly when approaching this material for the first time, even if it means that we actively challenge our definitions or delineations along the way. Chronology remains the first way we can ground our studies in something more concrete. As we have seen, 'modernist' can be used to describe both time period and artistic characteristics, while 'avant-garde' has been prefixed with either 'historical' or, indeed, 'modernist' to differentiate it from 'avant-garde' as an ethos or a non-period-specific approach. Yet it proves very difficult to provide definite dates for the beginning and end of the modernist avant-garde, as it is for any artistic movement. It did not appear overnight, nor did it disappear as the bells of New Year's Eve chimed. Many commentators attempt to construct chronological boundaries while often being aware of the dangers of such delineation. Modernism is, in general, perceived as having a longer lifespan than the historical avant-garde, with the latter sometimes being restricted to a relatively short time period ending with the rise of political dictatorship, first in Russia (Stalin began to take overall control in 1922), and then in Germany, Italy and Spain as the 1930s progressed.

In order to bring some clarity here we can say that we are looking at the period from approximately **1890 to 1945**, although it is vital to recognise the arbitrariness of these bookends. We go back to 1890 because the art of the late nineteenth century provided something for the twentieth-century practitioners to both build on and reject. Even more importantly, nineteenth-century changes in society (the creation of industrialised urbanism, scientific advancement and the forces of capitalism) continued into the twentieth century, affecting theatrical performance. Furthermore, as we will see, many of the practitioners of the late nineteenth century could be regarded as modernist, particularly those associated with naturalism and symbolism, two movements that provide the focus for Chapter 1. The year 1945 has been chosen simply because it marks the end of the Second World War, although we might just as easily have stopped in the early 1930s, when the rise of dictatorships meant that avant-garde innovations were frowned upon or even prohibited, or carry on until the mid 1950s when a number of playwrights challenged our notions of reason, comprehension and artistic value. As we progress through these performances, it must be remembered that many artists suffered under repressive governments – their work was rejected, they suffered imprisonment or displacement, and some, like Meyerhold, were even killed. 1945 was also the year when the atrocities of the Holocaust were exposed. How such a horrific event could be understood through art or whether, as Adorno maintained, this event forces us to dramatically reassess the nature of art remain extremely difficult issues to address. Often unjustly accused of silencing post-Holocaust artistic expression, Adorno actually simply rejected established methods of creating art, suggesting that 'these victims are used to create something, works of art, that are thrown to the consumption of the world which destroyed them' (Jameson 2007: 189). For many, the Holocaust marked the end of a modernist movement that had prided itself on scientific thought, as the systematic gassing of millions was actually based on rational study (eugenics) not irrational lunacy, however mad this rationality might seem.

While 'modernist' and 'avant-garde' can be understood as specifically connected to particular historical periods, the terms '**postmodernist**' and '**neo-avant-garde**' appear to break through chronological borders. But these terms prove as conflicted as their precursors. 'Postmodernism', of course, suggests a period and/or aesthetics that appeared after modernism. Though often overlooked, the relationship between the two, fraught and complex as it is, is vital to a thorough understanding of postmodernism, with Peter Brooker asserting that 'whether the set of contrasts means postmodernism disposes of or radicalises modernism is uncertain' (1992: 4). If modernism proves to be difficult to define, then postmodernism is even more so. To further complicate matters, the architect Charles Jencks coined the phrase 'late modernism' and, in so doing, drew attention to a troubling issue: what happened between modernism and postmodernism? How might we discern the transition? According to Jencks, late modernism 'took the theories and styles of their precursors to an extreme and in so doing produced an elaborated or mannered Modernism' (1980: 11). But this idea is not confined to buildings. Tyrus Miller, for example, notes that certain poets and prose writers could also be described as 'late modernist' as they focused on 'the survival of individual selves in a world of technological culture, mass politics and shock experience' (1999: 24). From the turn of the last century, another movement arose called 'remodernism', an attempt to return to the ideas and innovations of modernism in what was regarded (and forgive my sophomoric grandiloquence) as essentially a post-postmodern period. If read through all these definitions and redefinitions it becomes clear that not only is modernism difficult to pin down, it also has a tremendous relevance to the contemporary world.

The neo-avant-garde proves equally contentious. Peter Bürger rejected any notion of a neo-avant-garde by suggesting that the artwork of the 1960s and onwards was simply a pale imitation of the vibrancy of the historical avant-garde. His work has been rigorously questioned in recent years; Martin Puchner, for example, seeks to promote and study work dismissed by Bürger as 'anachronistic and empty repetitions without historical necessity of force' (Puchner 2005: 5). Postmodernism and neo-avant-gardism are not the focus of this book but they do represent an ongoing ethos that continues right up to twenty-first-century performances. That is not to say that more modern practitioners merely repeat the experiments of the early twentieth century. Indeed, Philip Auslander concludes that the models that appeared during the 1920s and 30s are not sufficient for more recent experimentation and that the 'project of political art must be reconceptualized in postmodern terms' (1997: 7). This is the difficult process of reimagining the objectives and characteristics of antagonistic art. Focusing on economics, Günter Berghaus suggests the term 'corporate Modernism' to refer to the way the 1950s responded to modernism, imagining it solely in monetary terms rather than artistic, dragging the uniquely marginal and antagonistic avant-garde into the mainstream capitalist systems of profit and commodities (2005a: 237). However, on a more positive note, he also suggests that avant-garde movements were not simply products of their time but 'were transferable to other times and cultures', giving us licence to reimagine them today (2005a: 238). So while recent work can be seen as part of a genealogy, it is by no means straightforward and the characteristics of the avant-garde ethos differ from period to period. This brief overview also enables us to ask a more troublesome question, one we will come back to in the Conclusion: in today's consumer-driven world, is there space and potential for an avant-garde?

All this is to say that, with its arbitrary borders, periodisation can be extremely difficult. In *The Cambridge Introduction to Theatre Historiography*, Thomas Postlewait gamely attempts to break through the errors and presumptions of historical scholarship. On the one hand, says Postlewait, 'each artistic work is in dialogue with the heritage', that is, all those conventions, techniques and artistic models that have gone before (2009: 14). Simultaneously, we occupy a privileged yet dangerous position: we know what happened next:

> Because of our belatedness, we subsequently fix it so that it becomes part of a developmental history – part of a plotted narrative. We turn it into something more than – if not other than – it was at the moment of occurrence, still open to the future.
>
> (Postlewait 2009: 20)

We only create chronologies after (often long after) the events. It is easy to forget, therefore, that history (theatrical or otherwise) does not stop and cannot be easily demarcated. The sheer number of different methods of dating the modernist avant-garde reveal the intrinsic problem of asserting a start and finish point. Yet our dates of 1890–1945 at least provide an initial focus, even if we find ourselves challenging them as we progress.

THE MODERNIST AVANT-GARDE AND GEOGRAPHY

As part of the new modernist studies debates, the relationship between modernism and geography has become increasingly fraught. Mao and Walkowitz refer to it as 'the diversification of modernism's places' (2008: 739). As part of this there has been an important turn from a focus on those quintessential centres of the modernist avant-garde (Paris, Berlin, London) towards the multiple peripheral avant-gardes that existed throughout the world. A range of other cities have been claimed as centres of avant-garde experiment: Zurich (dada), Milan and Turin (futurism), Moscow (futurism and constructivism) and New York which became a centre as the century progressed and artists moved from war-torn, dictator-dominated Europe to the US. Even as we place Europe and North America together in a problematically constructed 'West' we need to recognise the profound difference in experience within those areas 'Europe' and 'America', and between them. In his book *American Avant-Garde Theatre*, Arnold Aronson even suggests that, as a result of the proliferation of the American mythos and grand narratives of nationhood, it remains virtually impossible to use the term 'avant-garde' in an American context until much later: 'the rejection of narrative is essential for the development of an avant-garde' (2000: 13). Perhaps this is the reason that the avant-garde in America really came into its own in the post-Second World War period with the Happenings movement, the Living Theatre and the Wooster Group, among others.

However, James Harding and John Rouse challenge even this expanded collection of centre points. Actually, they insist, avant-garde performance was a far more global phenomenon 'whose territorial coordinates were always already heterogenous, dispersed, and diversely located in moments of contestation' (Harding and Rouse 2006: 27). What Harding and Rouse are *not* searching for is simply a collection of new geographical centres. Rather they dispel the idea of a centre entirely in favour of multiple peripheries – in their terms, a 'plurality of edges' (2006: 24).

Recent scholarship provides a significant attempt to understand the modernist avant-garde as a worldwide collection of experiments; in Andreas Huyssens's terms, this has led to a 'de-Westernization of modernism/modernity' (Eysteinsson and Liska 2007: 59). Older scholarship tended to overlook the innovations on continents other than Europe and America (by this scholars have generally meant western Europe and North America), not least because modernism is inextricably connected with the urban, industrial and technological. Applying this term across the world, therefore, becomes potentially problematic and, for the sake of clarity and brevity, in this book I rarely move outside Europe and the US. But, acknowledging my limited focus, it is vitally important to rediscover experiments on other continents to read alongside the North American and European scenes. A collection of new terms has arisen that enables the scholar to expand their geographical understanding of modernism. 'Transnational modernism' connotes the idea that artistic innovation was transmitted across typical national borders. More expansively, 'global modernism' suggests that art styles entirely transcended any sense of national differentiation. There are even 'planetary modernisms' that 'supplant concepts of modernist internationalism, which are typically based on binaries of Self-Other, modern-traditional, civilized-savage, high art-primitive art' (Stanford Friedman 2010: 483). All these terms are not without their problems, of course. Some who accept transnational modernism may be far more reticent about the idea of planetary modernisms. Some, like Huyssens, suggest that this sort of geographically expansive approach forces a reassessment of high and low culture (for what do these terms even mean in somewhere like India, for example) and the relationships between geographically specific modernisms across the globe (Brooker and Thacker 2005: 14–16). He even introduces another new phrase for us: 'alternative modernisms' (Brooker and Thacker 2005: 7). Creating new ways of understanding the relationship between modernism and geography simultaneously challenges the 1890–1945 genealogy I tentatively posited above. For different cultures and spaces have experienced (and continue to experience) modernity in different ways and at different times. This leads to what Stanford Friedman describes as '*plural* periods of modernisms, some of which overlap with each other and others of which have a different time period altogether'

(2006: 432). Spatial and temporal ways of understanding modernism are intricately intertwined.

THE CREATORS OF PERFORMANCE

As we shall see as we progress through this book, a range of diverse people created the performances of the modernist avant-garde: some were rich, some were poor; some were educated, some were not; some urbanites, some born in the countryside. They traced their histories through different classes and political backgrounds. Some formed small groups of like-minded individuals, others blazed their own trails. Some created movements, writing agitational manifestos that vehemently presented their ideas. In order to make sense of these groupings and collaborations, contemporary critics create complex networks of artists, from Mike Sell's concept of 'vectors of the radical' which 'moves and interacts with the people and places it encounters' (2011: 1) to Bonnie Kime Scott's map entitled 'A Tangled Mesh of Modernists' which graphically illustrates the connections between individuals (1990: 10). What these theoretical models illustrate is that, while artists certainly worked on projects and created movements together, relationships were far from straightforward with plenty of disagreements and splits along the way.

When looking at modernist avant-garde performance it can become easy to think that it was led and dominated by white, educated men. Ruth Hemus suggests that in the case of dada (and, I contend, across the modernist avant-garde), women artists have been overlooked in favour of their more well-documented lovers and husbands (2009: 3). However, recent scholarship, including Hemus's, casts doubt on the accepted patriarchal metanarratives and redeems a whole range of women who contributed to modernist art. Penny Farfan's 'kaleidoscopic . . . multi-faceted image' of modernist women's performance, for example, helps us to identify a range of performing women, diverse in their approaches and aesthetics, yet committed to producing challenging art (2004: 119). In a performance context, this includes figures such as Djuna Barnes, Gertrude Stein, Isadora Duncan, Elizabeth Robins and Ellen Terry.

Other critics have focused on modernism as a worldwide phenomenon: Urmila Seshagiri, for example, looks at how companies such as Sergei Diaghilev's Ballets Russes used non-Western forms as catalysts for performance, while Harding and Rouse examine lesser known innovations in places as varied as Japan, Mexico, the Middle East, Africa, Argentina and India. All this is to say that modernist performance was far more inclusive and multi-authored than might initially be imagined and, as the new commitment to transnational/global and gendered modernisms takes hold, many more examples of innovative performance methods may well come to light.

THE CHARACTERISTICS OF PERFORMANCE

So far we have focused less on performance and more on terminology and context. Now that we have an understanding (albeit fragmented) of the concepts and the period, we can turn to our primary focus. Given our rather fluid definitions up to this point, it is unsurprising that the performances were, often, not at all similar either in intention or aesthetics. It is very important to remember this and not to regard them all as belonging to one prescribed movement. However, in order to provide a way of understanding these diverse performances, there are a number of characteristics that could be seen in all of them in different ways.

In all there existed a commitment to **experimenting**, as Poggioli suggests, 'technically and formally' (1968: 131). This might have been extremely obvious, leading to performances that did not resemble any conventional view of theatre at all. Or this spirit of experimentation might simply have existed in the performing space or the inclusion of poetic dialogue or the questioning of typical narrative linearity. Sometimes this experimentation meant looking backwards and reworking techniques from *commedia dell'arte* or pantomime. Sometimes it led to engagement with popular culture such as comics or jazz. And sometimes practitioners looked forward to a world of futuristic machines and robotics. Over all, there hovers the sense that traditional, established ways of creating performance must be questioned, reworked or, even, destroyed altogether. If read as a series of experiments, genealogy becomes even more problematic, movements and ideas often appearing and disappearing with enormous speed. As Kirsten Shepherd-Barr suggests, 'the history of modernism on stage is a history of sudden arrivals and radical departures; of catastrophism rather than Darwinian gradualism' (Brooker et al. 2010: 132). This spirit of experimentation meant a constant searching for the new, an ongoing reworking of artistic ideas and a perpetual passing of the baton between groups, individuals and movements.

Modernist avant-garde art also created new diverse **worlds**, the imaginative liveness of performance lending itself to the production of multiple spaces with which the audience could interact. The agitprop experiments of the left-wing political groups, for example, presented utopian images of an emancipated future, free from class inequality, poverty and the constant drudge of mundane work. Yet there were an equal number of dystopic apparitions, such as the horrific, isolating worlds of the German expressionists, reeling from four years of total war. At times performances felt almost apocalyptic. Given that modernist avant-garde art was often defined as much by decreation as creation (Childs 2000: 1–2), as much by cutting, fragmenting and collapsing as designing or constructing, performances often seemed to be destroying rather than producing new worlds. Berghaus adroitly suggests that avant-garde art functioned like a 'bomb or a cleanser' (2005a: 38); either demolishing or totally purging artistic form and societal structures.

It would also be accurate to claim that **resistance** defined all modernist avant-garde performance. This might have been political resistance, fighting against shadowy hegemonies or particular movements and circumstances. Often there existed an anti-bourgeois feeling. Following Marxist proclamations, 'bourgeois' signifies the middle class, whereas 'proletariat' refers to the urban working class. However, the resistance centred not on the class *per se*, but rather on what that class distinction signified. 'Bourgeois' in this sense was not simply an economically identifying label but, rather, a derogatory term suggesting a lack of real cultural awareness or vibrancy. Challenging bourgeois values (economic gain and political power rather than art or creativity) united many contrasting avant-garde movements. Mike Sell provides a useful reading of the avant-garde's ability to resist hegemonic thought when he says that the 'avant-garde *challenges power* and that such a challenge is as varied as power itself' (2011: 4).

But it might just as easily have been aesthetic resistance, fighting against all that had come before. Again, these two types of resistance often appeared in the same place, form mirroring the content and vice versa. Repeatedly, as Berghaus suggests, these performers questioned 'grand narratives', generalised ways of making sense of the world, many of which had been established for many years: the uniqueness of the human, the sense of progress, the order of nature or appropriate societal roles (Berghaus 2005a: 32). This can, of course, be overstated, as many of these grand narratives continue to exist or else new generalised ways of describing experience have arisen. But it would certainly be true to suggest that with scientific learning coupled with the horrors of urban poverty and total war, the way society viewed the world certainly changed. The performances here reflected some of these changes and, indeed, in some cases actually directly impacted on them, affecting political decisions or the everyday lived experience of its audience.

HOW CAN WE UNDERSTAND THE MODERNIST AVANT-GARDE TODAY?

There are various ways we might seek to engage with the modernist avant-garde in our own scholarship and practice. In learning more about historical performance, what are we seeking to achieve and how can we respond to our studies in new and exciting ways? The following remain at the forefront of my, and hopefully your, intentions as we approach theatre history, and particularly the modernist avant-garde:

- Providing a sense of historical context – the researcher discovers a fascinating artistic rendering of the late nineteenth and early twentieth centuries. As a period defined by wars, class conflict, a questioning of spirituality, industrial expansion (and subsequent economic depression), the advent of modern feminism and the breakdown of empires, it is particularly noteworthy, providing a foundational epoch for contemporary society.
- Unearthing new/old performances – whereas the researcher often travels over the well-trodden path of theatre history (ancient Greeks, medieval Mystery Plays, Shakespeare and contemporaries, Restoration and so on), the modernist avant-garde remains far less familiar. There are some widely known, almost canonical performances. But many are less well known. This compels a spirit of scholarly adventure: an exciting prospect!
- Inspiring contemporary theatre – so often when we look at the modernist avant-garde we find precursors (active and acknowledged or, more often, simply interesting parallels) to the performances we see today. They help us to make new connections and prevent us falling into the trap of presuming that contemporary performance is entirely unique and without precedent.

THE AIM OF THIS BOOK

In recent years there has been a growing interest in new ways of understanding modernism and the avant-garde. All this scholarship has meant the rediscovery of lost works; the challenging of established ways of understanding more canonical examples; a questioning of assumptions about geography, race, class and gender; and an overcoming of the barriers between different artistic disciplines. Although these represent a welcome change of approach, the field can prove rather difficult to navigate. Furthermore, in these fascinatingly complex new discussions of modernism's legacy, performance (with some exceptions) seems to take on the role of a rather distant, overlooked cousin. This volume aims to form a bridge between new modernist scholarship and performance studies, smashing through the suspicion that often defines this relationship. Further, if we consider ourselves to be contemporary practitioners (in whatever capacity), we are left with an acute problem: what does this body of obscure, challenging work really have to say to us today? Here I hope to suggest ways that we, as twenty-first-century practitioners, might engage with this historical material.

HOW MIGHT THESE PERFORMANCES INSPIRE ME IN MY OWN PRACTICE?

This book is not simply a scholarly recording of modernist avant-garde performance. Rather, I hope the examples given provide new ideas for your own practice, whether you are an actor, performer, scholar, dancer, musician, director, designer, composer, choreographer, playwright or a fan of multimedia experimentation. As you read and use the practical explorations you will have the opportunity to ask 'how could this relate to my own practice?' and 'how could I create a new piece that engaged with the techniques I am exploring?' Many of the figures of the modernist avant-garde predicted the eventual overthrow of their own ideas by the thoughts and imaginings of a new generation. As twenty-first-century practitioners we have the opportunity to once again make the new, new!

HOW IS THE BOOK ORGANISED?

Rather than focus on a movement per chapter or separate the book into short studies of practitioners, we will instead progress through some themes and ideas that provide an accessible overview of both the historical period and the artwork. So each chapter mentions a range of performances, perhaps reading very different examples in parallel. This is not to ignore the differences but, rather, to supply a selection of interpretations of, say, the body or political engagement, thereby enabling us to think more easily about how these performances might relate to or inspire contemporary practice. Each chapter will also have play/performance examples, moments that could provide a blueprint for your studies. Most of these performances are relatively well known and students can access text-copies or at least find interesting photographic evidence or contemporaneous descriptions. They will be read in parallel with less accessible, less familiar examples that, I hope, will provide further models. The book, therefore, reassesses canonical plays and performances while trawling through the archives to find some unsung heroes of the modernist avant-garde. In addition, it provides an overview of secondary material relating to these performances. By and large, again, I use the most accessible, recent texts.

Chapter 1 introduces the conventions of modernist performance. It looks at some of the primary techniques and characteristics while also presenting some precursors and a critical examination of two ways of responding to modernity: symbolism and naturalism. In Chapter 2 we move on to look at four particular movements – expressionism, dada, surrealism and futurism – in order to construct a sense of what it meant to 'perform modernism'.

Political theatre provides the focus for Chapter 3. We look at both sides of the political spectrum, framing our argument with the contention that politics became performance while, simultaneously, performance became political. The body represented an extraordinarily important performance motif during this period, with innovations in dance and the growth of interest in the non-human, puppets and masks. This provides the theme for Chapter 4. The final chapter builds on the previous sections by examining the breakdown of disciplinary and generic borders. The performances refused easy definition, preferring instead to experiment with sound, music, visual art, film and radio. In the Conclusion we briefly look at a range of more recent performances that can be read as building on the innovations of the modernist avant-garde. At the end there is a glossary, providing definitions of words frequently used in this book, and some brief lists that can act as cue cards or pithy reminders of all the diverse ideas you will discover. Each chapter also has a concluding section entitled 'practical exploration'. These provide a selection of suggested activities, both performance-based and scholarly, that will help you to interact more fully with the material.

PRACTICAL EXPLORATION

The early decades of the twentieth century were defined by what Günter Berghaus has termed a 'feeling of cataclysmic commotion' (2005a: 26). So many new ideas, new perspectives and new experiences appeared throughout the nineteenth and early twentieth centuries that challenged typically held assumptions. Read a section of one or more of the following and determine why this might add to the feeling Berghaus describes:

Friedrich Nietzsche, Preface from *Human, All Too Human* (1878)
Karl Marx and Friedrich Engels, *The Communist Manifesto* (1848)
Charles Darwin, *The Origin of Species by Means of Natural Selection* (1859)
W.E.B. Dubois, *The Souls of Black Folks* (1903)
Sigmund Freud, *The Interpretation of Dreams* (1900)
Millicent Garrett, *Women's Suffrage* (1911)

Extracts from all of these works can be found in Kolocotroni, Goldman and Taxidou's *Modernism: An Anthology* (Edinburgh University Press, 1998). There are also portions online or you could simply dip into the original source material.

Consider how a) war, b) unemployment and c) new ways of understanding what it was to be human might have added to this feeling.

Return to the explanations of terminology in this section. Remembering that it is difficult to come up with conclusive definitions, what do you understand by the following terms – modern, modernity, modernism, avant-garde?

On pages 3 to 4 I list a number of questions that interrogate the relationship between politics and art, and query the objectives of creative work. Address each in turn and set up a debate: 'This House Believes that Art Should Remain Detached from Politics'. For all you competitive types, this task is less about winning the debate than about considering the issues involved.

Think about contemporary society. Are we also defined by a 'feeling of cataclysmic commotion'? How might this manifest itself? Tapping in to your own current understanding and experience of contemporary performance, how is art attempting to respond to or represent modernity? You might like to particularly consider the performance art movement and the latest turn towards verbatim theatre as two contrasting yet fruitful areas of enquiry.

CHAPTER I

The Conventions of Modernist Performance

UPDATING THEATRE HISTORY: THE MODERN AND THE HISTORICAL

If modernism should be understood as directly related to words such as 'modern' and 'modernity', terms that are intrinsically contemporary in nature, it follows that it should also connect with the idea of the 'new'. Robert Hughes's 1980 BBC series *The Shock of the New* and his subsequent book of the same title suggest that the avant-garde was defined by its newness, by its commitment to exploring uncharted artistic waters. This newness caused, as his title suggests, 'shock'. Hughes points to the 'ebullience, idealism, confidence, the belief that there was plenty of territory to explore' (1991: 9), all characteristics that can be seen in his examples – a 'vandalised' painting like Marcel Duchamp's *LHOOQ* (1919) or the architectural dynamism of the Eiffel Tower (built 1889).

Certainly an overwhelming sense of innovation defined much modernist artwork. However, the art of the late nineteenth/early twentieth century also confronted the perpetual problem of repetition. In this era, new technology led to new artistic genres, though many debated whether the results could be described as 'art'. Film and photography enabled artists to reproduce images exactly, albeit tinged with those recurrent aesthetic issues of perspective and bias. These new methods did not simply present images once as a landscape painting might, but could reproduce them infinitely. This meant, of course, that these images could be shared among more people, leading to a democratisation of art; you and I might even have copies on our own walls. As the member of the Frankfurt School Walter Benjamin put it in his seminal essay 'The Work of Art in the Age of Mechanical Reproduction' (1936), it also meant that the 'aura' of the artwork was lost; that uniqueness that makes an object 'art' disappeared, replaced by multiple versions. So, at one and the same time, these reproductive art forms revealed both a contemporary crisis and a potential revolution, a loss of art and an opening up of art.

It seems that modernism cannot be disconnected from newness, from technology, the urban or the scientific. However, in *Avant-Garde Theatre, 1892–1992*, Christopher Innes makes a startling claim. Avant-garde performance does not focus on the modern as much as what he terms the 'primitive' (1993: 3). The word 'primitive' is often regarded as derogatory, suggesting an 'uncivilised' Other in comparison with the 'civilised' West. However, during the early decades of the twentieth century there was a movement called primitivism that looked to myriad world cultures for inspiration. The artist Paul Gauguin's work exemplifies this movement, as does Pablo Picasso's famous painting *Les Demoiselles D'Avignon* (1907), portraying five Spanish prostitutes with one of the woman's faces replaced by an African-style mask. Looking at the avant-garde not as a historical period but as an ethos prevalent throughout the late nineteenth and early twentieth centuries, Innes suggests that primitivism manifests itself in a variety of ways but, as a general rule, 'the hallmark of avant-garde drama is an aspiration to transcendence, to the spiritual in its widest sense' (1993: 3). Thus, Innes concludes that avant-garde art responds to its context not by focusing on the material (industrialisation, class struggle or war, for example) but by attempting to find worlds and images beyond our everyday experience.

Primitivism does seem a rather odd concept for Innes to choose as the prevailing mood of the avant-garde. Given Hughes's focus on the new, Innes's definition – looking back to ancient civilisations and pre-industrial societies – feels a little archaic. But his theory does help us to realise that, for all its proclamations about contemporary society, the modernist avant-garde was often just as influenced by traditions and histories – 'artistic heritage' as Thomas Postlewait puts it (2009: 14) – even if that influence is often difficult to fully grasp. So here, at the very start of Chapter 1, we stumble upon a confusing tension: did the modernist avant-garde primarily celebrate modern technology or assimilate techniques from earlier theatre? Was it defined by newness or history, innovation or repetition? As we will see, the answers prove not at all straightforward and, more often than not, different practitioners proffered very different (often extremely forceful) responses. Performances regarded as modernist cannot be imagined as a homogeneous body of work and attitudes towards theatre history clearly illustrate the diversity of approach.

PERFORMATIVE MANIFESTOS

Often regarded as one of the doyens of Anglo-American modernism, in his *Canto LIII* the poet Ezra Pound coined a much-cited phrase. He advocated taking the old and 'making it new'. In artistic terms this meant transforming established techniques and forms for contemporary audiences, readers and spectators. The actual methods that artists used to 'make it new' and their responses to all that had gone before remained extremely diverse. One useful and entertaining way of determining modernism's relationship with history is to look at the various manifestos that appeared during this period. Manifestos have become an important focus of study, with books by Luca Somigli (2003), Martin Puchner (2005), Laura Winkiel (2007) and the publication of primary avant-garde documents in the 1998 Edinburgh University Press collection *Modernism: An Anthology of Sources and Documents* and the more recent Penguin book *100 Artists' Manifestos: From the Futurists to the Stuckists* (2011). Connecting the artwork and the manifesto, Puchner usefully claims an 'art forged in the image of the manifesto' (2005: 6), exhibiting aggression and polemical rhetoric, challenging aesthetics and societal norms. Both the manifestos and the art that reflected their claims embodied a violently antagonistic spirit.

We might imagine that these documents aimed to define movements, but as with today's General Election manifestos, the form actually walks a tightrope between fact and fiction, polemic and instruction. They are not detached analyses; rather they are full of amusing rhetoric, direct (often angry) responses to contemporaneous culture and society, and thought-provoking, at times impenetrable, images, like a modernist poem. They are also, importantly for us, inherently performative, that is, the words are active by design. Using the ideas of critical theorists J.L. Austin and Judith Butler, 'performative' here refers to the act of bringing something into existence. For Austin, words were not simply signs on a page; they could actually change our day-to-day experience: the 'I do' in a wedding service, for example, or the 'you are sentenced to . .' in a courtroom. Influenced by Austin's ideas, Butler investigated the way that gender is performed in *Gender Trouble*. She suggests that the gendered body is performative in the sense that 'it has no ontological status apart from various acts which constitute its reality' (2001: 2497). How might these ideas relate to the modernist manifesto? Well, we discover that it is not an objective explanatory mode, coolly commenting on artistic visions in a detached way. Instead manifestos are performative, presenting ideas as actions, creating new states of being rather than simply reflecting on them.

It must be remembered, then, that manifestos are inherently argumentative, designed to shake the reader or hearer to action. They are not reliable, impartial descriptions. That said, they remain an excellent starting point for our investigations. Many of the movements and practitioners mentioned in this book created their own manifestos: Wyndham Lewis's *BLAST* defined the vorticist movement (1914) and F.T. Marinetti's unrelenting *Futurist Manifesto* (1909) can still shock readers today, especially if read alongside Valentine de Saint-Point's *Manifesto of Futurist Women* (1912). Wassily Kandinsky's *Content and Form* (1910) and *Concerning the Spiritual in Art* (1911) paved the way for

expressionism, though perhaps they are better understood as artistic trea-
tises rather than manifestos. Then there was Tristan Tzara's *Dada Manifesto*
(1918), though Hugo Ball and Richard Huelsenbeck also wrote manifesto
definitions (or more accurately, given dada's rejection of logical description,
non-definitions) for this movement (1916 and 1918 respectively), as did artist
Francis Picabia (1920). Other manifestos included André Breton's *Manifesto
of Surrealism* (1924), Walter Gropius's manifesto for the Bauhaus movement
(1919) and Alexei Gan's definition of constructivism (1922). Even today, artists
often devise manifestos to define their projects (see Danchev 2011).

In keeping with our initial thoughts about newness and tradition, many
of the manifestos pointed to their author's opinion of the past. In their 1938
Manifesto: Towards a Free Revolutionary Art, Breton, the founder of sur-
realism, Mexican painter Diego Rivera and Russian revolutionary Leon
Trotsky maintained 'true art is unable *not* to be revolutionary, *not* to aspire
to a complete and radical reconstruction of society' (Danchev 2011: 297).
They rejected the status quo, both aesthetically and in terms of social history.
Likewise, Marinetti, the founder of futurism, asked 'why should we look back,
when what we want is to break down the mysterious doors of the impossible'
(Kolocotroni et al. 1998: 251). He advocated instead the destruction of all
established institutions including 'museums, libraries . . . [and] academies'.

In the *Manifesto of the Constructivist Group* (*c.* 1922), Alexander Rodchenko
presented another way of looking at the past. Actually, he suggested, constructivist art is less about destroying and rejecting the past than about changing the
way we perceive artistic elements. Squares, he proposed, have always existed
but, in the work of the constructivists, 'THEY WERE POINTED OUT./
THEY WERE ANNOUNCED' (Danchev 2011: 221). Rodchenko focused on
our perception of shapes, advocating a transformative change in the way we see
them, rather than destroying them altogether. This remodelling of the spectator's eye was an integral part of his broader 'IRRECONCILABLE WAR
AGAINST ART' (Danchev 2011: 221). For Rodchenko, it proved impossible
(and unnecessary) to entirely demolish the techniques or ideas of the past but
vital to challenge the way these ideas had been used or perceived.

Returning to Poggioli's definition as mentioned in the Introduction, the one
objective that unites all these manifestos is their antagonism. If, as Winkiel suggests, manifestos are poised 'between action and theory, politics and aesthetics,
and the new and the old' then this antagonism is embedded in the form (Winkiel
2007: 2). The manifesto automatically battles against established institutions,
traditional forms and assumptions about the nature of art. Its origins in politics
gives it this inherently antagonistic feel. Many political manifestos appeared
during the nineteenth and twentieth centuries, seeking to define a situation
and challenge readers to join the struggle. Works such as Marx and Engels's
Communist Manifesto (1848), Mina Loy's 1914 *Feminist Manifesto* and W.E.B.

Dubois's *Manifesto to the League of Nations* (1921) all advocated the rights of minority groups in the face of hegemonic powers. Again, the writers responded to the errors of previous generations, though this time the errors were not artistic but social, concerned with repressive forces and a search for equality rather than swirls of paint or poetic voices. The manifesto form, therefore, transcended the boundary between politics and art, the two becoming inextricably associated. Changing the world necessitates a change in culture too.

THEATRE HISTORY AS RAW MATERIAL

Practitioners used a variety of influences from theatre history in order to construct modern plays about modern issues. In doing so they largely ignored the high/low art debate I mentioned in the Introduction. They simply looked back to the performances that could be most helpful as raw material. Shakespeare enjoyed particular influence, especially in Britain, his brand of politically engaged, plot-driven poetic drama appealing to prostitutes and queens alike. Other practitioners looked to even older techniques. The ancient Greek theatre in particular was a vital precursor, particularly in its use of bare staging and masks. Italian *commedia dell'arte* was equally influential in its use of stock, comic characters such as Pantalone and Harlequin.

To attempt to provide a definitive case study for this claim that modernist practitioners often took inspiration from particular artistic heritages, I want to focus on the variety theatre mode (and other interconnected forms like music hall and cabaret), a genre that inspired a broad and remarkably diverse range of artists. The effect of the variety theatre could be clearly seen in the structure of these performances which were, by and large, non-linear, that is, they did not have a typical beginning–middle–end chronology. Variety theatre works in a similar way; it might start with a song, and then present a dancing troupe, before another song or a monologue or a comedian. It exhibits a uniquely episodic style which is less an aesthetic choice than an attempt to entertain an audience. The variety theatre also embraces an admirable sense of vibrancy that in the early decades of the twentieth century was often seen as a cure for the dull seriousness of bourgeois drama. Boredom proves virtually impossible in variety theatre because of the speed and diversity of performance. It is equally difficult to become totally immersed in a variety theatre performance as you constantly experience interruptions – the end of a song, the final flourish of the magician, the direct address of the MC – before moving on to another vignette that is probably unrelated to the previous one and may well have a very different tone.

Variety theatre certainly provided a blueprint for a range of modernist practitioners. Despite his proclamations against theatre history, Marinetti was a great advocate of variety theatre, claiming it provided a 'profitable showcase for countless inventive forces . . . [and] naturally generates what I call "the Futurist marvellous'" (Schumacher 1996: 42). The poet T.S. Eliot, who wrote a number of artistically experimental plays in a poetic drama tradition, including *Sweeney Agonistes* (1933) and *Murder in the Cathedral* (1935), also admired the variety theatre mode. Valorising the performance of English singer Marie Lloyd, Eliot claimed that the music hall could speak directly to audiences and reflect working-class experience, as the spectator 'joined in the chorus . . . [and] was himself performing part of the act' (1966: 458). This is a remarkable comment when one considers that Eliot is one of the most celebrated progenitors of high modernism. His case proves that intertextual references to Dante can sit next to variety theatre-style singalongs; his magnificent multivocal poem *The Waste Land* is witness to this. The German playwright Bertolt Brecht campaigned for an epic theatre that was politically engaging and entertaining. In doing so, he turned to cabaret where he claimed that, unlike 'serious music', songs are 'gestic' (Brecht 2001: 87). 'Gestic' here refers to a combination of a physical gesture and a social meaning, thereby preventing the audience from becoming too engrossed in the tune or lyrics. Gestus also enables particular issues or emotions to be tangibly revealed on the stage; attempting to avoid ambiguity, politics can be *shown* rather than merely *described*. Brecht also advocated the use of the revue, another variety theatre type, which demanded a non-linear narrative, again disrupting flow and compelling audiences to attend to the politics rather than the story (2001: 183). There were a number of other German figures who were interested in cabaret, including two of the earliest avant-garde figures, Max Reinhardt and Frank Wedekind (see chapter 2 in Kuhns 1997). The dadaists too created their brand of anarchic non-art at the Cabaret Voltaire in Zurich in 1916.

However, others were less complimentary. The Russian Vsevolod Meyerhold, for example, claimed that variety theatre lulled the working-class audience with its brand of escapist, titillating entertainment, even claiming it as a 'corrupting' influence (2008: 265). Possibly all the practitioners above would have partly concurred with Meyerhold's dismissal of variety theatre. Traditionally it certainly provided simple entertainment for mass audiences. However, by 'making it new', modernist avant-garde performers and directors could cherry-pick the form, taking the structures and attitudes of the variety show and transforming them into contemporary, challenging performances.

CREATING IMAGES:
SYMBOLISM FROM MAETERLINCK TO YEATS

Certainly a variety of practitioners 'made new' old established techniques from theatre history. But there were other theatrical moments that I want to claim not as influences or precursors, but as early flowerings of the avant-garde. These were nineteenth-century movements that, to some extent, paved the way, even if the later twentieth-century innovators often rejected many of their techniques. Two movements in particular influenced twentieth-century theatre and continue to inspire contemporary performance: symbolism and naturalism. These theatrical genres represented a starting point for the modernist avant-garde but also became a focus for the ire of the more antagonistic practitioners of the 1920s and 30s; one could accurately claim them as the first tentative steps of modernist experimentation and yet just as easily regard them as the final stand of nineteenth-century artistic methods of melodrama, the well-made play and a romantic sensibility. Despite the modernists' frequent cries to the contrary, I prefer to imagine them as the former, as early modernist avant-garde movements. It is interesting to read them in parallel for, in many ways, naturalism and symbolism represent two oppositional ways of dealing with the modern world in a performative sense. As we will see, however, they are not quite as antagonistic as one might at first presume.

Frantisek Deak categorises the avant-garde as a 'systematic, conscious, and radical attempt to reclaim through art the fullness of life – to bring onto the level of discourse those aspects of life that society chooses to neglect, disregard, or openly suppress' (1993: 132). Defining the avant-garde in this way, he focuses on symbolism as emblematic of this aim, not necessarily to be violently antagonistic but to cast light on unseen facets of human experience. Symbolism is also a key part of Innes's argument about primitivism, for he sees the aim of the movement as a search for a 'deeper level of reality than deceptive surface appearances' (1993: 19). So symbolism included a spiritual element, where 'spiritual' does not necessary mean 'religious' in any sense but simply an uncovering of something intangible or immaterial. It also represented a search for a new means of expression, emanating from a distrust of the word, or, as Berghaus puts it, a 'loss of faith in the ability of rational language' (2005a: 23). Language seemed unable to fully express the complexities of the modern world, particularly in light of contemporaneous psychological theories: how could words conjured up by an irrational, uncontrollable brain ever be fully reliable? This is not to say that symbolism was without language, but rather that the words were not really about explaining plot or constructing dialogue. Accordingly, the language became expressive, poetic, often incoherent, creating a feeling or mood. So, following on from my initial encouragement in the Introduction, when approaching these plays it is far better to ask 'what are the words doing?' than 'what do the words mean?' In 1896 the Belgian symbolist playwright Maurice Maeterlinck addressed the issue of symbolist language:

> One may even affirm that the poem draws the viewer to beauty and
> loftier truth in the measure that it eliminates words that merely explain

the action, and substitutes for them others that reveal, not the so-called 'soul state', but I know not what intangible and unceasing striving of the soul towards its own beauty and truth.

(Schumacher 1996: 93)

Maeterlinck's comments illustrate his interest in artistic beauty engendered by expressive, poetic words rather than by descriptive rationality. They also contain a sense that the soul strives towards an almost indefinable goal, that the destination might always be indistinct, shadowy and nebulous.

If we take a look at Maeterlinck's *The Intruder* or *The Blind* (both 1890), the language strikes us first. It is remarkably simple and yet strangely obscure. The words are easy to understand, the sentences less so. While the scenarios tell a story, there is generally very little action and no real sense of resolution. They are situated in defined, non-urban spaces such as the old country house of *The Intruder* or the forest of *The Blind*. Characters are difficult to understand, without individuality or definable personality. The challenges of these plays correspond to Maeterlinck's reservations about theatre as an art form in an 1890 essay. He suggested that art generally is symbolic in nature. A poem's complex syntax or a painting's misty landscapes exhibit a certain innate sense of symbolism whereas, for Maeterlinck, the play gives substance to these things, thereby reducing their mystical nature:

The stage is where masterpieces die, because the presentation of a masterpiece by *accidental* and *human* means is a contradiction. All masterpieces are symbols, and the symbol never withstands the active presence of man.

(Dorra 1994: 144)

With such a view of theatre it is surprising that Maeterlinck wrote any plays at all! He did not provide an answer to this conundrum, other than suggesting the elimination of the human from the stage. Whether a play with its sense of liveness, commitment to embodying theme and inescapable actor–audience connection could ever be symbolist in the same sense as a poem or a painting is an unresolved problem and worth considering. Counteracting Maeterlinck's concerns about performance, the critic Patrick McGuinness points to the symbolists' 'obsessive preoccupation with performance' (2000: 102). As so often in the modernist avant-garde, we find a Gordian knot; on the one hand the symbolists feared the materiality of the stage would destroy their attempts to explore the metaphysical, yet, on the other, they constantly presented their enquiries in performance. Martin Puchner refers to this sort of attitude as 'anti-theatricalism', confirming that 'a suspicion of the theater plays a constitutive role in the period of modernism, especially in modernist theater and drama' (2002: 1).

Another playwright associated with symbolism was the Irishman W.B. Yeats. Generally better known as a poet, his interest in the theatre led to the co-founding of the influential Abbey Theatre in Dublin in 1899. He also wrote many plays, defined by a sense of spirituality, ancient folk forms and Irish history. While there is always a story running through the plays, the realisation of these stories is often visually indistinct, with poetic language and symbolic or mythical characters. In his understanding of theatre, Yeats oscillated between clarity and indecision. One extremely clear aspect of his dramatic aesthetic was his staging:

> Painted scenery after all is unnecessary to my friends and to myself, for our imagination kept living by the arts can imagine a mountain covered with thorntrees in a drawing-room without any great trouble, and we have many quarrels with even good scene-painting.
>
> (Yeats 1921: 86)

Like many modernists, Yeats decluttered the stage, relying instead on the imagination of the audience. As we will go on to see, simple platform staging proved a unifying characteristic of the modernist avant-garde, although the intentions and objectives differed considerably.

Yeats looked to a number of different influences, not least Irish folklore. However, he was also fascinated by Noh theatre, a Japanese tradition from the fourteenth century. Noh, still a thriving art form in Japan today, relies on elaborate costumes, poetic diction, distinctive music and masks. Within this form exist a number of different play types, all expressing different moods, some spiritual, some with a more material focus. Yeats developed particular interest in the Noh dream play and, in fact, adapted this mode in his 1916 *The Dreaming of the Bones*, a play that combines ancient Irish stories of Diarmuid and Dervorgilla with contemporary soldiers' stories (Dorn 1984: 53). The action plays out against the backdrop of the 1916 Easter Rising, the Irish Republican rebellion against British rule. Ireland had been ruled by Britain since 1800, though many, particularly in the south of the country, resented their larger, more powerful colonial neighbour. In April 1916 a small Republican army proclaimed an independent Ireland in Dublin. Although British forces crushed the rebels, this event became a founding moment for later conflict and led to eventual Irish self-rule in 1921. *The Dreaming of the Bones* opens with the following stage directions:

> *The stage is any bare place in a room close to the wall. A screen, with a pattern of mountain and sky, can stand against the wall, or a curtain with a like pattern hang upon it, but the pattern must only symbolise or suggest.*
>
> (Yeats 1921)

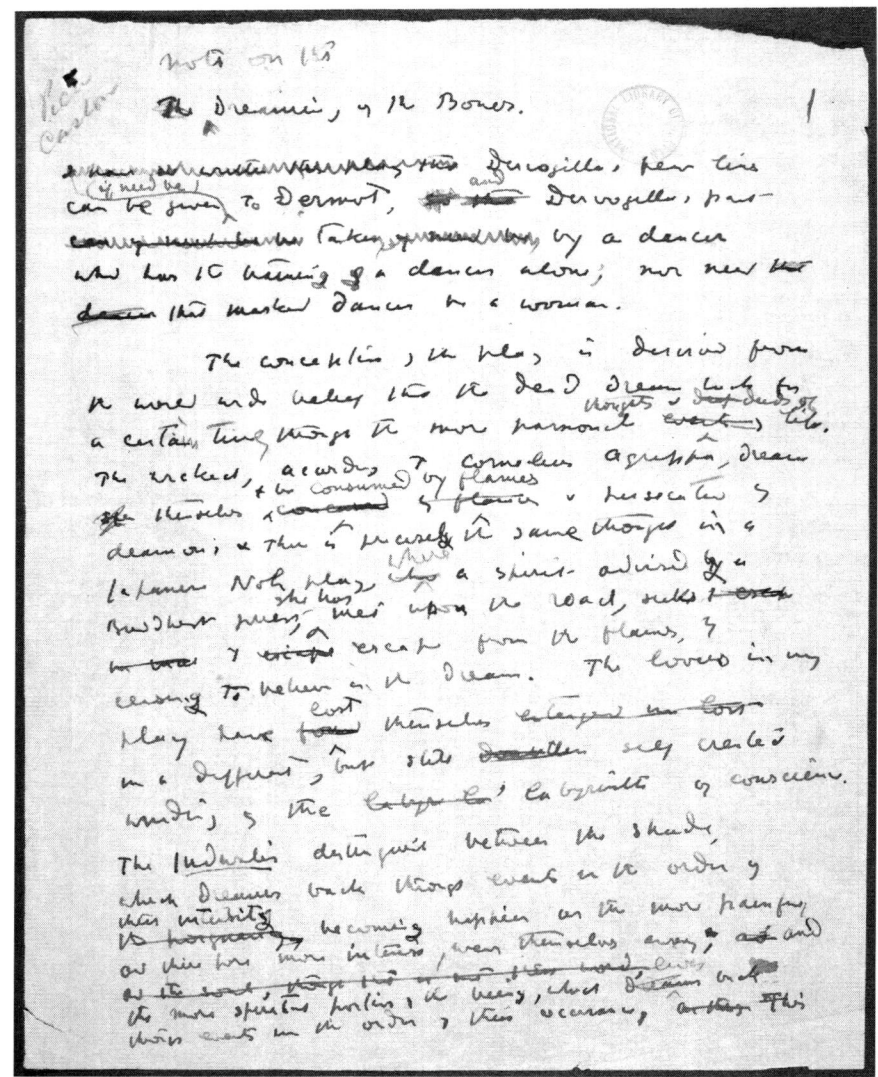

Figure 1 An image from W. B. Yeats's *Dreaming of the Bones*, 1916 © courtesy of the National Library of Ireland

Surprisingly, given its political undertones, the play occurs in no specified place. While it focuses on the events of the Easter Rising – 'I was in the Post Office, and if taken/ I shall be put against a wall and shot' (Yeats 1921) – there remains a constant suggestion that we are near the sea rather than in an urban Dublin setting. In transferring the action to an unspecified, shadowy space and in combining ancient mythical figures and unnamed modern participants in the Rising, Yeats's play becomes purposefully indistinct, reflecting the techniques of the symbolist movement.

In his search for an artistic symbolist mode, Yeats also incorporated dance elements into his plays. James Flannery suggests that it is difficult to discern quite what Yeats had in mind for his dances and I would certainly concur with that (1976: 208). Yeats admired the work of Ninette de Valois, a dancer with Sergei Diaghilev's Ballets Russes, even writing a selection of plays especially for her. Even his descriptions of his artistic vision seem clouded in uncertainty: 'The players must move a little stiffly and gravely like marionettes and, I think, to the accompaniment of drum taps' (Yeats 1921). The term 'marionette' reminds us of another important early modernist practitioner: Edward Gordon Craig. The similarities are not a coincidence as the two actually worked together between 1909 and 1912.

One of the most influential figures of twentieth-century theatre, Craig never really fully realised his own theatrical project. Despite differences (Yeats was a far more literary figure than Craig), they can be read in parallel, as 'both men were rooted in Romanticism and never quite came to terms with their modernity' (Taxidou 1998: 76). Once again, here are two figures wrestling with the relationship between the past and the contemporary. Craig stripped the stage bare, refusing to use unnecessary props and furniture. Instead he created mood through light, a medium that is as atmospheric as it is flexible. In fact light concerned many early modernist figures, including Swiss technician Adolphe Appia who designed many sets for Richard Wagner's operas. Appia differentiated between 'diffused light' which helps the audience to see the action and 'living light' which adds mood, atmosphere and theme. He even placed considerable emphasis on shadow as a lighting effect as opposed to merely an irritating by-product of a poorly set spot (Appia 1962: 74). Craig's 1905 *The Steps* exemplified his primary ideas. Constructed as four 'moods', *The Steps* contained no real story as such. It resembled instead four interlocking scenes where the rhythms and tones created by light and the position of human figures on the eponymous long flight of steps suggested different emotions. The audience was left with a series of impressions beginning with isolation and moving towards a hopeful promise for the future. Christopher Innes helpfully sums up Craig's intentions: 'each spectator is led to discover his inner nature, and to perceive his/her existence as an integral part of the cyclical patterns of nature' (1998: 140).

While Craig was not necessarily a symbolist *per se*, in *Avant-Garde Theatre, 1892–1992* Innes does go on to say that he can be read in parallel to the symbolists, particularly in his dismissal of stage illusion in favour of representative sets and figures. All four of these figures (Maeterlinck, Yeats, Craig and Appia) proposed differing projects and intentions but all united in their transformation of the stage through use of symbolic sets, acting styles, movement, language and music.

FOR AND AGAINST NATURALISM

Naturalism stands in sharp contrast to symbolism as a materialist rather than transcendental performance method, that is, focusing on actual everyday conditions of society as opposed to more spiritual or metaphysical matters. Whereas symbolist performances resembled dreams, naturalist plays concentrated on society, relationships (be they familial, romantic, work-based) and contemporary issues.

One mistake often made is to presume that naturalism and realism are the same and that these terms can be used synonymously. This is not the case, although the differences between the two are often difficult to disentangle. Realism can be applied to any performance that attempts to present an image or reflection of the 'real', the world outside the theatre walls. Realism, therefore, could describe many forms. Brecht's ideas, for example, are often referred to as 'epic realism'. His work was by no means naturalistic in approach but one cannot but read Brecht's playscripts as realist. Furthermore, when the Russian leader Josef Stalin decreed that socialist realism was the primary artistic method of communist Russia he advocated a straightforward linear story, coherent imagery but, in contrast to naturalism, an unequivocally optimistic positive resolution focusing on the potential of the proletariat. Despite associations with realism, these three forms (naturalism, epic realism and socialist realism) stand in sharp contrast to one another. Given these examples, perhaps we could argue that realism represents a perspective (a focus on the 'real') whereas naturalism, epic and socialist realism are ways of working out that perspective.

The Marxist critic Raymond Williams has many useful things to say about the similarities and differences between naturalism and realism. In his 1978 essay 'Realism, Naturalism and their Alternatives', he lays out some of the primary distinctions. Both, he suggests, originated not in aesthetics *per se*, but in different ways of looking at the world and from the sense that these societal changes should be reflected in art (1978: 2). If realism proclaimed a general move towards greater material engagement with the world, then naturalism declared something more specific. For naturalism directly reflected specific nineteenth-century developments: particular scientific advancement, the rise of the bourgeoisie, the growth of the urban landscape and political tensions. Williams goes on to say that naturalist dramatists 'insisted that it was impossible to understand character and action unless the full physical and social environment which shaped character and action was directly presented' (1978: 2).

So, the naturalists felt compelled to demonstrate a human figure at the centre of particular societal conditions. Naturalism intended to 'present a "slice of life" in all its harsh reality and to examine it as a scientist might examine a specimen under a microscope' (Hochman 1984: 245). Watching a naturalist play is akin to peering through a keyhole as, behind the door, people go about their business.

Naturalism sought after the real, rejecting falsities in favour of truth even if that truth was unpalatable, unpleasant or challenged artistic taste. Naturalist playwrights and practitioners showed gender imbalances, poverty-stricken families or urban squalor in order to fully comprehend the human character. They also directly reacted against two popular theatrical forms: the enjoyable yet escapist variety theatre and the well-made play. This latter form had the linear structures of naturalism and yet developed a distinct pattern from which it never wavered, with the plot generally relying on the eventual revelation of a secret and a subsequent tidy resolution. The well-made play became such an easy-to-follow pattern that the playwright Eugène Scribe was able to churn out over 350 plays between 1813 and 1861 (Innes 2000: 7). As well as responding to changes in science and the sociopolitical landscape, naturalism, then, also rejected the frameworks of its predecessors. Naturalism developed in the novel form through the work of nineteenth-century writers such as Honoré de Balzac, Henry James, Elizabeth Gaskell, Thomas Hardy, Victor Hugo, Charles Dickens and the Brontë sisters – Anne, Emily and Charlotte – among others. But the movement transitioned across to the theatre through the plays of Gerhart Hauptmann, Henrik Ibsen, August Strindberg, Anton Chekhov, George Bernard Shaw and the suffragette playwrights from both sides of the Atlantic.

While naturalism was most certainly a playwright-driven movement, it also profoundly influenced set design and theatrical acting. Sets accurately reflected real places. Gone were the painted backdrops, exposed as false stage effects as soon as the three-dimensional actor walked on. They were replaced by wardrobes that really opened, sofas that could be sat on and drinks cabinets that could provide real drinks, albeit generally cold tea rather than whisky. Costumes too were important, providing visual insight into a character's identity. Actors attempted to hone realistic on-stage voices that sounded far more like everyday conversation than the exaggerated speeches of melodrama or the predictable dialogue of the well-made play. French director André Antoine developed a particular interest in naturalist sets, creating mimetic scenography on his stage at the Théâtre Libre, Paris (established 1887). Antoine searched for a greater sense of the real, presenting not simply a box set but rather giving the impression of a larger, multifaceted space. He suggested 'in short the whole house – and not just the part in which the action takes place – should be sketched' (Innes 2000: 52). In this mimetic set Antoine placed props and objects that could transform an artificial stage set into a space that appeared to be a real, occupied house that the audience had the privilege of peeping into for a time. This led to some unusual stage devices such as rotting sides of beef for the 1888 *The Butchers* and real chickens for *The Earth* (1902). He connected this way of constructing set with the behaviour of the actors:

> Among so many objects, and with the complicated furnishings of our modern interiors, the performers' acting became, without their realizing it and almost in spite of themselves, more human, more intense, and more alive in attitude and gestures.
>
> (Innes 2000: 52)

For Antoine, then, an accurately simulated drawing room or factory floor could directly affect the efficacy of an actor's performance.

At this point, we must turn all too briefly to Konstantin Stanislavsky, a Russian theatre director whose work has influenced an immeasurable number of practitioners and who is rightly admired as one of the founding figures of modern drama. With Vladimir Nemirovich-Danchenko, Stanislavsky established the Moscow Art Theatre in 1898, now regarded as one of the most important performance spaces in theatre history. The theatre gained a reputation for serious dramatic art with versions of Chekhov's *The Seagull* (1898) and Maxim Gorky's *The Lower Depths* (1902). There is not space here to do justice to such a figure, but his importance merits a mention. Stanislavsky committed to creating a new type of theatre where actors did not merely pretend to be characters but actually *became* those characters, drawing on their own experiences in order to present true feelings and real emotion. This practice was called emotion memory. But what if the actor had never been in that particular position before or if personal emotions led to paralysis rather than creativity? In response to this problem, Stanislavsky created the 'magic if', a way of imagining how one *might* react in any given situation. Stanislavsky's justification for such an approach lay in his understanding of the actor who was 'under the obligation to live his part inwardly, and then to give to his experience an external embodiment' (1967: 15).

So, was Stanislavsky a naturalist? Certainly the connection is problematic if we look at him in parallel with prominent naturalist ideas. For, unlike many naturalists, Stanislavsky embraced many of the techniques and conventions of the established stage, particularly melodrama. His version of *The Seagull*, for example, was infused with the melodramatic, from the stereotypical damsel-in-distress interpretation of Nina to the tolling of bells in the background. In fact, according to J.L. Styan, 'Stanislavsky was using old stage trickery, and was not ashamed to say so' (1981a: 77). While other naturalists clearly appropriated melodramatic techniques, Stanislavsky's unequivocal acknowledgement of his indebtedness to melodrama does cast doubt on his identity as a naturalist. Furthermore, whereas naturalism was interested in the material everyday, Stanislavsky's method exhibited a greater sense of spirituality, focusing on the human mind. In fact Stanislavsky confronted this very issue in his handbook *An Actor Prepares*:

> Of significance to us is: *the reality of the inner life of a human spirit in a part and belief in that reality. We are not concerned with the actual naturalistic existence of what surrounds us on the stage, the reality of the material world!* This is of use only in so far as it supplies a general background for our feelings.
>
> (1967: 123)

Placing himself in the narrative under the alias Tortsov and using a discursive prose style, *An Actor Prepares* resembles one of the later avant-garde manifestos. Here Stanislavsky declared he was not a naturalist simply because he was far more interested in the human than the conditions of society. This inner emotion, this imaginative embodying of character, became Stanislavsky's notion of 'truth'. Acknowledging this, it is easy to see why Stanislavsky has been regarded as a vital figure in realism but far less easy to claim as a naturalist. Yet in other ways he became the naturalist *par excellence*, providing the most convincing theatrical illusions of the real of anyone in twentieth-century theatre history. Whichever way you look at it, the relationship between Stanislavsky and naturalism is a fraught one.

Many associated with the modernist avant-garde through the 1920s and 30s rejected naturalism and, in fact, this reaction became a defining characteristic, uniting a range of diverse experiments, from the antagonistic destructive futurists to workers' theatres to the theatrical work of a more establishment figure like W.H. Auden, who aimed for a drama that used a powerful mixture of poetry and prose in order to capture a sense of the zeitgeist. However, naturalism cannot simply be dismissed as a rather dull pre-avant-garde movement. Actually it has an extraordinarily contentious history and began with revolutionary fervour. The French journalist and playwright Émile Zola believed wholeheartedly in the power of naturalism to transform theatre and consistently advocated the genre in his writings. His *Naturalism in the Theatre* is imbued at once with a melancholy air of dejection at the state of contemporary drama and the hope for better days ahead. Like the later avant-gardists, he violently dismissed previous traditions, 'smashing the imposed patterns . . . [and] letting in through the backcloth the great, free air of reality' (Bentley 1979: 351). Zola wanted a 'revolution in theatre', performances 'pulsing with life' (Bentley 1979: 352 and 364). He imagined theatre that helped the audience to see properly, doing 'great things with the subjects and characters that our eyes, accustomed to the spectacle of the daily round, have come to see as small' (Bentley 1979: 364). Using the syntax of the trenches, he, like an avant-garde manifesto writer, expected a 'battle . . . [through] the melting slush of rhetoric and metaphysics' (Bentley 1979: 372).

The history of early theatrical naturalism certainly reflected Zola's impassioned prose. Performance premieres were often met with perplexed incredulity or surging anger. In London, for example, Henrik Ibsen's play *A Doll's House* (1879) caused near riots, while American critics attacked it as 'morbid, forced, repulsive' (Fischer-Lichte et al. 2011: 40). His later play *Hedda Gabler* (1890), a bleak work about academic rivalries, sex and suicide, met with a similar response. In Britain the *Daily Telegraph* described it as a 'hideous play' resembling 'a visit to the Morgue' (Innes 2000: 115). Raymond Williams eloquently describes the dangerous naturalist project: 'The new drama was low and vulgar or filthy; it threatened the standards of decent society by subversion of indifference to accepted norms' (Timms and Collier 1988: 311).

There is no doubt that naturalism was a form of revolutionary intent. It took on particularly importance in the discussion of women's rights in the early years of the twentieth century, not just in Ibsen's works, but in a range of other plays by men and women. Indeed in recent years, scholars have reassessed and resurrected turn-of-the-century plays about and by women, with the publication of collections such as Maggie Gale and Gilli Bush-Bailey's *Plays and Performance Texts by Women 1880–1930* (2012) and Naomi Paxton's edited *The Methuen Drama Book of Suffrage Plays* (2013). We are going to focus on two plays about women's experience: *Votes for Women* (1907) by Elizabeth Robins and August Strindberg's *Miss Julie* (1888). Why could these plays be described as naturalist? First there is a strong sense of story, a chronological progression that moves from the beginning to the middle to the end. Both are based in specific places: *Votes for Women* in Hertfordshire and London, *Miss Julie* on a Count's estate in Sweden. If, as Zola suggested, characters should be indivisible from their sociohistorical context and personal experiences, then such specificity of place is to be expected. *Miss Julie* has an extremely small cast of three, although a wedding party arrives on stage at one point and other characters are suggested either through dialogue or the wafting party noises or the Count's gloves and boots which are onstage throughout. In his horrifyingly misogynistic preface to *Miss Julie*, Strindberg questions the bourgeois concept of simple characters denoted by a wooden leg or a red nose. Rather, here we find 'modern characters . . . vacillating, out of joint, torn between the old and the new' (Strindberg 1992: xii). The characters of *Votes for Women* could be described in a similar way, although there are far more of them, including an unnumbered crowd. All the characters in both are recognisable as people (they have suitable costumes, speak in comprehensible dialogue, interact with others, respond with emotion) and are created by their societal circumstances.

In essence, what unites these plays is their focus on women's experience and sex. In circumstances akin to modern-day soap opera, the daughter of the Count, Miss Julie, falls for the servant Jean (John) who is engaged to fellow servant Christine. This proves explosive, culminating in an offstage sex scene and the potential that Jean and Julie might escape together to run a hotel. However, this is impossible and, instead, Julie exits with a razor blade, suggesting she will commit suicide. Strindberg asserted that the narrative for this play came from a real life story that struck him as tragic and worthy of a theatrical reworking (Strindberg 1992: x). *Votes for Women* focuses on Miss Levering, who had an abortion after being seduced and abandoned by a young man. The man was Stoner, now a parliamentarian, engaged to be married to the naive but spirited Jean. Moving from the Hertfordshire countryside to London, the play focuses on the suffragette movement, calling for women to have the vote. In the final scene, Stoner and Miss Levering meet again. Stoner is remorseful, Miss Levering forgiving and the play ends with the hopeful suggestion that women will indeed receive the freedoms that the suffragettes desire.

What are the aims of these two plays? Strindberg summed up his own position as follows: 'We [naturalists] love to call a spade a spade, and we believe that societies will collapse unless sincerity, the first covenant on which societies rest, is restored' (Schumacher 1996: 298). For both plays, it is this spirit of sincerity that proves the driving force. In keeping with the techniques of naturalism, the plays also balance personal trauma with broader social issues. The themes are difficult and upsetting, even more so for contemporaneous audiences used to jolly evenings at the music hall or the expected patterns of the well-made play.

Thus, our initial enquiries would suggest that these two plays are certainly examples of the linear, society-based naturalism that Zola so eloquently described. While this is true, naturalism is rarely as straightforward as one might first imagine. Actually both of these plays contain moments that disrupt naturalistic patterns. In *Votes for Women* the women's suffrage rally stands out. This scene retains a naturalistic feel but simultaneously transports the audience outside to a political event. As might be expected, the language moves from dialogue to political rhetoric and there is even the suggestion that much of it was taken from real women's suffrage events (Gale and Bush-Bailey 2012: 207). When the rally begins the play suddenly turns into a political agitprop piece, a form that dominated workers' theatre throughout the world, rejecting the linear illusions of naturalism in favour of slogans, declamatory statements and polemic. The setting of the scene in the 1907 version placed the speakers at the back of the stage facing out, while the onstage crowd listened (or otherwise) with their backs to the audience. This transformed the audience from passive spectator into active member of the crowd (Gale and Bush-Bailey 2012: 239). Often accused of hiding behind the proscenium, actually natural-ism constantly makes the transition into the auditorium through soliloquies, stage settings (as in this case) or simply by compelling its audience to look intently at a particular moment or event.

Miss Julie too breaks the naturalistic mould with two short scenes that are almost symbolist in design. Strindberg described them as being 'resting-places for the public and the actors, without letting the public escape from the illusion induced' (Strindberg 1992: xvii). The first, a self-proclaimed 'pantomime', focuses on Christine who continues to work in the kitchen while Julie and Jean go to dance at the party. In one way this scene could be described as almost hyper-naturalism, with Christine performing everyday tasks. Strindberg's stage directions cast further light:

> *She should not look in the direction of the spectators, and she should not hurry as if fearful that they might become impatient.*
>
> (1992: 5)

A conscious lack of actor–audience interaction and a commitment to authenticity – she *actually* washes the plate and *actually* curls her hair – slows theatrical time to the pace of everyday time; that is, time as understood on the stage, often necessarily quicker and more loaded with action, suddenly resem-bles the way we comprehend time outside the theatre walls – seconds, minutes, days. On the other hand, she picks up the handkerchief Julie has left behind and *'begins to stretch it, smooth it, fold it up and so forth'* (1992: 5). The handkerchief becomes a symbol of Julie's predicament; Christine manipulates it because she has no control over the actual situation. As in Shakespeare's *Othello*, there are many symbolic ways of reading a handkerchief. The second moment of inter-ruption places a group rather than an individual at its centre, with the wedding party entering to perform a dance and a song, leaving before the lead characters return. It momentarily fragments the linear narrative with celebratory choreog-raphy. When Julie and Jean return it is obvious that they have had sex and the naive ballet sequence becomes a poignant comment on innocence and infidelity.

Even in a form with such a strong sense of chronology and linear story-telling, there exist numerous exceptions, moments of interruption. In fact we might even claim that naturalism and symbolism are far less oppositional than we initially thought. Naturalism, in fact, relies heavily on symbols. As an example, the eponymous doll's house became an emblem for Ibsen, a symbol of repression, of the position of the childlike woman, of an inability to break free. And what about his 1881 play *Ghosts*? What are the ghosts? They are not real apparitions, even if such characters were possible in a naturalist play, associated as they are with a mythic intangibility; they are, rather, a symbolic nod to the past, to things that haunt, to inescapable fate and the lingering influence of a long-dead father. They pre-empt the future when Oswald gradually fades away, spectre-like under the sentence of his father's indiscretions.

The plays of J.B. Priestley provide another (later) example. Containing naturalistic dialogue, character and set, a play such as *Time and the Conways* (1937) nevertheless uses time as a symbol. The opening act is based in 1919, the middle act in 1937 and the final act back in 1919. This resembles, of course, how human beings actually perceive time; one minute we are engaged in rehearsals, the next we are thinking of this evening's dinner and the next a childhood experience. Our consciousness does not interact with the world in a linear fashion and *Time and the Conways* reflects this, despite its naturalistic conventions.

As Claude Schumacher suggests, 'it becomes obvious that naturalism and symbolism are as indissociable as the fingers on one's hand, and these age-old traditions (renewed by generation after generation) enrich each other in every successful work of art' (1996: 7). Robert Leach pushes this still further in *Makers of Modern Theatre*, which examines Stanislavsky alongside Meyerhold, Brecht and Artaud. He claims that 'the starting point is to be found in their understanding that the theatre is always symbolic. It assumes that everything that happens on stage *stands for* something else' (2004: 2). It is also interesting that our lead protagonists in the naturalist movement also wrote a number of plays that defy easy classification; before *A Doll's House* and *Ghosts*, Ibsen penned *Peer Gynt* (1876), a fragmented folktale which seems to have moments of graphic realism on the one hand and dreamlike imagination on the other. Strindberg is perhaps better known for his later plays *To Damascus* (1900) and *A Dream Play* (1902), which paved the way for expressionism with their dislocated narratives and focus on the unconscious. *Mrs Warren's Profession* (1893) is clearly a naturalist play, but Shaw also wrote *Man and Superman*, a peculiar 1903 work that combines naturalistic sequences, Friedrich Nietzsche's idea of the *Übermensch* ('superman') and a journey into hell. It is, therefore, very difficult to claim a playwright as a naturalist; artists change as careers develop and often the inherently creative aspect of art leads them down a range of (sometimes conflicting) avenues.

Naturalism was, then, a revolutionary movement. However, much of the modernist avant-garde rebelled against its conventions, rejecting both its commitment to mimetic realism (its characterisation, sense of place, authentic set design and costume) and its linear structure. The turn towards a more fragmented style can be seen in one of the most influential plays of the modernist avant-garde: Luigi Pirandello's *Six Characters in Search of an Author* (1921). This play is, in essence, a caricature of naturalism, a satirical jab at the conventions of linear realism. It takes place in a rehearsal which is interrupted by six Characters who have a story to tell but no author to tell it. They approach the Director in the hope that, through an improvisatory process, he might be able to present their story. However, it becomes evident that the narrative is simply impossible to stage, or at least impossible to stage in a naturalist sense. The Director feels compelled to add lines, to change the order of events and to include new scenes in order to turn the 'real' story into theatre. Whispers, by their nature heard by only a select group of people in real life, have to be louder for the audience's sake; names have to be changed. The search for truth, that central commitment of naturalism, is seen as an impossible task not only because there are too many truths to deal with but also because the truth (or, more accurately, *mimetic* truth – truth seen directly in a mirror as a full reflection of the image) is simply unstageable, particularly the shocking narrative of prostitution, incest and child death that the Characters present. The Father sums up the problem:

> What I actually mean is that your art is a kind of game, in which you try very hard to present – as the gentleman says – a perfect illusion of reality.
>
> (Pirandello 1922: act 3)

The Father here inadvertently suggests that the naturalist project is inherently flawed, as the nature of theatre means that the mirror held up to reality always distorts. The reflection will never be entirely accurate. Accordingly, for the later avant-garde practitioners, naturalism became an impossible project.

Six Characters in Search of an Author is overtly theatrical, drawing attention to itself as theatre rather than giving any illusion of real life. In doing so it becomes what Lionel Abel describes as 'metatheatre', plays that 'have truth in them, not because they convince us of real occurrences of existing persons, but because they show the reality of the dramatic imagination' (1969: 59). Citing Shakespeare's *Hamlet* as a model, the most obvious example of metatheatre, according to Abel, is the play-within-a-play trope. Pirandello employs this technique in his play, too, to break down any sense of illusion or coherence, not allowing his audience to forget that theatre is an artistic construct. The idea of metatheatre recurs frequently across the modernist avant-garde, appearing as overt references to rehearsals, narrative interruptions, actors playing multiple characters or directly addressing the audience, or using prologues to tell the whole story at the beginning. The modes of metatheatre enable practitioners to present theatre as constructed art and therefore prove useful for those seeking to challenge aesthetic conventions or address the audience for political reasons.

This is not the last time we will discover the techniques and ideas of naturalism and symbolism, even though the modernist avant-garde set itself up

largely as an attempt to destroy past traditions. These two movements represented transitional points, leading to the transformative experiments of later
years and continuing to influence today's performance traditions.

PRACTICAL EXPLORATION

In 'The Modern Theatre is Epic Theatre', Bertolt Brecht provides a useful
template for understanding the differences between dramatic and epic
theatre. His footnote confirms 'this table does not show absolute antitheses
but mere shifts of accent'; it is not that dramatic and epic are binary oppo-
sites but that they exist in a kind of chain of difference (Brecht 2001: 37).
Create a 'shifts of accent' table for your explorations through the modernist avant-garde, starting with naturalism and symbolism. This table can be
revisited often and revised or added to when necessary.

The manifesto form remains a fascinating, polemic, performative mode.
Write a new manifesto for a twenty-first-century theatre company of your
own creation. Consider the importance of defining aesthetics, engaging
with contemporary society in some way and creating a piece that inspires
the reader/hearer.

Read through Maeterlinck's *The Blind* or Yeats's *The Dreaming of the Bones*.
Explore a short extract in a workshop setting. How might you a) stage the
play, particularly given the lighting ideas detailed above, and b) act the play,
given Craig's concept of the *Übermarionette*?

Émile Zola confirmed that 'today the naturalistic thinkers are telling us that
the truth does not need clothing; it can walk naked' (Bentley 1979: 362).
Read one of the naturalistic plays mentioned above – what is the truth the
playwright is seeking to reveal?

Next take the play and look at a) narrative structure – what sort of story arc
does it create? – and b) stage directions – what kind of backdrop is required? It
often helps to draw a groundplan and imagine the way the scene might look.

Take a short extract from the play (perhaps the final scene of *Ghosts*, the
opening sequence of *Miss Julie* or the end of *Votes for Women*) and try acting
it out. Zola criticised 'theatre language', the stereotypical way of speaking
on stage. Instead he wanted actors to show characters with 'their individual
ways of thinking and expressing themselves' (Bentley 1979: 371). How
might this transform the way you act a scene?

Compare your experiences of workshopping the extracts. As an actor/director/designer, what are the primary differences or similarities between the ways you approach naturalism and symbolism?

Read *Six Characters in Search of an Author*. How does it differ from the other play extracts you have worked with during this chapter? In light of this play, what do you understand by the term 'metatheatre'? Can you think of some examples from your own experience?

CHAPTER 2

Performing Modernisms: Expressionism, Dada, Surrealism and Futurism

MOVING '-ISMS'

The avant-garde is often understood in terms of movements or '–isms': constructivism, cubism, fauvism, surrealism, suprematism etc. Sometimes the artistic communities performed under the banner of a particular movement. At other times critics position artists retrospectively. Occasionally we read artists as part of particular movements even though they actively resisted being categorised as such. These movement titles are useful; they enable us to approach artwork and performances with particular expectations and allow us to make some sense at least of their occasional impenetrability. However, they can also bring more confusion, forcing us to find defining characteristics or theatrical genealogies that simply do not exist. Again, the idea of 'movement' immediately compels us to take a performative stance; while I am conscious of stating the obvious, 'movement' is an action, bringing something into existence; when I kick a football I (perhaps) score a goal. Our reading of 'movement' benefits from Mike Sell's overarching idea: 'if the avant-garde is a "movement", it is a movement that goes in many different directions' (2011: 10). He connects two definitions of movement ('movement' as category and 'movement' as action) together to produce a term that means both simultaneously. By using 'movement' in this way we can also connect our theoretical framework to the modernist avant-garde's obsession with the moving body, a topic we will return to in Chapter 4.

If movement was a defining characteristic of the movements, then the borders between movements were far more permeable than might be expected; they merged into or subsumed one another or else acted as a precursor to new movements. Berghaus addresses this issue, confirming that 'we tend to under-estimate the osmosis and cross-currents between different avant-garde movements at the beginning of this century' (2000: 271). This is most certainly true. Dada and surrealism shared many similar characteristics and personnel; Russian and Italian futurists were well aware of one another; dada and futurism exhibited comparable contempt for established aesthetics and pursued an anti-art instead; futurism in Russia influenced constructivism, the latter indebted to the revolutionary intentions of the former. Do not be tempted to imagine that these movements existed in isolation with clearly defined identities and incontestable beginnings and ends.

The four we are focusing on here were particularly bewildering, all dominated by ideas of destruction: a noisy, savage process. Sometimes this destruction was dramatic, creating an overwhelming sense of nothingness. If art is the act of imaginative creation then it seems rather odd, even subversive, to discover movements that smash things to bits as a matter of course. Yet simultaneously they committed to a redefinition of art – a creative, inventive demarcation of new genres, methods and perspectives. Futurism, expressionism, dada and (read here in an uneasy conjunction with the latter) surrealism provide interesting examples of this movement-led avant-garde because they denote so many different experiments, political positions and artistic decisions. Two pieces designated 'expressionist', for example, might have had very different objectives and only faintly resemble one another. Dissension became one of the defining characteristics of avant-garde movements, and fallouts and disagreements plagued many of them.

Futurism was predominantly an Italian movement, though a fruitful Russian version existed too. The relationship between the Italian and Russian futurists proves difficult to discern, though the two groups were certainly in contact (Berghaus 2000: 75). In Italy the movement began in 1909 when Parisian newspaper *Le Figaro* published Italian poet F.T. Marinetti's *Futurist Manifesto*. This document represents one of the most fascinating examples of the manifesto form; frightening and challenging, it makes strong claims for potential future directions of humanity both artistically and socially. As might be expected from the title, futurism looked forward with disdain for the past, and a love of action, rapid movement and dynamism. The manifesto's declarations include the destruction of institutions such as museums, the 'beauty of speed', the glorification of war as a cleanser and a valorisation of railways, planes, shipyards and factories (Kolocotroni et al. 1998: 251). Futurism advocated not simply an artistic revolution but the entire restructuring of modern life. It also included the infamously misogynistic 'scorn for women'. Here Marinetti rejected the feminisation of society, leading fellow futurist Valentine de Saint-Point to write a manifesto-based response in 1912 entitled *Manifesto of Futurist Women*. In it she called on women to regain warrior instincts largely lost in the civilisation process:

WOMEN, TOO LONG CORRUPTED BY MORALS AND
CONVENTIONS, RETURN TO YOUR SUBLIME INSTINCT;
TO VIOLENCE AND TO CRUELTY.

(Rainey et al. 2009: 109)

Marinetti and Saint-Point rebelled against the same practice of taming human personality. They rejected society's civilising project and instead advocated a return to something more primeval and essential. Saint-Point also wrote the startling *Futurist Manifesto of Lust* (1913), encouraging visceral physical responses to one another rather than sentimental, moralistic relationships. Saint-Point even seemed to condone rape as a consequence of soldiers' victories in war (Danchev 2011: 39). By concluding with 'LUST IS A FORCE', Saint-Point connected lust with dramatic movement, untrammelled desire with speed (Danchev 2011: 42). For a movement that prided itself on a rejection of the past and a unilateral focus on the modern, there remained an almost oxymoronic preoccupation with discovering a lost primordial instinct.

None of these movements had a particularly strong showing in Britain, although there were certainly many examples of avant-garde performance moments, even if they did not form movements as such (see Warden 2012). Vorticism remains the one notable exception to this, a movement often associated with futurism, although the protagonists questioned the connection. Ezra Pound coined the term 'vorticism' and fellow poet and artist Wyndham Lewis wrote the manifesto, published in the movement's journal *BLAST* in 1914. The vorticist experiment lasted only a year or two as the pressures of the war took their toll. *BLAST* is an antagonistic piece of work, 'blessing' things such as ports, machinery, English humour and castor oil while 'blasting' the politeness of England, 'sentimental gallic gush' and sport (Lewis 1914: Manifesto 1). It both blasts and blesses England and France, its most fervent cursing reserved for emblems of bourgeois snobbery. Lewis challenged futurist ideas and, although futurism and vorticism have similarities, it must be remembered that he claimed 'AUTOMOBILISM (Marinetteism) bores us' (Lewis 1914: 'Long Live the Vortex'). Given vorticism's persistent antagonism it can be difficult to see what it actually advocated – a problem for many of the movements discussed in this book. Perhaps it can best be read through Lewis's proclamation: 'WE ONLY WANT THE WORLD TO LIVE, and to feel its crude energy flowing through us' (1914: 'Long Live the Vortex'). Dynamic antagonism towards bourgeois sensibilities and an iteration of action and vitality occupied the centre of this movement.

Since it was such a short-lived movement there was very little opportunity to explore the ideas of vorticism in performance, with a couple of notable exceptions, including Lewis's *Enemy of the Stars* published in *BLAST* alongside the manifesto (there was also a later, more theatrical 1932 version). It remains a fascinating, troubling piece of performative prose with two characters, Hanp and Arghol, but no real dialogue or directions. *Enemy of the Stars* is far less about story and narrative than action and linguistic revolution. It includes an underlying violence, culminating in a bloody fight between the two protagonists; this also affects the language, the dialogue resembling a linguistic battle. Unperformed until much later, it would prove an interesting challenge for contemporary practitioners.

In 1916, as futurism stuttered, its pro-war message tainted by the horrors of battle raging across Europe, dada appeared in Zurich, orchestrated by Hugo Ball and Tristan Tzara, alongside figures such as Richard Huelsenbeck and Emmy Hennings. Like the futurists, the dadaists constructed a number of manifestos; Tzara, Ball, Huelsenbeck and Francis Picabia all wrote antagonistic documents of intent. However, one could be forgiven for coming away from these manifestos feeling more confused than illuminated. Tzara's 1918 *Dada Manifesto* starts in an unpromising way – 'I won't explain myself because I hate common sense' (Tzara 1992: 14). In fact it is notoriously difficult to work out exactly what dada was, a problem embodied in the movement's very name, which remained undefined. It might be the French for 'hobby horse' but it might just as easily be an imitation of childish nonsense language. Even the use of the word 'movement' or terms such as 'artist' or 'artwork' seem strangely incongruous when exploring dada. It certainly exhibited a hostile approach to art (or at least established ideas of art), just as futurism did, with Tzara claiming, 'there is a great, destructive, negative work to be done. To sweep, to clean' (Tzara 1992: 12). However, it was not clear how dada might provide any answers. Instead the manifesto contains noisy proclamations such as this:

> Liberty: **DADA DADA DADA**; – the roar of contorted pains,
> the interweaving of contraries and of all contradictions, freaks and
> irrelevancies: LIFE.
>
> (Tzara 1992: 13)

After the war, dada moved from Zurich to Berlin and Paris, although versions appeared in a number of other European and American cities. In Paris the group was joined by André Breton and continued until the mid 1920s when it split, with Breton going on to form the surrealist movement.

It is customary to see dada and surrealism as inextricably linked, though incorrect to imagine that surrealism was simply a continuation of dada or that the two had the same impulse. Clearly Breton forms an obvious link between them and there were aesthetic similarities. Despite dada's obsession with destruction, the movement did exhibit a creative impulse. However, the dadaists had the onerous task of stripping away the past before they could for-mulate new art. The surrealists could reap the benefits of this; having already disposed of tradition and established techniques, they now had the freedom to forge new aesthetic pathways. In his 1924 *First Manifesto of Surrealism*, Breton explained the movement: 'I believe in the future resolution of these two states, dream and reality, which are seemingly so contradictory, into a kind of absolute reality, a *surreality*, if one may so speak' (Kolocotroni et al. 1998: 308). This manifesto retains the unusual (often nonsensical) perspec-tive of dada but is far more affirmative, presenting actual definitions of the movement. It focuses on the subjective, the unfathomable nature of the mind, but nevertheless commits to deciphering reality rather than wallowing in nothingness. In this way the intention is the same as the realists but with very different effect.

Expressionism retained an important place in German culture from the turn of the century to the rise of the Nazis. In the theatre, its earli-est manifestation is generally regarded as artist Oskar Kokoschka's 1909 *Murderer Hope of Womankind* (although plays by Wedekind and Strindberg most certainly provide earlier examples of an expressionist style, namely the former's 1891 *Spring Awakening* and the latter's 1898–1901 trilogy *To Damascus*). The movement paralleled a particularly traumatic period of German history, from the defeat of the First World War, through the ulti-mately flawed Weimar Republic to the rise of the Nazi party. It is no wonder then that expressionism was defined by fragmentation, brutal imagery and screaming (the *Schrei*). As well as addressing and presenting the local German context, the movement became intricately intertwined with the general anxieties of modern experience; as Richard Murphy suggests 'the harmoni-ous world has also vanished, along with the conventional orienting notions of time, space and causality' (1999: 20). By the mid 1930s the Nazis were decry-ing expressionism as decadent nonsense. In 1937 they even organised the Degenerate Art Exhibition, displaying expressionist paintings for visitors to mock. Fritz Kaiser's *Guide to the Degenerate Art Exhibition* clearly articulates the exhibition's intentions:

It wants, at the beginning of a new era for the German people, to give a general insight, by means of original documents, into the dreadful final chapter of the cultural degeneration of the last decades before the great turning process.

(Washton Long 1995: 308)

The curators split the artwork into sections, each given an explanation. The final group 'takes in the largest space of the exhibition and contains a cross-section through the abortions of all the "Isms"' (Washton Long 1995: 308).

This event only serves to show the perceived threat that these movements posed to authoritarian regimes.

While expressionism remained a predominantly Germanic movement, many practitioners (particularly playwrights) from across the world used a form of expressionism. It seemed to typify contemporary trends and worries. There arose a strong American expressionism (Sophie Treadwell, Eugene O'Neill, Elmer Rice), an Irish version in the later plays of Sean O'Casey (*The Silver Tassie* in 1927 and *The Star Turns Red* in 1940) and British examples in works such as Stephen Spender's *Trial of a Judge* (1938) or Ewan MacColl's *The Other Animals* (1945). Yet the connections between these manifestations of an expressionist sensibility seem nebulous. Certainly the American scene claimed independence, with O'Neill maintaining that *The Emperor Jones* and *The Hairy Ape* were written 'long before I had ever heard of Expressionism' (Walker 2005: 4). Hence, expressionism flowered in a number of locales without necessarily stemming from a single German root. This is one of the most interesting aspects of transnational modernism: artists were not necessarily in direct contact but, responding to similar desires, tensions and contexts (both sociopolitical and artistic), they created works that strongly resembled one another. Focusing on these figures might at first suggest that playwrights drove expressionism. This is most certainly not the case; expressionistic movements and acting styles became even more influential than the plays, reappearing in various guises throughout the modernist avant-garde and beyond. As we will see later, many choreographers and dancers are often associated with expressionism (as some are with dada), although the connection proves uneasy and not altogether clear.

All these movements appeared in a variety of artistic manifestations: paintings, sculpture, collage, prose, film and poetry, as well as live performance. Many of the movements were highly interdisciplinary so it is useful to examine the range of artwork associated with them. Paintings such as Giacomo Balla's *Dynamism of a Dog on a Leash* (1912) reveal the speed and movement of futurism while the Norwegian Edvard Munch's 1885 *The Scream* illustrates the pain and isolation of the expressionist figure. Sculptures by Jacob Epstein display a clear vorticist sense of the moving machine while Marcel Duchamp's infamous readymade, the 1917 *Fountain* (a signed urinal), visually reveals dada's contempt for established art and desire to destroy bourgeois notions of taste and artistic worth. There are vibrant poems by Vladimir Mayakovsky (Russian futurism) and Tristan Tzara (dada), and strange films such as the expressionistic *The Cabinet of Dr Caligari* (1920) and *Un Chien Andalou* (1929), a surrealist piece by Salvador Dalí and Luis Buñuel with a notorious eye-slicing scene. Given the mixed-media characteristics of these movements, it is useful to get a sense of these unfamiliar, fantastical worlds through the varied artwork that appeared.

MOVEMENTS IN PERFORMANCE: FUTURIST BOOING

Despite the 'antiperformative bias' that Harding and Rouse identify, all of these movements, to a greater or lesser extent, exhibited an interest in performance. Again, returning to our definitions of 'performative' in the Introduction, it is clear to see why movements committed to change and action might be interested in art forms (like theatre, dance and music) that have a sense of liveness and immediacy at their heart. Indeed, if we think again about Mike Sell's definition of the avant-garde as moving in many different directions, here are movements defined by movement, by the performances and actions of live bodies.

The futurists proclaimed performance as a necessary artistic mode:

> War, which is intensified Futurism, demands that we march and not that we moulder in libraries and reading rooms. **Hence we think that the only way that Italy can be influenced today is through the theatre.**
>
> (Rainey et al. 2009: 204)

The exciting live action of theatre could be an antidote to the art of staid institutions. As authors of this document, *The Futurist Synthetic Theater* (1915), Marinetti, Emilio Settimelli and Bruno Corra had a specific theatre in mind. This theatre was to be 'synthetic' (reducing situations to a few words or images), 'atechnical' (rejecting the restrictive techniques of the establishment stage), 'dynamic' and 'unreal' (Rainey et al. 2009: 204–7). Gone were the bourgeois-supported operas; in fact, as Berghaus documents, Marinetti and his futurist compatriots created scandal by interrupting establishment theatre performances with their own 'action theatre' events such as burning foreign flags and shouting antagonistic slogans (2005a: 97–8). Futurist plays, in contrast to opera, compressed many ideas or grand themes into short theatrical vignettes. They exhibited no compulsion to maintain logical structures or linear narratives, or create character or tell a story. Ideas could be simply combined together without necessarily relating to one another. This variety theatre-influenced form was dynamic and quick, moving rapidly between scenes, places and circumstances. With no need for illusion, artwork maintained its independence as artwork rather than trying to present recognisable drawing rooms or lifelike romantic relationships.

Futurist designers such as Enrico Prampolini simultaneously overhauled stage settings. In his essay *Futurist Stage Design*, Prampolini rejected painted scenery in favour of effective lighting, bringing a sense of moving dynamism to the stage. This forced actors to behave differently:

> *Gas-actors* rustling, hissing sharply, producing bizarre noises, will easily endow works with unprecedented interpretive meanings,

Figure 2 Enrico Prampolini, set design for Filippo Tommaso Marinetti's play *Cocktail*, 1927
© Yale University Library, Beinecke Digital Collections

express variegated emotive totalities far more efficiently that some celebrated actor.

(Rainey et al. 2009: 215)

In his description of 'Gas-actors', Prampolini connected the human figure directly with the performing space; his stage was full of vibrant colour and light created by combining fluorine with 'other gases and salts' leading to 'quivering and luminous forms (produced by electrical currents + colored gases)' (Rainey et al. 2009: 215). Subsequently, merging the actor with the playing space, 'the *gas-actor*, perhaps vanishing into the void, or perhaps multiplying himself, will reply by emitting a highly disagreeable odor and an equivocal hiss' (2009: 215).

The futurists also experimented with language, transforming it from a comprehensible system into a collection of unexpected noises and images. In their 1914 manifesto *Weights, Measures and Prices of Artistic Genius*, Corra and Settimelli claimed:

THE WORK OF ART IS SIMPLY AN ACCUMULATOR OF CEREBRAL ENERGY; CREATING A SYMPHONY OR POEM MEANS TAKING A CERTAIN NUMBER OF SOUNDS OR WORDS, WIPING THEM WITH INTELLECTUAL FORCES, AND STICKING THEM TOGETHER.

(Rainey et al. 2009: 186)

Connecting music and poetry so resolutely revealed the futurists' commitment to creating dynamically experimental and not necessarily logical language. Simply 'sticking them together' rather than considering sentence flow or structure meant that words became part of a creative, unpredictable aesthetic experiment. Marinetti played with this idea in creating his sound poems, describing them as 'words in freedom'.

And how might the audience respond to these productions? Marinetti and his co-writer Francesco Cangiullo suggested a 'theatre of surprise', a mode that shocked and astonished the audience. They suggested (as did other practitioners we will encounter on our journey) that artists impose their work on the audience, startling spectators and even causing them to feel uncomfortable or dissatisfied. In 1911 Marinetti wrote the imaginatively named manifesto *The Pleasure of Being Booed*, a meditation on the importance of unpopularity. Authors must 'despise its audience' rather than drawing them into a pleasurable story. His reasoning proves enlightening:

> Not everything booed is beautiful or new. But everything applauded immediately is certainly no better than the average intelligence and is therefore *something mediocre, dull, regurgitated or too well digested.*
>
> (Schumacher 1996: 42)

A provocatively new way of looking at theatre and a great encouragement to us all! However, such contempt for the audience should be tempered by Marinetti, Corra and Settimelli's claim that '**Through unbroken contact, create between us and the crowd a current of mutuality without solemnity, in order to instil in our audiences the dynamic vivacity of a new Futurist theatricality**' (Rainey et al. 2009: 209). The futurists simultaneously rejected a particular audience while embracing a different type of spectator who espoused the futurist vision.

Futurist plays are short and intense experiences, with few directions or assistance for a potential performer. Yet they are also exciting and quick. Two interesting Italian examples help to ground the manifesto proclamations in something more concrete. Umberto Boccioni's *Genius and Culture* (1916) is one of the longer examples and retains some semblance of story. The three characters (the Woman, the Critic and the Artist) enact a debate about the nature of art. The Critic presumes the Artist is mad, producing his art through hectic fever rather than quiet contemplation. He contrasts traditional ways of creating art, peacefully waiting for the Muse, with futurist methods: dynamic, active, frantic. When the Artist dies at the end, the Critic responds:

The Artist is really dead! Ah! I can breathe easy. I'll write a
monograph . . . Around 1915 a marvellous artist was flourishing
in Italy. Like all great gentlemen, he was 1 meter 68 in height.

(Rainey et al. 2009: 489)

The Critic remains unable to interact with the excitement of real artistic
creation and, instead, can only write a book about the artist that combines dull
dates with unimportant objective facts.

Our second example – Mina Della Pergola's 1917 *Fidelity* – consists of
two scenes. The first is a typical scene of a couple parting. In the second She
runs to her lover, Maestro, while He goes to his lover, Donnina. They receive
letters from each other apologising in romantic terms for their delay in returning. They both rip up the letters and go back to their respective lovers. This
is infidelity accelerated. In *The Pleasure of Being Booed*, Marinetti championed
theatrical originality and categorically denounced 'love affairs' (Schumacher
1996: 471). Pergola's play reimagines a relationship in futurist terms. It is
remarkably brief with no long character development or painful discussions
about who will get the book collection; the audience witness the affair and the
play abruptly ends. Its brevity shocks as it leads to a profoundly unnatural lack
of emotion. And yet the meaning remains clear. The title, *Fidelity*, seems an
unusual choice given that the play focuses on infidelity. Yet, in keeping with
the futurist dismissal of bourgeois constructs such as marriage and courtship,
the title becomes a satirical twist; these characters remain faithful to their
visceral instincts rather than society's expectations, rejecting marriage as 'the
intangible domain of the conjugal police' as Marinetti put it in a 1910 speech
to the Lyceum Club of London (Rainey et al. 2009: 72).

In Russia, Vladimir Mayakovsky dominated the futurist drama scene. In
1917 he co-authored (with David Burliuk, Alexei Kruchenykh and Velimir
Khlebnikov) an essay entitled *A Slap in the Face of Public Taste*, a piece that
by its very heading chimed with Marinetti's work of two years earlier. It
contains the proclamation, 'stand on the rock of "we" amidst the sea of boos
and outrage', a statement that once again pointed to the unpopular nature of
futurist art (Mayakovsky et al. 1917). But Mayakovsky's interest in futurist
aesthetics began some years earlier. He performed his first play (entitled, in
a remarkably narcissistic gesture, *Vladimir Mayakovsky*) in 1913. The play
resembles in all respects a one-man show despite the multiple characters.
It explores the recesses of the poet's mind and is described as a 'tragedy',
although it is far more comedic than tragic. The futurist characteristics of this
short play can be seen in his focus on the genius of the individual poet and
contempt for his audience, described as 'poor drudges!' (Mayakovsky 1995:
38). The play's setting resembles a futurist dream: 'a city with its spider web
of streets' (Mayakovsky 1995: 23). In the first performance, a collection of

Figure 3 The backdrop for Vladimir Mayakovsky's *Vladimir Mayakovsky. A Tragedy*, 1913, painted in cubo-futurist style by Iosif Shkolnik and Pavel Filonov © Northwestern University

rectangular boxes formed the city, yet the painted backdrop also suggested the sense of speed and dynamism that would be expected from a futurist performance, the buildings transformed as they are when you whizz past a landscape on train. The play, performed first at Luna Park Theatre in St Petersburg before touring, caused enormous confusion for the audience and was often booed or heckled. In both Russia and Italy, audiences seemed utterly perplexed and disturbed by the futurist performances.

MOVEMENTS IN PERFORMANCE: DADAIST AND SURREALIST VISIONS

Although 1916 marked a starting point for dada, the spirit of dada and the surreal appeared some years earlier in the Frenchman Alfred Jarry's *Ubu Roi* (1896), a scatological tale of the grotesque Pa Ubu which challenged bourgeois ideas of taste. Pa and Ma Ubu's usurpation of King Wenceslas, their murder of the population and their focus on riches clearly comment on the immorality of the powerful. However, their subjects also seem to be money-obsessed, unmoved by ideas of community. Despite its fantastical narrative, it is the play's rather frightening sense of the real that lingers. This was central to Jarry's intentions; he described the play as an 'exaggerating mirror' (1980: 83). Reminiscent of the naturalist project, Jarry wanted to show the audience to themselves. Yet he differentiated between *Ubu Roi* and, say, *A Doll's House* by focusing on the audience response. The audience, he suggested, missed Ibsen's brutal onslaught because 'the public are a mass – inert, obtuse, and passive – that . . . need to be shaken up from time to time' (1980: 84). For Jarry, naturalism allowed the audience to be far too comfortable. Evocative of Marinetti's *The Pleasure of Being Booed*, Jarry also questioned the appropriate audience response:

> But paid applause is a kind of stage direction for the audience;
> in a theatre which is really a theatre and where a play is being done
> which . . . etc, we believe, along with Monsieur Maeterlinck, that
> applause of silence is the only kind that counts.
>
> (1980: 90)

Clapping is a capitalist construct and therefore to be avoided, replaced by the oxymoronic silent applause. Despite Jarry's originality, then (and not wanting to make problematic connections), his project chimes with the naturalists and, in his mention of Maeterlinck, the symbolists.

As dada progressed, the chief instigator Tzara wrote a number of plays, including *The Gas Heart* (1921) and *Handkerchief of Stars* (1924). But, by and large, plays were superseded by performance in a more fluid, fragmented sense. This meant focusing on the actor's antics rather than falling back on predetermined text. In her book *Dada and Surrealist Performance*, Annabelle Melzer provides a useful description of the dada actor as an 'anti-actor':

> All craft is ignored. He uses his unskilled body and a spirit capable of spontaneous emanations, allows himself manifestoes and poems, some pots and bells, cardboard and paint, a chair or two and perhaps a bed sheet.
>
> (1994: 59)

There remained an anarchistic democracy to the dadaist movement, an overwhelming sense that either the performances meant nothing at all or else the audience were missing something.

Performance events juxtaposed a number of different elements, resembling variety theatre or, in dadaist parlance, cabaret. During these theatrical evenings, contributors performed in short bursts of fevered activity. Take, for example, the evening of 22 January 1920 at the Palais des Fête in Paris where the French art critic André Salmon presented a lecture entitled 'The Crisis of Change' which was interrupted by poems, songs, chanting people in masks and a blackboard painting by Breton, until eventually Tzara arrived on stage only to be drowned out by bell-ringers hiding secretly in the wings. The audience 'reacted with outrage: whistles, shouts of "Enough, enough" and insulting invectives' (Melzer 1994: 6).

These short performance fragments took many forms. Hugo Ball's 1916 *Karawane* was one such element, with the author/performer dressed in a cardboard suit with a tall, coned hat and large wings. *Karawane* was a *Verse ohne Worte* ('verse without words'), replacing logical sentences with strange noises resembling Marinetti's 'sound poems'. Both Ball's and Marinetti's poetic ensembles were emblematic of a larger avant-garde distrust of established language. We use words, by and large, in an attempt to make sense of the world, to explain circumstances and ideas in logical, coherent ways. Dada counteracted this with sounds, rhythms and voice effects. Listening to *Karawane* and Ball's other *Verse ohne Worte* remains a somewhat perplexing, even humorous experience. The works play with vowels: sometimes they are long, sometimes clipped and sometimes, as with his 1916 *Katzen und Pfauen* ('Cats and Peacocks') they resemble the noises of animals rather than humans. The works challenge logic and established ideas of art. They even exhibit an almost religious quality, echoing shamanistic incantations and bringing us back to Christopher Innes's contention that primitivism defined modernist avant-garde performance.

Following Ball, other dadaist figures also experimented with sounds and words. Kurt Schwitters, for example, constructed *Ursonate* (written between 1922 and 1932), one of the most fascinating and bewildering examples of the sound poem genre. Structured in four parts, it is simply a collection of sounds pronounced with German enunciation. Like any sonata, it returns to repeated phrases, often building to crescendo. The tone changes throughout, slowing down and speeding up, quietening to soft vowels before becoming louder and more dynamic, particularly with the successions of rolled 'r's.

Like these poems, Tzara's play *The Gas Heart* gave plenty of scope for unusual speech. It narrates an illogical story, anthropomorphising parts of the body; the ear, the nose, the mouth and so on are all characterised, able to speak and interact. In the opening directions, Tzara described it as the 'greatest three-act hoax of the century', once again deconstructing the nature of theatre and revealing contempt for an audience gullible enough to take it seriously (Cardullo and Knopf 2001: 272). To describe the conversation that ensues as 'dialogue' is inaccurate, for it is simply a collection of words and repetitive phrases. Recurring statements such as 'I'm killing myself Madelaine Madelaine' and 'The conversation is lagging, isn't it?' turn the play into a piece of unusual word music, the human body parts occasionally responding to each other as an echo and, at other times, pronouncing disconnected phrases. It concludes with Mouth mimicking a horse called Clytemnestra and the promise of a marriage with Eye. Logic, Aristotelian linearity and dramatic momentum rejected, *The Gas Heart* remains as perplexing for modern audiences as it was for our predecessors in the 1920s.

Like Ball's outfit for his poems, in the original production of *The Gas Heart* the characters wore cardboard costumes designed by Sonia Delaunay. They were similar to those designed a year later by Ivo Pannaggi and Vinicio Paladini for the 1922 *Futurist Mechanical Dance* in Rome which were also constructed out of cardboard and metallic paper (Rainey et al. 2009: 326). In *The Gas Heart* they proved restrictive, turning a play that certainly has scope for imaginative movement into a fairly static piece. The play also marked the birth of surrealism or at least the split between Tzara and Breton. The latter violently interrupted the performance, which led to fights and the arrival of the police (Berghaus 2005a: 166). Tzara was furious, Breton unrepentant and the two went their separate ways.

While it would be incorrect to state that surrealism was merely the next step in the dadaist project, the two were inextricably connected, not merely through personnel but also in terms of aesthetics. Although dada focused on the destruction of art history and its institutions, and it could be claimed that surrealism was more constructive and creative, it is too simplistic merely to presume that dada attacked art while surrealism developed new aesthetic methods; the strategies of both left behind interesting, challenging aesthetic experiments. Indeed, although dada meant nothing (or perhaps everything), it was paradoxically not without meaning, a contention Richard Huelsenbeck made clear in his *Memoirs of a Dada Drummer*:

> If the spirit of the personality and of the inner order is not accepted,
> then there will be no art. This is the deeper significance of dada and
> of all related thoughts. Dada's true goal is a revision in the face of the
> human ideal that makes all art a mere symbol.
>
> (1969: 88)

Yes, dada often felt like a childish game, but actually it also addressed the state of art in a capitalist society which had turned all art into a commodity: who owns it? how can we buy it? how can we create it quickly and cheaply? what is it worth? In this sense dada certainly had a political objective, a project surrealism built on.

The word 'surrealist' first appeared in a performance context in the introduction to Guillaume Apollinaire's play *The Breasts of Tiresias* (1917). Apollinaire's play tells the tale of Therese/Tiresias, who becomes a man, her breasts floating away. Her husband then gives birth to thousands of children (Benedikt and Wellwarth 1964: 56–62). This strange narrative can surprisingly be read alongside work by those stalwarts of British high modernism, T.S. Eliot and Virginia Woolf (in *The Waste Land* and *Orlando*, respectively), who also used the ancient Greek figure of Tiresias, the blind prophet of antiquity. Placing this character at its centre, Apollinaire created a play that not only displays the unusual images of surrealism, but also questions the stability of gender definitions, pre-empting the work of later gender theorists such as Judith Butler. A blind prophet proves an interesting, almost oxymoronic figure; he can see into the future but cannot see the everyday. Tiresias enjoys a unique perspective on the world; like many avant-garde practitioners he looks forward but also sees past or through the mundane everyday to truths that lie beneath, in the modernist case, howling factories, the commodification of people and the general untrammelled materialism of the modern world.

One figure associated with the surrealist movement (although difficult to unambiguously claim as a surrealist) was Antonin Artaud. His influential essay collection *The Theatre and its Double* (1938), his film scenario *The Seashell and the Clergyman* (1928) and his plays *A Spurt of Blood* (1925) and *Cenci* (1935) defined his central idea: the Theatre of Cruelty. This concept is regularly misunderstood as simply the creation of shocking theatre and has been used as a justification for many a dull performance of screaming curses and fake blood from the joke shop. Certainly Artaud's ideas remain shocking but they are far more nuanced than that. Artaud began *The Theatre and its Double* with a long, grim description of the plague. He then compared the conditions of plague times to the theatre, and here lies the crux of his argument. During periods of plague social order collapses entirely; there are no laws, no moral expectations, no sense of maintaining respectability. Unburied bodies lie in the streets and, knowing they will probably die anyway, people behave exactly as they wish. The structures of society turn to rubble revealing the underlying cruelty of human beings:

> If fundamental theatre is like the plague, this is not because it is contagious, but because like the plague it is revelation, urging forwards the exteriorization of a latent undercurrent of cruelty through which all the perversity of which the mind is capable, whether in a person or a nation becomes localized.
>
> (Artaud 2010: 20)

Artaud's theatre did not shock simply in order to make audiences feel uncomfortable or actors feel they are 'cutting edge'. Rather, just as the plague makes us see ourselves as we really are (even if that is a terrifying vision), theatre too should reveal truth rather than be content with established conventions. Clearly this stripped bare revelation of humanity will indeed be a shocking experience.

As with Ball's *Verse ohne Worte* and Marinetti's sound poems, Artaud similarly distrusted the logic of language. He advocated a theatre that relied less on dialogue than on the senses, connecting with emotions and feelings. Art should reveal a latent raw truth yet remember that 'obvious ideas, in theatre as in all else, are dead and finished' (2010: 28). His work exhibits a dream-like quality and a focus on the body (and the connected ideas of the erotic and death) rather than language. It may well be bloody, violent or disturbing but only because the Theatre of Cruelty breaks through established façades rather than because it is inherently so.

A Spurt of Blood is a provocative, challenging example of this mode. As might be expected, Artaud largely advocated a move away from written plays. However, he also developed new ways of constructing the text: 'The reduced role given to understanding leads to drastic curtailment of the script, while the active role given to dark poetic feeling necessitates tangible signs' (2010: 62). As with the symbolists, Artaud remained far less interested in what words *mean* that what words *do*. This approach is integral to *A Spurt of Blood*, the words only adding to the collection of images rather than bringing clarity to them. It is a short play with no real narrative, a cast of representative characters and an unusual, surprising, disturbing selection of images, including naked bodies, corpses, deflating breasts, scorpions and swelling vaginas. These unfamiliar (yet uncannily familiar) images connect Artaud's experiment to ideas of surrealism. However, it must be noted that he was actually expelled from the surrealists in 1926. While the surrealists dabbled with communism, Artaud remained resolutely independent, refusing to allow his art to be part of any political project (Leach 2004: 158). Such an ardent apolitical stance has led to accusations that he drew on fascist ideologies and aesthetics, claims upheld in a study by Kimberley Jannarone, *Artaud and his Doubles* (2010).

There are some practitioners who are notoriously difficult to define generically. In fact, avant-garde scholarship's obsession with movements often means that we can place practitioners amid artistic traditions that do not accurately reflect their body of work. One such figure is Gertrude Stein, an American poet who moved to Paris. The French capital became a centre for many women of the modernist avant-garde, including the novelist Djuna Barnes and the activist poet Nancy Cunard (Benstock 1987). Stein's theatre work is extraordinarily cryptic and troublesome to interpret. The vibrant yet perplexing images she created might place her as part of a symbolist tradition. Equally, her most famous performance script, the 1938 *Dr Faustus Lights the Light*, mixes dada sceptism about the machine, the surrealist unconscious and a futurist 'fascination with technology' (Bay-Cheng 2004: 22). In their *Theater of the Avant-Garde*, Bert Cardullo and Robert Knopf suggest that she represents an 'American Dada and Surrealism' (2001: 421–3). So for ease (and recognising that the fit is not a straightforward one), I will follow their lead and mention her in this dada and surrealism section. Stein's plays are rather awkward collections of images, often fantastical yet grounded in a sense of recognisable reality. They represent a fascinating contribution to our understanding of an American modernist avant-garde, particularly because, as Marc Robinson notes in his interrogation of traditional genealogies of American theatre, she 'shed the baggage that most playwrights haul about' (1997: 11). Certainly her plays reflect her scepticism about script, language, narrative and story, and it is for this reason that she can be placed alongside the dadaists or surrealists.

Useful for any potential playwright, Stein's notion of the landscape play maintains that any given landscape is constructed relationally. It is not active like a vehicle or a machine; instead its dynamism comes from the relationship between the sky, the fields, the hills. The landscape provides a visual description of Stein's playwrighting methods. With little real action her plays resemble a selection of interconnected images. Using a characteristic absence of grammar, she suggested 'a landscape does not move nothing really moves in a landscape but things are there, and I put into the plays the things that were there' (Cardullo and Knopf 2001: 463). In focusing on landscape, Stein's work can be read in parallel to simultaneous scientific work by figures such as Albert Einstein. Stein's plays, like Einstein's theory of relativity, deal with space and time, shifting focus from 'a plodding time-bound narrative to a spatial construct in which all components are equally interesting and the contemplation of the work is controlled by the spectator' (Aronson 2000: 29).

Stein's plays continue to provide perfect raw material for contemporary performance, combining obscure difficulty with an innate sense of theatrical freedom. In fact Sarah Bay-Cheng suggests that Stein is 'probably best considered as a kind of cultural prism through which the European avant-garde theater and film of the 1920s was filtered to become the American avant-garde of the 1960s' (2004: 118). Of all the figures we are studying, Stein represents one of the most enduringly influential. To choose just one example, her 1922 *Do Let Us Go Away* juxtaposes a variety of odd, unsettling images, making it increasingly difficult to ask the question 'what does it mean?' A short speech from one of the undefined characters, Maggie, illustrates the point:

> I will tell you about Eugenia. She moved the table and hopes to be married. I do not think so because I do not think she is attractive. There is not a family in which some do not embroider. It is a great industry.
>
> The wind
> There is wind every day. (Stein 1922: 219)

And yet, as with many poems or musical symphonies, beneath its obscurity appear recurring pronouncements on going and coming, staying and leaving, moving or keeping still: 'They are not going today', 'They came unexpectedly. They will not go away suddenly' (1922: 225). It ends with uncertainty:

> Jane: Jenny give me the keys. Oh yes. I am waiting.
> Nicholas: Follow me.
> The Lawyer: Stay to play
>
> The End
>
> Yes I have a brother.
> Sitting at a café. (1922: 226)

Do they go away? Do they stay? Are they unable to go or even unable to move? What are the keys for? Who says the final lines, uttered after the official end of the play? Does the café represent staying (e.g. sitting) or going (where is the café)? These and many other questions puzzle us. And yet Stein's conglomerations of images connect with the innovations of the symbolists, dadaists and surrealists in their poetical impenetrability.

We should not progress further without briefly considering the way that these two early twentieth-century movements – dada and surrealism – influenced mid-century plays. For there were a number of playwrights whose work can be read as part of a (albeit fragmented) genealogy. Their plays mark a transition from modernist to 'after modernist' or 'late modernist', though I would be loath to claim them as postmodernist as they clearly exhibit more of the qualities of the modernist canon than anything else. These include all those associated with Martin Esslin's idea of the Theatre of the Absurd. Plays such as Samuel Beckett's *Waiting for Godot* (1952) or *Endgame* (1957), Harold Pinter's *The Dumb Waiter* (1959) and Eugene Ionesco's *The Chairs* (1952) or *Rhinoceros* (1959) all continued the conventions of the dadaists and surrealists. Esslin claims that these later plays form an experimental theatre genealogy beginning with Jarry's *Ubu Roi* and moving through dadaist and surrealist experiments. The Theatre of the Absurd, he suggests, remains part of this tradition, differing most significantly in its reception: in Beckett, Ionesco and Pinter, 'for the first time this approach has met with a wide response from a broadly based public' (Esslin 1968: 388). The plays that Esslin presents under this banner all exhibit certain characteristics: a reliance on poetic imagery rather than accurate, objective pictures of reality, a preoccupation with questions rather than solutions, and a purposeful facing up to a world of uncertainty where the established systems of reason have collapsed. For Esslin, these plays represent the 'psychological reality expressed in images that are the outward projection of states of mind, fears, dreams, nightmares and conflicts within the personality of the author' (Esslin 1968: 405). Such a focus on the author when the Author (that is, any sense of God) has been purposefully rejected by the playwrights does seem rather odd and incongruous. Yet Esslin's analysis does point us towards one factor central to this current volume: the plays of Ionesco, Beckett and others can certainly be understood as a continuation of modernist ideas in the post-war epoch.

MOVEMENTS IN PERFORMANCE: EXPRESSIONIST SCREAMING

While language combusted into sounds and rhythms, in expressionism it erupted in cries of agony. *Der Schrei* ('the scream'), visually presented in Munch's painting, proved a recurring moment in expressionist drama as a declaration of personal pain, isolation and torment. Whereas futurism looked with hopeful expectation to a machine-filled, war-driven destiny, and dada and surrealism maintained a sense of humour, expressionism seemed rather bleak. At its centre appeared an isolated figure, routinely (though not universally) a man. While he often existed in a community or society, he stood apart from them, ostracised by his peers or detached through his own choice. This figure usually despaired over the state of the world or his own inabilities, hence the importance of the *Schrei* – an audible symbol of unresolved distress.

Expressionism was partly defined by the troublesome issue of human identity. If we can no longer truly know ourselves, if we have an innate irrational element in our brains, how can we make sense of the world around us? And what of the human self in the brutalising arenas of war or oppressive factories of industry? Psychologists of the period (for example, Freud and Jung) attempted to understand the human psyche while concurrently pointing to its ineffable unknowability, but expressionists rejected their scientific ruminations and search for logical answers while simultaneously commending this new focus on the extraordinary unpredictability of the mind. In focusing on identity, the expressionists also moved away from the objective materialism of naturalism towards a far more subjective view of the world. This complex personal perspective could not be understood or explained even by the most eminent of modern scientists. Richard Murphy describes this as rewriting 'the world as a construction of human consciousness, thereby liberating it from inherited values and perceptions' (1999: 65).

The expressionists' focus on dreams indicated this, whether it be dramatising the protagonists' dreams (initially seen in Strindberg's *The Dream Play* but recurring in plays such as Ernst Toller's 1919 *Transformation*) or structuring the entire narrative in dream sequences (Toller's 1921 *Masses Man*). The expressionists even followed the soul beyond death in plays such as Elmer Rice's naturalist-infused *The Adding Machine* (1923). Indeed, the expressionist playwright Paul Kornfeld coined the phrase 'drama of the soul'. He maintained that realistic acting could never fully express the human soul which was connected with heaven rather than earth (Styan 1981b: 5). The intangible elements of human identity became central to expressionist thinking, leading to the rejection of traditional methods of characterisation and a focus instead on the subjective, inner life. Expressionist performances, therefore, resembled the earlier experiments of the symbolists.

In later plays, expressionism's bleakness can be attributed to the horrors of the First World War, with scenes dominated by skeletons and body parts. They directly questioned the physical and psychological identity of the human and such enquiries became just as obvious in the way performers approached these plays. Berghaus describes the expressionist technique as a 'jerky and convulsive style of acting, with jolting movements, quivering gestures, and sudden thrusts of the head' (2005a: 65). The body exhibited a sense of the irrational. Tapping into the modernist interest in masks, expressionist actors also often painted their faces and bodies. While expressionist plays, unlike symbolist works, generally place an actor at the very centre, the imagery and movement styles constantly challenge conventional ways of understanding human physicality.

In his book *German Expressionist Theatre*, David Kuhns identifies three different expressionist acting styles: the *Schrei* (scream), the *Geist* (spiritual) and 'emblematic performance' acting, known elsewhere as the *Ich* (the I) (1997: 17). All three required different skills; the *Schrei* approach meant that actors had to control breathing and create a powerful vocal and physical performance. The *Schrei* might be just a momentary scream but it might also define an entire play, the whole performance enacted in a state of intense painful emotion. Whereas *Schrei* acting isolated the protagonist from the audience, *Geist* acting was far more collegiate, a 'communion, a sharing between actors and audience' (Kuhns 1997: 141). While *Schrei* acting exhibited an explosive power, *Geist* acting developed sensitivity to inner experience. Again, as in symbolism, these performances often had a mystical spirituality, affecting all aspects of the stage apparatus, from the way actors conducted themselves to the lighting and set design. 'Emblematic performance' differed considerably in that it 'curtailed ambiguity by reinforcing a single dominant issue' (Kuhns 1997: 173). This latter style was often seen in late expressionism when war and economic/political turmoil made the hazy imagery of the early expressionists, revelling in dreamlike states, almost untenable. All three methods not only show the great variations within the broader movement of expressionism but also provide uniquely challenging scenarios for the actor.

If expressionist acting styles differed considerably, the plays are equally diverse. Like many modernist avant-garde performance texts, they challenge the linearity of naturalism by presenting a fragmented narrative form, influenced by the idea of pictures hung on a wall or individual movements in a piece of music or by the Catholic notion of the Stations of the Cross. Drawing on the latter, these plays are often referred to as *Stationendrama*, moving the protagonist from one position to the next with each 'station' (scene) focusing, in some way, on pain and suffering. This religious element reappears frequently in expressionism, although, by and large, the means of redemption or salvation are not explicitly revealed. The playwrights usually adopted a poetic form, creating symbols and images rather than constructing recognisable dialogue, although sometimes almost naturalistic scenes would be juxtaposed with impenetrable symbolic vignettes. Structuring plays in this spiritual, metaphysical way led to extremely fragmented narratives where the focus was less upon plot resolution than the 'meaning embodied by the semiotically intensified tableau' (Murphy 1999: 175).

Differing from much of the modernist avant-garde, expressionism actually became a mainstream artistic movement with a high profile, particularly

Figure 4 Poster by Oskar Kokoschka advertising the première of his play *Murderer Hope of Womankind*, 1907, image in the public domain

in Germany. Three diverse examples give a sense of the movement: Oskar Kokoschka's *Murderer Hope of Womankind* (1907), Sophie Treadwell's *Machinal* (1928) and Ernst Toller's *Masses Man* (1919). The painter Kokoschka's 1907 play is often regarded as the earliest example of expressionist theatre. Without any sense of logic or coherence, *Murderer Hope of Womankind* resembles a collection of 'visionary explosions' (Sokel 1963: 11). It focuses on the relationship between a Man and a Woman. As the short play progresses, the action becomes more extreme: the Woman's dress is torn and she is branded by the Old Man. Subsequently the Woman cuts the Man with a knife, imprisoning him until the final scene when he rips open the cage, killing the warriors and maidens before departing in flames (Ritchie and Garten 1980: 29–32). Generically the play resembles a tragedy and yet, depending on performance methods, it proves difficult not to find its extreme emotion comedic. In its use of grotesque imagery (perhaps best illustrated by Kokoschka's own advertising poster for this production, which pictures the Woman with the flayed, bloodied body of the Man in the style of a *Pietà*, the recurring Christian image of the Virgin Mary cradling the dead Christ), it recalls moments in many other German expressionist plays, such as the bloody death of the Sister in Georg Kaiser's *The Protagonist* (1921). Murder became a central expressionist motif, either the death of the central protagonist (for example, the murder of the eponymous Judge in Stephen Spender's 1938 play) or murders committed by the central figure, such as the Son's killing of his Father in Walter Hasenclaver's 1916 *The Son* or Mr Zero's murder of his boss in Rice's *The Adding Machine*.

One of the intrinsic difficulties with *Murderer Hope of Womankind* remains its disturbing misogyny. The Woman is terrifying, a violent challenge to masculinity. The illustrations from the 1916 published version illustrate the troublesome sexual politics. The tattooed nude figures fight for pre-eminence, threatening each other with knives. In the final illustrations, the Man seems to have gained control, towering over the Woman, holding her in a violent position of subordination. Sophie Treadwell's *Machinal* is an altogether different play, although it also centres its action on a cage/prison (a recurring emblem throughout the modernist avant-garde but particularly in expressionist performances). Focusing again on the relationship between a man and a woman, what is especially interesting about this play is its connection with life outside the theatre. As a journalist, Treadwell took inspiration from the case of Ruth Snyder, accused of murdering her husband (Walker 2005: 212). In terms of thematic focus, then, Treadwell adopted a similar approach to Ibsen or Shaw; while displaying expressionistic characteristics, *Machinal* attempts to connect with real lived existence. The play suggests two primary potential critiques: the economic, analysing the inequalities of capitalism, and the feminist, focusing on the position of women in this economically driven society. In typical expressionist fashion, Treadwell wrote *Machinal* as a series of episodes, although it certainly promotes a more linear, sequential story than many other expressionist plays. In keeping with expressionist conventions, the play exhibits *Schrei* moments, for example at the end when the Young Woman, sentenced to death, is speaking with a Priest:

YOUNG WOMAN: *(her calm shattered)*. Father, Father!
Why was I born?

(Treadwell 2012: 79)

The Young Woman's struggles seem to be focused against her husband who selects a particular role for her to fulfil, but also her mother who is as implicated in the unequal gender hierarchy. The mother's detached pragmatism, encouraging the Young Woman to marry for economics, reveals the way that women potentially contribute to their own subjugation (Treadwell 2012: 17).

Two stills from the 1928 production exhibit these dual themes of economic and gender inequality. The first, an office scene, shows workers pinned behind imposing desks and the entrance of the boss, an omnipresent figure of power. The image clearly shows the hierarchy; all the workers are engaged in tasks, holding items in their hands whereas the boss merely stands as a spectator, powerful yet detached from physical labour (Walker 2005: 214). The second shows the Young Woman sitting in bed with her lover. Gone is the utilitarian office space, replaced by a quintessential romance scene

Figure 5 Zita Johann and Clark Gable in Sophie Treadwell's *Machinal*, 1928 © courtesy Billy Rose Performing Arts Collection, New York Public Library

(Walker 2005: 234). The dialogue of this episode adds to the change in tone; the repetitive numbers replaced by dreams about seashells and sung nursery rhymes (Treadwell 2012: 45–7). In 1993 *Machinal* was performed in Britain for the first time under its original title, with Fiona Shaw in the lead role, and it remains one of the most regularly performed plays of the modernist avant-garde canon due to its contemporary themes, gripping story and tremendous opportunity for female actors.

Ernst Toller's *Masses Man* also features a prison and an incarcerated woman. However, in this case her commitment to left-wing politics leads to her incarceration. Of all the expressionist playwrights, Toller was perhaps the most politically engaged, even participating in a failed attempt to set up a socialist state in Bavaria. Imprisoned for his involvement, doubtless this experience influenced *Masses Man*; though a fictional account, the play recalls the failure of the revolution and the pain of Toller's own detention. Even in his incarceration, Toller maintained his revolutionary stance:

Barbarism, moral and spiritual rottenness, lies, hypocrisy and profiteering are triumphant. But Socialism is not beaten. One can throw revolutionaries into prison. But the idea for which they fight – is that slain by such methods?

(1936: 179)

Toller's resoundingly inspirational calls from prison remind us of the power of theatre and the strong (though, of course, varied) convictions of many modernist avant-garde practitioners.

Sonia is the lead character in *Masses Man*, an unusual figure in German expressionism's male-dominated world. A socialist revolutionary, she is eventually imprisoned for her beliefs and shot. The piece is structured as a particularly fascinating fragmented collection of pictures, some of which are based around recognisable dialogue while others are imaginative flights, 'the visionary beyond of a dream' (Toller 2000: 131). Hans Strohbach designed the 1921 version as terrifying and oppressive, with cage bars and looming shadows. The lighting proved particularly innovative, suggesting a 'twilight of the soul by an elusive blending of the limelight rays' (Toller 2000: 190). This mixing of ethereal lights and severe architecture created a performance piece as arresting visually as it was politically. Sonia's dignified death comes after a conversation with the Nameless where she maintains 'Man in Masses must be freed,/ Community in Masses must be freed' (Toller 2000: 182). The innovation of the designs and the power of the poetic voice are all subsumed by the hopeful political message of this play.

These three plays represent a cross-section of expressionist theatre, giving some sense of the political, structural and thematic differences within the movement, while simultaneously providing intriguing challenges for us as practitioners in terms of set (all require a prison backdrop), acting style (how best to negotiate the changes in tone) and direction (maintaining rhythm and tempo).

TROUBLESOME POLITICS

These movements represent very different ways of creating art, yet all are emblematic of that fluid category, the 'modernist avant-garde'. Practitioners' intentions were also extremely diverse, spanning the entirety of the political spectrum. While many modernist avant-garde movements and practitioners stood resolutely on the political left, futurism is often associated with extreme right-wing politics, particularly Italian fascism. Marinetti became a keen supporter of Benito Mussolini and the latter, in turn, absorbed the futurist devotion to war and the machine into his own political project. And yet the relationship between futurism and fascism was never straightforward; fallouts and arguments occurred and, in 1926, the Italian police force even classified Marinetti as 'anti-fascist' (Berghaus 2000: 11). Clearly futurism was not inherently fascistic, a contention clarified by the Russian version of the movement, which supported the communist revolution. Mayakovsky, admired by the Party, became a strong advocate for a popular Bolshevik culture. Later he worked with Vsevolod Meyerhold, one of the major figures of Russian constructivism, a movement firmly associated with the Revolution. In Italy, futurism's valorisation of war, the machine and the celebration of violent revolution made it a precursor to the rise of fascism. In Russia, practitioners followed the opposite path. That such extremes came from the same movement (though in different geographical spaces) indicates the troublesome relationship between the modernist avant-garde and politics.

The politics of expressionism also retained a certain ambivalence. Rejected by the incoming Nazi party and denounced as decadent, it would be easy to associate this movement firmly with left-wing politics. Certainly figures such as Toller and the Irish socialist O'Casey strongly pronounced their left-wing views. But expressionism has also been described as apolitical, that is, lacking any distinct political leaning. Despite the Nazi rejection of it, expressionism has perversely even been associated with fascism. Indeed, Joseph Goebbels, the Nazi Minister for Propaganda, actually wrote expressionist plays. Like futurism, expressionism exhibited some of the primary interests and desires of both sides of the political divide.

And what of the political leanings of the dadaists and surrealists? Certainly the dadaist manifestation in Berlin was more political than its original renderings in Zurich, allying firmly with the left in the aftermath of a world war that left poverty and a power vacuum in its wake. Artistically it sought to destroy the foundations of bourgeois art, exhibiting an anarchistic approach – logic became the focus of its ire. This attack on material logic might well have been the reason for Tzara's disdain for Marxism (Berghaus 2005a: 158). Even then, dada's contempt for audiences aligns it with futurism. How could a movement so innately dismissive of its audience ever really connect with political movements that focused so completely on the people as a revolutionary force? Surrealism maintained the dada spirit of anarchism. In 1952 Breton reflected on the relationship between surrealism and anarchism in his *To the Lighthouse*: 'it was in the black mirror of anarchism that surrealism first recognized itself' (Graham 2009: 130). While Breton meditated on the lack of successful merging of surrealist and anarchist thought and the regrettable alliance of some of its members with Stalinist authoritarianism, he remained convinced that surrealism and anarchism shared similar objectives and concerns: freedom, challenge to accepted morality and establishment institutions, and generous solidarity.

In a period of wars, economic depression, class struggles and the rise of the dictator, political tension remained a defining factor of these decades. These tensions cannot be restricted to party politics or simplistic political spectrums; rather, movements (and individuals associated with those movements) demonstrated an extraordinary array of beliefs and convictions. In *The Invention of Politics in the European Avant-Garde* (2006), Sascha Bru and Gunther Martens suggest three ways that the avant-garde engaged with politics. First, some works were aesthetically political, challenging the conventions of art. Some dealt with politics as a theme, and finally some artworks aligned with particular ideas and vehemently advocated their political positions (Bru and Martens 2006: 11). In this light, politics seems a defining factor of the modernist avant-garde. In the next chapter we will examine the political context, exploring some of the exciting revolutionary theatre that appeared while constantly questioning straightforward understandings of the tricky relationship between politics and art.

PRACTICAL EXPLORATION

While this book is particularly interested in exploring modernist aesthetics through contemporary performance, it is useful to understand something of their context. There are a number of books that provide a helpful overview of twentieth-century history, including Routledge's edited introduction *International History of the Twentieth Century and Beyond*, A.J.P. Taylor's classic *The Origins of the Second World War* or J.A.S. Grenville's *A History of the World: from the 20th to the 21st Century*. There are many other volumes that focus on particular periods or events. The best way of discovering more about modernist culture is to explore the Modernist Journals Project or Ubuweb, both of which are committed to allowing greater access to original source material. It is also useful to contextualise modernist avant-garde performance within broader cultural genealogies. Reading introductions such as John Russell Brown's *The Oxford Illustrated History of Theatre* or Philip Zarrilli, Bruce McConachie and Gary Williams's *Theatre Histories* will provide some sense of how these movements relate to the history of theatre. As part of your ongoing enquiries explore some of these sources, asking yourself a) how does this provide a greater understanding of twentieth-century context and b) how might these aesthetic or sociopolitical histories impact upon the modernist avant-garde in performance?

Tristan Tzara understood poetry like this:

> *To make a Dadaist poem:*
> - *Take a newspaper.*
> - *Take a pair of scissors.*
> - *Choose an article as long as you are planning to make your poem.*
> - *Cut out the article.*
> - *Then cut out each of the words that make up this article and put them in a bag.*

- *Shake it gently.*
- *Then take out the scraps one after the other in the order in which they left the bag.*
- *Copy conscientiously.*
- *The poem will be like you.*

And here are you a writer, infinitely original and endowed with a sensibility that is charming though beyond the understanding of the vulgar.

Create your own poetry by following his instructions. How does this connect with the dada project?

During dadaist evenings at the Cabaret Voltaire, performers would read out manifestos. Turn to *Twenty-Three Manifestos of the Dada Movement* in Alex Danchev's edited collection *100 Artists' Manifestos* (or alternatively to Tzara's *Dadaist Manifesto* if it is more accessible) and choose a section to read aloud. Particularly consider the role and intention of the manifesto form as you perform it.

André Breton created a range of surrealist games, including 'Exquisite Corpse'. Take a sheet of paper in a group of four. The first person should draw a head and fold down the paper so the next person cannot see the drawing before passing it on. The second should draw the torso, the third the legs and the fourth the feet, repeating the process of folding the paper each time. Once everyone has drawn, the paper should be unfolded and the picture admired.

Breton also promoted the use of automatic writing. Sit with a sheet of paper in front of you and simply write or draw whatever comes into your head. He suggested this as a way into the subconscious mind. How might these two tasks relate to the surrealist project?

Read Samuel Beckett's *Endgame*. Perform a couple of pages from it and imagine how it might be a) staged and b) performed. Consider a potential back story: what has happened? Why are they together? Where are they? What is outside? Also interrogate it through Esslin's idea of Theatre of the Absurd. What is absurd about *Endgame*? Is it funny?

Artaud's ideas are as challenging as they are influential. It is well worth engaging more fully with *The Theatre and its Double*. As you read, note down any particularly striking ways of creating theatre. Take *A Spurt of*

Blood and examine how it relates to Artaud's broader project. This play is often deemed virtually unperformable. How might you perform it?

Read Wyndham Lewis's short play *Enemy of the Stars* (http://dl.lib.brown. edu/pdfs/1143209523824858.pdf) published in the 1914 *BLAST*. Is this a play? Why, or why not?

Given that futurist plays are short and dynamic, they provide a useful model to follow. Write your own futurist play based on the objectives of the movement and on the conventions displayed in the works mentioned above. Stage your new play.

Take a short section of an expressionist play (the three we focused on above are good examples, as are *The Star Turns Red* by Sean O'Casey, *The Hairy Ape* by Eugene O'Neill or *From Morn to Midnight* by Georg Kaiser) and explore it through performance. Focus particularly on the moments of heightened emotion and how these might be staged.

All these movements endeavour to make audiences feel uncomfortable in some way. Why might this be a unifying focus? How do you think the examples mentioned above might make an audience feel? How might we make audiences feel uncomfortable as we create theatre in its image (and why might this be desirable)?

CHAPTER 3

Politics and Performance

THE AVANT-GARDE AND POLITICS

In 1938, as fascism took hold in Europe and Stalin's purge trials sentenced many Russians to death, a conversation arose between two philosophers, Ernst Bloch and Georg Lukács. The dialogue, published in English translation in Fredric Jameson's collection *Aesthetics and Politics* (2007), focused on the importance of artistic form. Convinced of the vitality of avant-garde aesthetics, Bloch endorsed the significance and relevance of expressionism. By contrast, Lukács rejected expressionism as decadent, destroying art and confusing the general population with its obscurity: 'one needs a certain "knack" to see just what their game is' (Jameson 2007: 57). Instead, he plumped for realism, a mode that was certainly not naturalism (which, with its decidedly melancholic and often melodramatic feel, he rejected as part of modernist decadence) but nevertheless focused on real situations in a wholly objective way. Only then could art really engage with politics and the modern world. He cited the novelists Thomas Mann and Honoré de Balzac (ironically both of whom have been described as naturalists) as examples of the first stage of this realist project: critical realism. Lukács forcefully rejected avant-garde art, admiring the intentions of a limited number of avant-garde practitioners but, by and large, condemning them all outright as elitist. Bloch disagreed wholeheartedly. Connecting aesthetic experiment and political radicalism, Bloch maintained that expressionism 'undermined the schematic routines and academicism to which the "values of art" had been reduced' (Jameson 2007: 23). What better form than expressionism, thought Bloch, to challenge conventional (economically driven) ways of creating art and engage fully with the world in all its fragmented, complex intricacies?

The fierce argument between Bloch and Lukács points us towards an ongoing issue in the avant-garde. Can avant-garde art be political at all? Can

art that Lukács rejected as incomprehensibly baffling engage with everyday
political issues? The Marxist critic Raymond Williams attempts to decipher
the avant-garde's complex politics, discerning anarchism, nihilism and revolutionary socialism as being the strongest affiliations (1989). And yet, as mentioned in the previous chapter, some artists turned the opposite way towards
fascism and a number of others remained in the centre, rejecting the extremes.
This diversity in political opinion is one of the primary reasons why the mixed
term 'modernist avant-garde' can be so troublesome at times; what indeed do
Anglo-Catholic playwright T.S. Eliot and communist set designer Vsevolod
Meyerhold have in common when it comes to politics? Williams suggests that
the 'political ambiguities' appeared because of 'the commitment to a violent
break with the past' (1989: 58). As the history of European politics proves,
dramatic disruptions often lead to myriad political positions, as past hierarchies and systems are thrown out. With dramatic transformations it is always
difficult to predict resolutions, to guess which political direction such revolutionary tendencies might lead. The same is true in the theatre.

POLITICAL CHANGES

Some of the most dramatic political changes in history occurred in the early
decades of the twentieth century. In some countries these changes were significant but limited. In others, the entire political landscape was reshaped. Russia,
for example, witnessed the violent demonstrations of the 1905 Revolution, the
end of the monarchy, a new government and, from the October Revolution in
1917 onwards, the rise of a new communist state. Soviet communism began
with Lenin's hopeful fanfare and disintegrated into autocratic Stalinism as
the century progressed with the murder of millions, including many cultural
figures. In Germany the bitter defeat of the First World War led to the abdica-
tion of the Kaiser, the establishment of the Weimar Republic and, later, the
rise of Nazism. Beginning as an attempt to regain some of Germany's pride,
Nazism rose to prominence with a transformative, patriotic message. However,
it ended in defeat and the uncovering of the systematic annihilation of the death
camps. Many killed there were of Jewish descent, blamed as scapegoats for
the demise of the German nation. However, many others died in the camps,
including the disabled, homosexuals, other minority ethnicities and artists.
Fascism also became the prevailing political order in Spain, under Franco, after
a bloody civil war in 1936. In Italy Benito Mussolini led the fascist government
from 1923 until 1943. This proliferation of political extremes and the dangers
they posed to theatre practitioners meant that many artists moved to countries deemed safer and more democratic. Switzerland, the USA and Britain in
particular benefited from these artistic immigrants. France was governed by a

succession of republics but, due to its proximity to the fascist states, became increasingly dangerous as the Second World War began. It joined the Allies (at first Britain and the Commonwealth, and Poland, and, by 1941, the Soviet Union and the United States) in defeating the fascist expansion.

And what of the USA and Britain? Neither experienced dictatorship, and yet political changes did occur. Most significantly the USA entered two wars and significantly changed the fortunes of the Allied forces. As the century progressed the USA (for good or ill) became the twentieth-century super-power, beginning a project of interventionism (particularly in countries with oil reserves or where there was a perceived threat of communism), a foreign policy which continues to haunt current administrations. The greatest change in Britain occurred as its empire disintegrated. In the nineteenth century many European nations (including Belgium, Portugal, France, Germany and Italy) inordinately expanded their global borders, taking over areas in Africa, Australasia, South America and Asia, and drawing new (often entirely arbi-trary) national boundaries. Gradually these empires fractured as countries demanded independence. Nowhere was this change more significant than in Britain where an enormous empire gradually diminished until it became a col-lection of (mostly) independent nations.

Economics so often drives politics. This was particularly true of the nineteenth-century Industrial Revolution, engendering the rise of capitalism, a system where production was centralised, market forces dominated and profit became the prevailing concern. This meant a disproportionate growth in the urban population as people moved to the cities to find work. A popula-tion crammed together in poor housing while the smoke pollution from the factories whirled around them made for unsanitary conditions. However, these new cities also became spaces of learning, education and culture. The capitalist economic system rests on the establishment of two groups: those who own the means of production and those who do not, those who make profit and those who live a hand-to-mouth existence, their position dependent on supply and demand. Unsurprisingly, as the twentieth century progressed these two groups clashed. In Russia this led to the overthrow of the bourgeoisie (the middle classes) by the proletariat. In Britain it meant hunger marches from coalmines and factories to London, the seat of governmental power. In 1929 the entire system (temporarily) imploded, leading to the Wall Street Crash, an event that shook economic foundations across the world and meant that in many countries savings became virtually worthless overnight.

However, politics should not simply be seen in economic or party terms. The early decades of the twentieth century also witnessed tremendous changes in gender politics, with the advent of the suffragette movement and the grant-ing of the vote to women for the first time in many countries. Women rose to prominence still further during the world wars, when they were often relied upon to continue work while the men were away fighting. This movement of women into the workplace was an important change in the social order. Coupled with this, the First World War left a generation of young men dead or maimed, physically and/or psychologically. The effects of this war cannot be overstated; its devastation led to extremes in politics, in society with the rise of the 'lost generation' whose parties and decadent lifestyles F. Scott Fitzgerald so poignantly imagined in *The Great Gatsby*, and in sexual relationships which became more permissive, for a time. Furthermore, one of the defining events of the turn-of-the-century period occurred amid huge press interest at the Old Bailey in London in 1895: the trial of the Irish playwright and poet Oscar Wilde for gross indecency. Homosexuality was brought to public attention in the most dramatic of ways, paving the way for later changes in the law.

As imperial empires broke down, new countries appeared, subjugated peoples rose up and the power of ruling states started to diminish; subsequently, to borrow Bill Ashcroft, Gareth Griffiths and Helen Tiffin's phrase, the empire began to 'write back' using culture to explore issues of colonial and postcolonial identity. This posed particular challenges: should populations previously under colonial rule return to a pre-colonial identity (something which was often difficult to distinguish from the colonial situation) or should they adopt a modern, new identity? What of language or tribal customs or religion?

This necessarily brief general overview at least provides some context. Suffice to say, the first half of the twentieth century was a period of great sociopolitical upheaval across the world. While I have only really focused on Europe (and mostly western Europe) and North America, to a greater or lesser extent all modernist performance throughout the world came out of the spirit of crisis indicated by my brief historical overview above. As Michael Levenson suggests, 'the century had scarcely got used to its own name, before it learned the twentieth century would be the epoch of crisis, real and manufactured, physical and metaphysical, material and symbolic' (Levenson 1999: 4). The question for theatre makers was how best to engage with the political changes. How could art contribute, challenge, document and/or support?

In the Introduction we briefly looked at the challenge of presenting politics on the stage through the arguments of Theodor Adorno and Bertolt Brecht. The disagreement between them leaves us with many questions. Is it possible to really discuss politics on stage? Should art disconnect itself from politics? Are aesthetics more important than political didacticism? Are some artistic forms inherently political? Is it possible to create art that is not political? Should political art simply document events? Is it obliged to make engaged comments on these events or encourage audience members to contribute to political struggles outside the theatre walls? These are difficult, troubling questions and no doubt you will already have strong opinions. In the last chapter I argued that movements such as expressionism, futurism, dada and surrealism expressed particular (and varied) responses to context despite often appearing nonsensical. In this chapter we will discover a selection of overtly self-proclaimed political artworks and movements. Some are well known, some have been largely overlooked, but all provide models that might be useful for contemporary performance as well as illustrating the tremendous political (and subsequently artistic) turbulence of the early-to-mid twentieth century.

PERFORMING POLITICS: RALLIES, PAGEANTS AND MASS SPECTACLES

By 1934 Adolf Hitler had been Chancellor of Germany for a year but was still attempting to centralise power. Part of this project, the yearly Nuremberg rallies, brought Nazi supporters together in support of the Führer. The 1934 gathering was immortalised in Leni Riefenstahl's ambitious and aesthetically groundbreaking film *Triumph of the Will* (1935). The film captures the adulation of the crowd, attempting to present the Nazis as the popular party as well as uniting the nation under the swastika banner. The lines of SA (*Sturmabteilung*) soldiers and the iconography make for an impressive display. Riefenstahl also captures Hitler's closing speech, punctuated with images of various other high-profile Nazi figures sitting in the audience, panning back to provide pictures of the enormous, fervent crowd. The speech is noticeable for its performative qualities, which Riefenstahl ably transfers to film. Hitler begins with a dramatic pause as if preparing for a scene in the theatre. He leaves orchestrated gaps for clapping and cheers, and infuses his voice with forced emotion. The tone varies from quiet reflection to thunderous, motivational encouragement. His use of gesture is fascinating, employing both a vigorous pointed finger and gesticulations of unity (moving his hands to his heart or aping an embrace). The whole speech might be a rehearsed performance for the cinema or, indeed, the stage.

It might seem odd to focus on Hitler in a book about predominantly left-wing avant-garde art. I am certainly not claiming him as an avant-garde theatre practitioner. But his performance does create a precedent. As the twentieth century progressed, politicians across the political spectrum became far more concerned with the way their speeches were performed. With the advent of cinema and more accessible news outlets, politics became performative in the extreme. Here lies a precursor to the contemporary spin-laden political scene.

While politics took on a distinctly performative air, the reverse was also true: many theatrical performances might easily have been mistaken for political rallies. The early decades of the twentieth century witnessed an unprecedented number of large-scale pageants and mass celebrations that sat right on the tricky border between performance and rally, theatre and (for want of a better phrase) 'real life'. Nuremberg was not a unique event, although its methods of documentation mark it as particularly revolutionary. Large political events (whether in support of the prevailing governmental system or against it, and whether centrally organised happenings or spontaneous outbursts) reappeared time and again throughout the nineteenth and twentieth centuries. Some were fairly peaceful affairs; some were not, such as the 1819 Peterloo Massacre in Manchester (a city at the centre of much Marxist scholarship and debate), which led to running battles, eleven deaths and many injuries at the hands of the charging cavalry (O'Brien and Quinault 1993: 195). The infamous New York Astor Place Riots of 1849, for example, were 'part of a populist attempt to overthrow imported elitist arts, manners, and customs' (Aronson 2000: 11). Amazingly, this riot arose over performances of Shakespeare's *Macbeth* by English actor William MacCready at the exclusive Astor Place Opera House and, simultaneously, by American actor Edwin Forrest whose working-class supporters interrupted MacCready's performance, calling for egalitarian national art rather than elitist English imports. With twenty-two killed and over one hundred injured, this theatre-based confrontation had broader repercussions and intentions (Butsch 2008: 29). Some events, such as the 1848 European revolutions, changed the entire history of the world, despite their initial defeat. As Karl Marx put it in his *Eighteenth Brumaire of Louis Bonaparte*, in 1848 the concept of a social republic 'was drowned in the blood of the Paris proletariat, but it haunts the subsequent acts of the drama like a ghost' (1852: 60). His notably theatrical description points to the recurrent influence of mid nineteenth-century events over ensuing history.

The spirit of mass protest continued throughout the twentieth century, making its way from the street to the stage. Many of these built on a form with a long history, right back to the medieval Church: the pageant. Once again we have stumbled across a method that is not modernist at all, another movement that forces us to question modernism's proclamations of newness, innovation and experimentalism. In the modernist avant-garde the pageant found new impetus, inflected with the tumultuous politics of the period. Erika Fischer-Lichte describes this resurrected form as 'contradictory. From the very beginning, pageants combined a faith in progress with distinctive anti-modernist traits; they pledged creative innovation but enacted traditional civil and religious rituals' (Fischer-Lichte and Wihstutz 2013: 226). While significantly different in terms of intention and aesthetics, examples include Cicely Hamilton's 1910 *Pageant of Great Women*, performed at the Scala Theatre London by Edith Craig's (sister of Edward Gordon) feminist group the Pioneer Players; W.E.B. Dubois's *The Star of Ethiopia* (New York, 1913), which transported spectators back to a pre-slavery African landscape; and the 1933 *Romance of a People* performed at the Chicago World's Fair, a timely celebration of Jewish identity and a proclamation of 'America and the Jewish Nation as twin pillars of democracy' (Love 2011: 57). All these examples exhibited the primary characteristics of the pageant form: interdisciplinary performance, large casts, an extolling of particular people groups and a compelling sense of solidarity.

One of the most prominent pageants was the *Paterson Strike Pageant* performed in Madison Square Garden in New York in 1913. With 1,200 actual striking silk workers as actors, the pageant re-enacted the events surrounding their decision to strike, real life and theatrical performance merging with the express aim of drawing attention to the workers' plight while creating a performance that corresponded with Edward Gordon Craig's ideas of a simple, bare stage (Murphy 2005: 6). Avant-garde aesthetics and political necessity combined. Craig's ideas are not typically viewed as particularly political. However, the *Paterson Strike Pageant* provides an encouraging example for us; modernist avant-garde conventions can be used in a variety of settings for a variety of different purposes.

These pageants reflected an interest in mass performance that transcended usual political and geographical divides; large-scale performance events appeared across the world in a variety of different contexts. Of these, the most famous is Nikolai Evreinov's *The Storming of the Winter Palace* (1920), in which 6,000 actors, 500 musicians and 100,000 spectators gathered in the Winter Palace Square in Petrograd to celebrate and re-enact the events of the 1917 October Revolution. Like the pageants in America and Britain, *The Storming of the Winter Palace* combined modernist avant-garde aesthetics (namely constructivist staging, an idea we will return to later in this chapter) with a nod to established forms, in this case traditional Russian travelling players and folk tradition (Baer 1992: 74). In re-enacting an actual event, *The Storming of the Winter Palace*, like the *Paterson Strike Pageant*, also seemed to transcend art and resemble a journalistic enterprise; the relationship between the 'theatrical' and the 'real' became extremely complex. *The Storming of the Winter Palace* was clearly not a mimetic replay of the original events. One doubts that, amid the chaos of 1917, groups paused for choreographed choral singing or watched in awe as iconographic red stars blazed out from the palace windows. Accuracy was, of course, not the point of this event; rather, 'the need to elevate and embellish reality, to impart to it visual grandeur, over-powered everyone' (Rudnitsky 2000: 45). Political unity rather than factual authenticity drove the performance.

But while the Russians used mass performance to celebrate their communist revolution, nearly two decades later the fascist governments in Italy and Germany employed a very similar form. In Italy, 20,000 spectators watched *18BL* (Florence, 1934), a mass spectacle that gave the principal role to a truck (Schnapp 1996). Meanwhile in Germany, the Nazi government had responsibility for the Olympic Games in 1936; the opening ceremony represented one of the twentieth century's most impressive examples of the mass performance form, with dance, music, speeches and striking swastika iconography. This built on the growing *Thingspiele* tradition, performances presented outside that encouraged community (rather than any sense of the individual) through *Sprechchor* (declamatory singing) and dance (London 2000: 18–19). Despite coming from different political systems, these mass performance events proved strikingly similar, artistically and in intention.

But what, if anything, do these diverse performances have to say to us today as contemporary performers? Are they simply historical examples of interest? Well, this modernist tradition continues apace in the twenty-first century, most noticeably with events such as the opening ceremony for the London 2012 Olympic Games, a theatrical celebration extraordinaire orchestrated, interestingly, by film director Danny Boyle. They also teach us about the intricate relationship between politics and theatre in the modernist period, the two becoming almost inextricable in these ambitious mass performances. While it is unwise to claim all the above as avant-garde, the mass performance genre does enable us to examine the performance of politics and theatre's potential as a force to uphold or challenge prevailing systems.

PERFORMING (FOR) THE PEOPLE

In 1903 the French novelist and playwright Romain Rolland confronted a vital question, one that occupies (or at least should occupy) all performers: who is our performance for? Rolland came up with three requisites for what he termed 'the people's theatre': 1) it must be a recreation, giving pleasure to the spectator; 2) it must be a source of energy, leading to action; and 3) it must be a 'guiding light to the intelligence' (Krasner 2008: 62). Rolland points to three essentials for a people's theatre; all the practitioners in the subsequent discussion of workers' theatres confronted these issues as they sought to create a theatrical form and tradition that would engage with people perhaps unused to the trappings of the theatre.

During the early decades of the twentieth century, a range of practitioners and companies sought to narrate political issues (particularly those buried by hegemonic systems) and encourage spectators to be participators, to join the struggle outside the theatre doors. In retrospect, these performances are often not regarded as part of the modernist avant-garde. Partly this is due to their marginality – many were regional, playing to small, working-class audiences – and partly to their personnel, as many were organised by amateur groups rather than more prominent theatre practitioners. Furthermore some of these political theatre groups had, by their own admission, very little practical theatre experience, viewing theatre as a potent weapon in the class struggle rather than an artistic medium. This led to accusations that those involved were far more interested in the political message than the aesthetics, that events were more slogan-driven rants than theatre. While slogans were indeed popular and these performances may not have employed the conventions of bourgeois theatre (curtains, actors, sets, scripts, silent auditoria), they do represent a fascinating contribution to the modernist cultural scene. More than this, their passion, enthusiasm and flexibility remain infectious, meaning that they provide interesting source material for anyone working in political drama today.

Although these small political performances sprang up all over the world, it can be difficult to bring any sense of unity, mostly because of their localism. However, these performances all exhibited the primary characteristics of agitprop. 'Agitprop', an abbreviated term, brings together two important ideas: agitation and propaganda. That is, agitprop happenings educate an audience and incite them to action. It is a form of 'adaptability, immediacy, topicality' (Clark et al. 1979: 223), a flexible genre that can change daily depending on circumstances and utilise any available skills: dancing, acting, singing, playing music, writing sketches and giving speeches. Richard Bodek argues for its relevancy and functionality: 'Agitprop was more than theater, rather it was truth: the proletariat's feelings, thoughts, struggles, sorrows, and class consciousness were the core of its performance' (1997: 120). Hence, it reflects and responds to a specific audience. It also aims for truth, like so many of the movements and practitioners mentioned in this book. For the naturalists, 'truth' meant that compelling combination of real-life situation and human experience in context; for the expressionists, presenting 'truth' necessitated an exploration of the human mind, even if the world created necessarily became a collection of fragmented images. The agitprop groups argued that their 'truth' was the 'facts', the real objective story behind the hegemonic constructs; here were the actual events beneath the smiling spokespeople of the growing multinational conglomerates or the biased headlines of the mainstream press. Yet this newly discovered truth was not presented in purely objective terms. Rather, these groups retained an unambiguously polemical, didactic stance; facts and political argument, education and entertainment merged together.

These agitprop performers presented on plain, empty stages, designed to enable audiences to see and hear rather than suggest any illusory sense of place. Sometimes they performed outside, simply using the steps and pavements of the cities; modern industrial spaces transfigured into theatrical arenas. Other performers acted their sketches in spaces unused to theatre such as workingmen's clubs, village halls or factory floors. Rather than requiring working-class audiences to visit established theatre buildings, these flexible sketches could be taken to them. Costumes were basic, often simply the working clothes of the performers who usually had other full-time jobs or were suffering the poverty of unemployment.

These simple outfits provided the name for one of the most influential collections of these groups: the Blue Blouses. They had a presence in Germany and Russia, both countries with a strong agitprop scene. Using plain platform stages, these groups performed short sketches that were as effective outside as they were inside (Leach 1994: 172). This made the plays tremendously flexible. The sketches relied on the abilities of the human body, on voice projection and disciplined movements. Using limited props, the groups travelled from audience to audience (Bradby and McCormick 1978: 47). The 1925 Blue Blouse publication 'Simple Advice to Participants' made the groups' objectives clear; on the stage should be 'only things necessary for demonstration', performers should 'learn to work with industrial tempo, the march-parade, a definite beat' and the performance should be a construction of real life, not a mirror, influencing the 'brain of the spectator', 'preparing him for the perception of the new social condition' (Drain 1995: 181–2).

While agitprop gained most prominence in Germany and Russia, Britain also experienced a turn towards flexible, working-class performance. The Workers' Theatre Movement (WTM), a countrywide collection of regional groups, committed to present politics on stage in a way that would challenge and engage the working class. Established in the mid 1920s when smaller groups began to identify with one another, it realised, in the true spirit of a proletarian organisation, that in a larger, unified group, individual voices would be considerably louder. In the 1932 document *The Basis and Development of the WTM*, this collective sought to define their position as a weapon in the class struggle. For a time, agitprop became the primary method of presentation and this collaborative document points to the three benefits of this form: 1) its flexibility, 2) its use of the real experience of the worker-'actors' rather than compelling them to train in any traditional conservatoire sense and 3) the closeness of the audience which 'is of great value in making the worker audience feel that the players are part of them' (Samuel et al. 1985: 102).

The US also witnessed the growth of workers' theatre. As in Britain, the American groups did not simply copy the more established Russian or German versions but used a form of agitprop to focus on national and regional issues. However, we should resist simply lumping the British and American scenes together. As Stuart Cosgrove suggests, as a result of issues of ethnicity and race, they differed quite considerably, with Britain largely dominated by an indigenous white working class while America had disenfranchised black workers and a range of other ethnic groups (Samuel et al. 1985: 260). This meant that American workers' theatre often explored influences from other parts of the world.

The American and British agitprop groups adopted a similar style to the German and Russian versions, with slogans, short scenes, non-naturalistic structures and direct challenges to the audience. A piece like the *15-Minute Red Revue*, for example, presented by the Prolet Buehne in New York in 1932, is structured around rhythmic patterns, both in the disciplined, almost regimented movement style and in the way the dialogue and slogans should be spoken. It celebrates the Soviet Union and condemns the capitalist system. Given that Prolet Buehne presented this sketch in 1932, a year of horrendous famine in Russia, its politics are, in hindsight, problematic and naive. And yet it illustrates the unambiguous stance of much workers' theatre around the world in the period. A similar 'them and us' attitude appears in the British sketch *Meerut* from 1933, in which British workers are asked to ally with workers in India. Unity does not derive from national borders but, mirroring the final contentions of Karl Marx and Friedrich Engels in *The Communist Manifesto*, should exist between classes regardless of nationality; a British worker has a good deal more in common with an Indian worker than with his or her British employer. In both pieces the staging and performance style are important. In the 1930s, the *15-Minute Red Revue* played on a blank platform stage with a map of the Soviet Union as a backcloth. *Meerut* required a similarly plain space on which the performers used poles to symbolise a prison. Both were distinctly polemic, *Meerut* concluding with 'COMRADES – SMASH THE BARS!' and the *15-Minute Red Revue* with 'Therefore fight FOR THE SOVIET UNION!' (Samuel et al. 1985: 117 and 315). Performers spoke in their natural dialects and speech patterns, infused with the fervour that spontaneously arises when we speak passionately about our concerns.

This sort of argumentative didacticism remained even when these groups attempted script-based plays. In 1935, for example, the workers' theatres in New York collaborated with the professional company Group Theatre in a performance of Clifford Odets' *Waiting for Lefty*, a play about a New York taxi strike in February 1934. While it promotes more rounded characters and everyday dialogue, the playscript ends with the distinctly agitprop statement 'WE'RE STORMBIRDS OF THE WORKING CLASS. WORKERS OF THE WORLD . . . OUR BONES AND BLOOD!' (Samuel et al. 1985: 351). It also retains the familiar crowds of workers and, in the character of Harry Fatt, the typical representative of capitalism who was such an important reviled figure in earlier agitprop experiments. Harold Clurman reflected on the play's appeal:

> Deep laughter, hot assent, a kind of joyous fervor seemed to sweep the audience toward the stage. The actors no longer performed; they were being carried along as if by an exultancy of communication such as I have never witnessed in the theatre before. Audience and actors had become one.

> (1967: 138)

Agitprop groups appeared throughout the world, including China and Japan (Taxidou 2007: 200). Although many political theatre companies gradually moved away from the blunt hammer of agitprop, its structures, slogans and (particularly) its fervour remained. Very few workers' theatre scripts survive, mostly due to their inherently ephemeral nature – they changed nightly, they were not written down, they relied on improvisation. However, agit-prop's energetic movements, commitment to interdisciplinary performance and unencumbered dedication to educating and enthusing the working class still mark it as one of the most important and lively genres of the modernist avant-garde.

NEWSPAPERS ON THE STAGE

Another form, increasingly prominent in Germany and Russia, was the living newspaper. This theatrical method emerged from the agitprop tradition, maintaining the spirit of immediacy, flexibility and didacticism. Yet living newspapers often exhibit a more pronounced sense of theatricality, combining dialogue with slogans, rounded characters with stereotypes. Like any newspaper they contain a mixture of serious reportage and more trivial issues, focusing on both large-scale world events and the micronarratives of individuals. This form contributes to a vibrant history of documentary theatre, a style that continues to impact the contemporary theatre scene across the world. Again, this genre searches for a truth. Janelle Reinelt exposes the identity of this truth: 'The value of a document is predicated on a realist epistemology, but the experience of documentary is dependent on phenomenological engagement' (Forsyth and Megson 2009: 7). Certainly a document (and living newspapers use a range of documents as raw material for performance) can possess an innate sense of the truth and yet the way we read them or watch them or search through them relies on our own constructions of that truth. This is what Reinelt is suggesting in her description of 'realist epistemology' and 'phenomenological engagement'. However, as well as disseminating information, Derek Paget contends, living newspapers employ 'an operational concept of "pleasurable learning"' (Forsyth and Megson 2009: 228). This touches on a recurring issue for creators of politically engaged theatre: how can we make facts and documents into performances that might entertain an audience?

In Germany theatre groups toured round the country bringing their brand of inflammatory living newspaper to disparate communities. The playwright and doctor Friedrich Wolf saw the importance of connecting the theatre of the Weimar Republic with everyday experience and events; in his own words, 'every page of the newspaper, if read properly, daily contains tragedies that cry out for the stage' (Kaes et al. 1994: 542). Judging by the twenty-first-century explosion of documentary theatre, many contemporary practitioners concur with Wolf's assessment. Britain's living newspaper scene was particularly varied and interesting, with companies using a range of different modes, including the indigenous pantomime. Unity Theatre, an organisation with its origins in the WTM, had local companies in many major British cities including Glasgow, Bristol, Liverpool and London. Along with Joan Littlewood and Ewan MacColl's Theatre Workshop (or at least its Manchester-based earlier incarnations), Unity created some of the most innovative examples of the genre, plays such as the 1936 *Busmen* which examined the events of the busmen's strike. Theatre Union, a precursor to Theatre Workshop, produced pieces such as *Last Edition* (1940), taking the circumstances leading up to the Second World War (the rise of fascism, continued unemployment on the home front) and dramatising them through a fragmented newspaper-style format. *Busmen* and *Last Edition* represent two slightly different ways of constructing living newspapers. The former uses a fairly straightforward linear narrative, albeit with a collection of small vignettes which could successfully stand alone. *Last Edition*, on the other hand, focuses on a range of different issues and events without really seeking to connect them at all, except, of course, under the banner of working-class experience.

However, the most mature and established tradition of the living newspaper appeared not in Europe but in the USA. Still attempting to recover from the events of the 1929 Wall Street Crash, poverty and unemployment affected an enormous section of the American population. Artists experienced this economic downturn as acutely as any other sector. President Franklin Roosevelt committed to economic growth with the establishment of the New Deal project, a collection of initiatives that aimed to give relief to those in need and kick-start economic prosperity. The Federal Theatre Project (FTP) represented just one incarnation of this New Deal. Established in 1935, it proclaimed a twofold aim: 'the re-employment of theatre workers now on the relief rolls' and 'the establishment of theatres so vital to community life that they will continue to function after the program of the Federal Project is completed' (FTP 1935: 2). Orchestrated by Hallie Flanagan, one of the most prominent female contributors to modernist theatre, the FTP included groups from across America: from New York, Los Angeles, Chicago, Seattle and elsewhere (Flanagan 1936: 3–4).

The FTP produced many different types of performances – plays for young people, comedic entertainment, classics from Ibsen and Chekhov (among others) – as well as promoting the groundbreaking Negro Theatre. But it is perhaps best remembered for its living newspaper experiments, which Flanagan described as a 'terse, cinematic, hard hitting dramatic form' and, often, 'controversial' (1936: 8). The FTP performed a number of these plays, including *Triple A Plowed Under* (1936), *Power* (1937), *One Third of a Nation* (1938) and *Spirochete* (1939). Each play focused on a contemporary issue, from struggles in agriculture to the development of the electricity grid, from the

Figure 6 A photograph of masks from the end of *Power*, 1937 © New Deal Network

need for housing to the increase in sexually transmitted diseases. Bringing these innovative, challenging plays to the stage led to many experiments in design, including the projection of *Triple A Plowed Under* and the intricate housing block setting of *One Third of a Nation*, in which four large boxes contained separate scenes.

The extant playscripts provide useful renderings of the FTP's living newspaper form. *Power*, for example, narrated the struggle between a private company and a public enterprise for control over Seattle's electricity. It remains a typical issue in capitalist societies: should utilities be provided for monetary gain or for the not-for-profit advantage of the population? Written by Arthur Arent and first produced in New York in 1937, *Power* narrates an educative yet polemic account of this struggle, concluding with a scene in which all the contrasting voices are brought together: the Man on Street who wants reduced bills, the Stockholder demanding dividends, the Judges who can't agree. The finale uses a Loudspeaker voice, a common apparition in the living newspaper, and points to the importance of this decision: 'upon it will rest the social and economic welfare of the people of the Tennessee Valley' (Arent 1937: act 2, sc 6). While the play clearly has an ending, it is, again in typical living newspaper style, an undetermined one, with the final note confirming '*the foregoing finale is subject to change when the TVA issue is finally decided by the United States Supreme Court*' (Arent 1937: act 2, sc 6). Such an open-ended conclusion brings an innate dynamism to the play. In the New York version, the entire company, dressed in everyday wear, performed on a fairly sparse platform stage, enabling the actors to address the audience directly. However, it still nodded to many of the avant-garde techniques we have already examined. For example, rather than using actors for the Supreme Court judges, they were represented by nine masks in an almost symbolist or expressionist rendering (Arent 1937). Suddenly *Power* can be read alongside other avant-garde performances; as Derek Paget suggests, 'in its use of a wide vocabulary of technical devices, the Living Newspaper has obvious connections with the radical theatrical movements in Europe' (1990: 55).

CONSTRUCTIVIST REVOLUTIONS

While the American government established the FTP, a decade earlier the new Russian government had endorsed constructivism, an artistic movement that chimed with the intentions and values of the communist project. The designer and artist Alexander Rodchenko defined the movement in his 1922 *Manifesto of the Constructivist Group*, declaring an 'IRRECONCILABLE WAR AGAINST ART' and advocating a new art, reflecting the changes in society where 'everything throughout is being constructed of *lines and grids*' (Danchev 2011: 221). One need only look at Rodchenko's utopian graphic posters or Lyubov Popova's use of mixed textiles to get a strong sense of the movement. Constructivism valorised the machine (providing a connection with futurism which, it must be remembered, was far more left-wing in Russia than in Italy), geometrical shapes and dynamism, and promoted the role of art in the revolutionary state as at the service of the newly emancipated working class.

In fact, Popova provides our way into constructivist theatre as, in 1922, she provided the set for Vsevolod Meyerhold's version of Ferdnand Crommelynk's *The Magnanimous Cuckold*. Meyerhold had been a student of Stanislavsky but the two had fallen out (aesthetically if not personally) when the former challenged the latter's commitment to naturalist staging. However, despite the obvious differences, Meyerhold and Stanislavsky should not be seen as oppositional, for the two shared many concerns, most noticeably the need for actors to use their bodies effectively. Indeed, encouraging actors to perform physically in a convincing way provides a bridge between Stanislavsky and Meyerhold which we will come back to in the next chapter.

Rather than creating a mirror image of a room or a factory, Meyerhold's productions, while remaining wholly committed to examining the real on the stage and bringing 'to art your own vision of the world' (Gladkov 1997: 96), revelled in modern geometric shapes. The sets resembled the factories of the modern city or a playground for the newly emancipated worker to enjoy. *The Magnanimous Cuckold* provides a case in point. In her manifesto *On Organizing Anew*, designer Popova, like Rodchenko, rejected old ways of creating art. Instead she reduced her new art to an equation: '(Form + colour + texture + rhythm + material + etc) × ideology (the need to organize) = our art' (Danchev 2011: 197). Notably Popova focused on the elements of aesthetic production and the philosophical notion of solidarity in order to create constructivist art. The stage for *The Magnanimous Cuckold* comprised multiple platforms connected by stairs and slopes. Three wheel structures provided the backdrop with an additional stylised windmill stage right. Despite its overtly modern setting, it seemed rather an odd choice of play; *The Magnanimous Cuckold* is the peculiar tale of jealous Bruno and his beautiful wife Stella, whom he presumes to be unfaithful (Braun 1998: 180). It is hardly an earnest political play.

However, it reflects Meyerhold's interest in humour and entertainment; he admired the *commedia dell'arte* tradition and, as a student, was even a partner in a cabaret theatre known as Comedian's Rest (Leach 1993: 10). Some years before *The Magnanimous Cuckold*, Meyerhold had produced Aleksandr Blok's *The Fairground Booth* (1906), which resembled popular variety theatre with its 'audience involvement, riotous action, unashamed theatricality' (Pitches 2003: 17). He also admired American film actor Charlie Chaplin. Suffice to say, for Meyerhold, politics and political engagement did not negate the need to create entertaining, comedic theatre. Once again I hope to break through a commonly held misunderstanding that political theatre necessarily equals dry, shouted polemic.

Many other Russian theatre practitioners followed the constructivist lead. Constructivist-influenced productions included Alexander Tairov's version of Eugene O'Neill's *The Hairy Ape* (1926) and Evgeny Vakhtangov's 1922 *Princess Turandot*, not to mention Meyerhold's other productions such as *The Death of Tarelkin* (1922) and *The Earth in Turmoil* (1923). These productions represent different responses to the constructivist mission, despite the proliferation of geometric shapes, pillars and platforms. Indeed, not all artists who claimed to be constructivist saw eye to eye about their methods and approaches. Meyerhold cheekily retorted 'I would sooner agree to be St Basil's neighbor than Tairov's' (Gladkov 1997: 97), while Rodchenko rejected '"new" constructivists' who took the ideas and made 'junk' (Danchev 2011: 221). It would be true to say, however, that the theatre became one of the spaces where the constructivist project was best expressed. For on this geometric stage actors appeared, bringing a sense of movement and liveness to static space; we will come to this in the next chapter.

By 1933 the aesthetics of the worldwide workers' theatre movements were changing. Gone were the vibrant sloganising and powerful shouts for unity, replaced by less experimental (and arguably – though certainly not universally – far more dull) forms. The Soviet Union's growing disapproval of agitprop filtered down to many national workers' theatres. At a 1933 theatre competition in Russia, the British delegation was condemned for a perceived lack of aesthetic maturity (Stourac and McCreery 1986: 239). In 1939 the American government withdrew the FTP's funding, Flanagan's experiment undermined by politicians' concerns about its plays; they were too polemic, too revolutionary. Meyerhold's theatre closed in 1938 after Stalin committed to socialist realism rather than avant-garde art. Socialist realism maintained a strong linear narrative, focusing directly on everyday issues. It was unambiguous, patriotic, furthering the aims of those in power, defined by 'typicality, optimism and revolutionary romanticism' (Leach 2004: 22). Whereas naturalist realism may well have an unhappy, bleak finale (think of Ibsen's *Ghosts*), socialist realism had to end positively, for only then could revolutionary potential be realised.

Meyerhold's brand of constructivist, imaginative, anarchic avant-gardism simply did not fit into this model. In 1940 a Soviet-endorsed firing squad executed Meyerhold, who was accused of spying. Although their fates clearly differed, Flanagan and Meyerhold came up against a similar issue: when the government is involved in art, support depends entirely on the whims, fashions and intentions of those in power.

BERTOLT BRECHT AND EPIC THEATRE

German playwright Bertolt Brecht remains one of the best-known and most popular figures of twentieth-century political theatre. However, some might question mentioning him at all in a book about the modernist avant-garde. Certainly, although he admired the avant-garde's commitment to challenging established artistic methods, he was vocal against particular movements, referring to expressionism as aesthetically challenging but 'incapable of shedding light on the world as an object of human activity' (Brecht 2001: 132). This despite his youthful experiments with expressionist techniques in his 1923 *Baal*. But a chapter on early twentieth-century political theatre cannot entirely ignore Brecht's ideas even if, by necessity, we must deal with him all too briefly.

As with many other theatre practitioners and movements, it can be easy to jump to simplistic conclusions about Brecht's project. Perhaps you have incorrectly been told that Brecht did not want his audience to feel emotion or that he wanted to 'alienate' his audience. In supplying a brief overview of his project, I encourage you to return to Brecht's useful proclamations about his ideas with an open mind, endeavouring to break through misguided assumptions. Brecht created a theatrical mode that could connect with contemporary society and philosophy. He wanted a theatre that engaged his audience, not only with the play itself but also the issues the play identified in the hope that a night out at the theatre might actually change audience opinions. Epic theatre was the result of his enquiries. He advocated a theatre that forced his spectators to respond in a certain way, making the familiar unfamiliar, while compelling the audience to look (and that is *really* look) at the world again, as created by social forces engendered by humans. For Brecht, the world was not static; rather, it was constructed by human forces and consequently changed all the time. Seeking to avoid captivating his audience with intricate stories and compelling characters, Brecht rejected empathetic emotion, although engaged emotion (feeling angry about injustice, feeling furious at warmongering generals etc.) remained central to his aesthetic.

Form reflected the fragmented, ever-changing nature of the world. In Brecht's plays, songs or scene changes interrupt deaths and tragedies, forcing the audience to respond critically to the politics and not simply have a jolly night out at the theatre. Epic theatre constantly surprises its audience – there is 'nothing obvious in it' (Brecht 2001: 71) – while cutting through misconceptions or ignorance. However, for Brecht, this learning experience was enjoyable, in fact more enjoyable than attending a theatrical event that merely entertains. Reminding us of Derek Paget's later proclamations about the living newspaper cited above, Brecht wanted 'pleasurable learning, cheerful and militant learning' (2001: 73). Accordingly, Brecht's theatre used music, placards, direct audience address and ways of revealing the story before it occurred in order to prevent his audience from simply being drawn into the action. There was no need to cover up lighting apparatus or conceal the rehearsal process or dress the stage manager in black in a vain attempt to make him or her invisible: 'No attempt was made to put it [the audience] in a trance and give it the illusion of watching an ordinary unrehearsed event' (Brecht 2001: 136). Brecht's theatre maintained no illusion. In fact he dismissed illusory theatre, particularly when engaging with politics, for how can methods that 'make the audience see rats where there aren't any . . . really be all that suitable for disseminating the truth?' (2001: 142).

In enabling his audience to really analyse the material conditions of the world in his theatre, Brecht created the *Verfremdungs-Effekt*, often (perhaps unhelpfully) translated as 'alienation effect'. 'Alienation', of course, suggests pushing the audience away, separating spectators from the stage and each other. This was not Brecht's intention. Rather, he wanted to create an element of distance, preventing his audience from being swept along by emotion or story or character and enabling them to approach the play in a new way, in a more critical, more engaged, (paradoxically) more involved way.

Such a brief overview of Brecht's intentions would suggest that his ideas entirely rejected the premises of naturalism. This is certainly true. However (here we return to that thorny issue of realism), Brecht did seek to present the real on the stage. In fact he used the term 'realism', although he maintained 'before it can be applied we must spring-clean it' (2001: 108). Brecht's realism cut through the illusions of naturalism as, for Brecht, 'restoring the theatre's reality as theatre is now a precondition for any possibility of arriving at realistic images of human life' (2001: 219). Indeed, despite the profound differences in form, Brecht's plays, like those of the naturalists before them, focus on contemporary issues like war, social inequality and economic deprivation.

Although his fate was not as tragic as Meyerhold's, Brecht also suffered for creating his brand of socialist, engaged art. Fearful of the Nazis, he left Germany in 1933, eventually heading to America. However, in 1947 he was called to appear in front of the US Congressional House Committee on Unamerican Activities (HUAC). HUAC claimed that the American film industry had been infiltrated by communists and, at the opening salvos of the

Cold War, they determined to root them out. Freed and found to be a 'good witness', Brecht left for France the next day (Mumford 2009: 36).

Brecht's plays are among the most performed dramatic texts of the modernist avant-garde and many provide fascinating challenges for the contemporary performer. *Mother Courage and Her Children* (1939), for instance, exemplifies many of Brecht's foremost innovations. It discusses an important theme, particularly in the 1939 context: war. However, Brecht's focus on the Thirty Years War (1618–48) creates that important feeling of distance; Brecht did not intend to confront the contemporaneous threatened war (although of course this acts as an inescapable backdrop) but war in general, illustrating the universal truth that conflict devastates those lowest in society's hierarchy while making those in charge very rich and very powerful. Considering this serious message, it is initially surprising to find plenty of songs (some very funny) and humour. Part of Brecht's epic theatre project, this disturbs the linearity of the plot, thereby creating a narrative of interruptions. While subsequent audience reactions depend on staging choices, clearly the script leaves no time to be sad or to wallow in cathartic emotion. You are forced to examine the scene critically, as one would conduct a scientific experiment. A clear example can be seen in the transition from scene 6 to scene 7. At the end of scene 6 Mother Courage, a travelling saleswoman moving from regiment to regiment selling her wares, laments the scarring of her dumb daughter Kattrin, the death of one son (the oddly named Swiss Cheese) and the disappearance of the other (Eilif). The war has devastated her family and she concludes scene 6 with an appropriate and expected phrase: 'War be damned' (Brecht 2000: 59). However, scene 7 opens with the tagline 'Mother Courage at the peak of her business career' (telling the full story before events have unfolded is one of Brecht's other *Verfremdungs-Effekt* conventions) and her remarkable statement 'And war gives people a better deal' (2000: 59). Which of her proclamations does she believe? The answer is that it does not really matter; Brecht wants to present various opinions of war for our scientific analysis. The inconsistency in Mother Courage's reaction simply draws attention to two of these opinions in a memorable and intentionally disjointed way. Typical theatrical methods of constructing character and engendering pity in the audience disappear entirely in this timely (and still wholly relevant) play. The play has little in the way of conclusion, being structured in a cyclical pattern; Mother Courage's final speech ends 'Wherever life has not died out/ It staggers to its feet again' (2000: 88). One imagines that the whole play might simply start again from the beginning and, as audience members, we too are trapped in this cyclical structure. Only by challenging the system might we escape from the seeming inevitability of new destructive wars.

Throughout this chapter I have claimed that the relationship between politics and performance, always tensely reciprocal right back to the ancient

Greeks, was reworked, reimagined and problematised in the modernist avant-garde. Nowhere is this clearer than in Brecht's 1941 *The Resistible Rise of Arturo Ui*. The play looks satirically at the rise of the Nazi party, displacing (or distancing) the action to Chicago where mobs fight for control over the cauliflower industry. In scene 6 Ui (the wannabe dictator) employs an actor to teach him to perform; Ui is a poor speaker and an awkward physical presence. His actor-teacher performs in 'the classical manner', that is, with overtly theatrical gesture and flowery expression. What follows is Ui's hilarious re-learning of the art of standing, walking, sitting and speaking and, in Ui's words, creating 'the little man's image of his master' (Brecht 1998: 157). The scene concludes with the actor leading Ui in the reading of Mark Antony's famous speech from Shakespeare's *Julius Caesar* ('Friends, Romans, countrymen' etc.). Ui continues the speech by himself and suddenly the atmosphere changes from the slapstick humour of the acting lesson to the serious political challenge of the speech: 'ambition should be made of sterner stuff' (1998: 160). Before our eyes Ui transforms from a bumbling thug to a respectable statesman, performing his leadership role with all the theatrical gravitas of the ham actor who has taught him.

Whereas Brecht considered this play to be politically challenging, Theodor Adorno rejected it as a crass and ineffective piece of theatre, stating that 'for the sake of political commitment, political reality is trivialized' (Jameson 2007: 184–5). No doubt *The Resistible Rise of Arturo Ui* provides an admirable anti-Nazi message, but, for Adorno, the humour, the farcical focus on the cauliflower industry and the innate connections with the seductive 1920s gangster scene meant it could never be effective politics.

This chapter began with Hitler as a performer and the rally as a performance act and ends with an actor pretending to be a thinly veiled caricature of Hitler simultaneously pretending to learn how to be a dictator. As this cyclical structure reveals, politics and performance share a complex, interdependent relationship. But *The Resistible Rise of Arturo Ui* leaves us with difficult questions: can theatre be political? And if so what does political theatre look like? Raymond Williams resists reducing the complex relationship between avant-garde aesthetics and politics to an easy equation, preferring to conclude that the avant-garde 'has also been, in its own ways, a politics. It has continued to shock and to challenge' (Timms and Collier 1988: 319). Perhaps this is as definitive and conclusive as we can be.

PRACTICAL EXPLORATION

Get hold of a copy of a famous speech (Emmeline Pankhurst's 'Freedom or Death' speech from autumn 1913, Winston Churchill's 'Fight Them on the

Beaches' or Franklin D. Roosevelt's 1933 Commencement Speech). Within your group take it in turns to read a section. Imagine you are a) simply speaking it to a friend, b) presenting it before a large supportive crowd and c) presenting it before an angry, disgruntled crowd (the other members of the group can act as the crowd). What are the different tones, speech patterns and emphases that you need to employ?

Many agitprop performances were presented outside, forced to contend with the noisy background of the city. What difference might this make to your performance methods? Walk around your city or town looking for suitable performing spaces: what makes them suitable?

Take a look at the Workers' Theatre Movement's short sketch *Meerut* (www.wcml.org.uk/contents/international/india/meerut--the-workers-theatre-movement-play/). What are the defining characteristics of this play and how might you perform it?

The scripts of many FTP living newspaper productions are now in online archives. Read through some of the examples at http://memory.loc. gov/ammem/fedtp/fthome.html and consider the accompanying pictures. What effect might these works have had on a 1930s' American audience?

Take a recent newspaper story and create a short sketch that might successfully engage an audience. Consider the passion and political intensity of agitprop, and the mixed genre approach of many living newspapers.

Look through the images from Meyerhold's *The Magnanimous Cuckold* at http://max.mmlc.northwestern.edu/~mdenner/Drama/plays/constructivist/constructivist.html. What is the effect of these images? Design a groundplan for your agitprop piece that employs constructivist ideas. It might even be possible to put these into action.

Watch some recordings of the 1936 Munich Olympic Games opening ceremony (readily available on YouTube). What is your impression of this groundbreaking event? Using this as your starting point, why do you think practitioners from all sides of the political spectrum used the festival pageant form?

Take scene 6 from Brecht's *The Resistible Rise of Arturo Ui*. Perform it with friends, considering the way that Ui might change in response to the actor's advice. What is the tone of this scene? Is it funny or sinister? Or both?

Should governments fund theatrical performance or should they stay well out of it? Give justification for your decision.

CHAPTER 4

The Modernist Body

SPLITS, FRAGMENTS, DESTRUCTION AND FREEDOM: THE BODY EXPLODING

Let us start this chapter with a philosophical question, one that you can throw into late-night conversations in your university halls: what makes a human being human? Is it that I have a body and that this body is present in the world? Is it that I have a mind that can make sense of this world? Is it that I can reason or communicate or love or that I have ambitions? Are human beings defined by their ability to create, to make or to destroy? What if, as theorist Peggy Phelan has suggested 'the formation of the "I" cannot be witnessed by the "eye"', that is we imagine that we can understand selfhood by comprehending various facets of that selfhood' (1993: 5). Following Phelan's rather troubling yet strangely liberating assertion, what if the defining characteristics of humanity have become perplexingly unreliable and indistinct? What if the 'I' proves increasingly difficult to see with the 'eye'?

In her 2007 book *Modernism and Performance: From Jarry to Brecht*, Olga Taxidou reconnects the two concepts at the centre of this book: 'modernist' and 'avant-garde'. She focuses on the body in performance: 'as actor/philosopher/director, the modernist performer emerges as the privileged site on and through whom modernist experimentation takes form' (2007: 9). In so doing she not only traverses (and indeed lessens) the gap between 'modernist' and 'avant-garde' but also between 'text' and 'material', and between 'the word' and 'the body' (2007: 213). This body is not neutral but rather makes us consider issues of gender, race and the mechanisation of the world. As Colette Conroy asserts, 'the questions that are asked about theatre and the body, of theatre and bodies, then, become a central and absorbing guide to theatre-goers who intend to analyse the connections between the theatrical matter and the real lived cultural matter of their lives' (2010: 75). However odd, strange, disturbing or otherworldly a piece of theatre might be, if there is a body moving on the stage then audience members always have something familiar to identify with. Indeed sometimes the fact we all have bodies is our only point of connection.

So far we have seen the dramatic changes over the course of the twentieth century in perceptions of art, in the use of language, in the relationship between actor and audience, in the intentions and objectives of performance and in the multiplicity of voices (marginal and mainstream, revolutionary and reactionary). However, one of the most substantial developments was in the way scientists (and subsequently artists) perceived the human body. We might think back for a moment to Tzara's dada extravaganza *The Gas Heart* (1921), in which parts of the human body become characters. Marinetti, too, showed a keen interest in this fractured body, writing his 1915 play *Feet* in which '*the public sees only legs in action*', which ends with a 'man who is running away' and 'a foot that is kicking at him' (Cardullo and Knopf 2001: 199–200). The American e.e. cummings's 1927 play *Him* contains the recurring image of a picture with two holes through which heads appear, apparently detached from their respective bodies. Later in his career Samuel Beckett, whom we have discussed as the quintessential late modernist playwright, wrote *Not I* (1972), giving the central role to the Mouth. Beckett's *Endgame* (written some fifteen years earlier) also plays with the fragmented body, placing Nagg and Nell in bins so the audience only ever see their faces and hands. Tzara, Marinetti, cummings and Beckett shattered the human body, making it strangely unrecognisable and unreal by focusing on it in bits rather than as a whole. We identify the bits, of course, but disconnecting the hand or the mouth from the body as a whole makes these bits appear otherworldly.

If the body became an unfathomable object, the same was true for the human mind. Contemporary science had given artists licence to reimagine the mind not as a space of reason, nor as representative of an individual's spirituality, nor even as the central defining characteristic of individual identity. Rather, like the body, it split apart. Many plays illustrated this change, none more dramatically than the Russian Nikolai Evreinov's *Theatre of the Soul* (1915). Evreinov is, of course, better known for his post-Revolutionary recreation of the October Revolution, *The Storming of the Winter Palace*. Again, we are reminded not to unequivocally claim theatre practitioners as intrinsically symbolist or expressionist or part of the mass performance tradition. Often modernist practitioners embarked on creative journeys that took them in a variety of directions, much as our own studies and practices do today.

In this play the central character is split into three warring elements: the Rational, the Emotional and the Subliminal. Clearly this mirrors Freud's concepts of the Ego, the Id and the Superego. Acknowledging the way we subjectively create the world (and infusing the play with a rather disagreeable sense of male voyeurism), the play contains two concepts of the Wife and two concepts of the Dancer, female figures constructed entirely differently by the Rational and Emotional entities. For all its peculiar symbolist fuzziness, Evreinov's play actually represents a situation we find ourselves in every day as the rational and the emotional fight for pre-eminence, with the subliminal occasionally throwing in its unwanted contribution. In performance, translator Christopher St John (to be clear, she was actually a woman) described the set used by Edith Craig's Pioneer Players in their version of the play:

> Miss Edith Craig used queer and fascinating machinery, of the simplest kind, by which little was seen of the three entities of the soul beyond their faces appearing at different levels. The heart was represented by a glowing red space which appeared to pulsate owing to the effect of light.
>
> (Evreinov 1915)

Craig's production simultaneously split apart the mind and the body, compelling the audience to understand the physical and mental in a new, potentially frightening, way.

No longer was the body a straightforward container of this increasingly fragmented human soul (if it ever really was); the modern world caused the body to split apart, to suffer, to be an emblem of freedom or incarceration, joy or horror. Many aspects of contemporary society affected the body. Industry suppressed it, causing it to become a dislocated part of an economically driven machine. Industrial production was standardised by systems such as Fordism (named after Henry Ford, the car manufacturer) in which workers with little skill could do a simple repetitive task on an assembly line, thereby bringing down the cost of production and enabling the workers to buy the products they contributed to: capitalism at its most efficient! Politically the body could be both the site of freedom (as participator in a rally or strike) and a reminder of hierarchies and hegemonies (imprisoned or tortured). Often artists' bodies experienced both; practitioners such as Ernst Toller and Vsevolod Meyerhold protested or represented liberty and freedom before physically experiencing the effects of hegemonic forces, with Toller imprisoned for his role in a socialist uprising and Meyerhold murdered by Stalin's regime. Chaotic battlefields destroyed bodies, torturing them with gas or gunfire; extermination camps and gulags annihilated whole populations. Yet, simultaneously, people found a new sense of bodily freedom in dance halls and in the early manifestations of a sexual revolution that would later smash through societal expectations during the 1960s.

Of course it is extremely important to note that men's and women's bodies are ingrained with different political symbolism; this was as true during the early years of the twentieth century as it is today. As we saw when we looked at Robins, Ibsen and Strindberg in Chapter 1, the 'woman question' preoccupied many theatre makers. This focus on woman's experience was not the sole province of naturalist playwrights but reappeared in the work of groups such as Edith Craig's Pioneer Players or the important acting roles taken by Zinaida Raikh and Helene Weigel (in Meyerhold's and Brecht's theatre, respectively). As Taxidou confirms, 'naturalism's interest in the "woman question" on a thematic level is matched by the broader formal experiments in representing the female body' (2007: 56). Women's bodies in the modernist avant-garde were ambivalent, at times challenging patriarchal hegemony, at times disturbingly suppressed by male dramatists, playwrights, directors and actors. In her study of recent performance art, *The Explicit Body in Performance*, Rebecca Schneider contends that the origins of the later 'explicit body' lie in the historical avant-garde (1997: 2). In contemporary performance the woman's body becomes a complex, fractured place of sexual exploration and political suppression/freedom. But important changes in the perception of women's bodies can be seen throughout the modernist avant-garde; as Linda Nochlin persuasively claims, the 'body-in-pieces' (her term) is inextricably linked with modernity:

> On the one hand, the bodily fragment – female – may function as a sign of the marvellous in Surrealist production . . . on the other hand, reassembled in the form of horrific photographs of mutilated dolls, female body parts may serve as the site of transgressive questioning of both sexuality and the body as a unified entity.
>
> (2001: 53)

Presented as particularly ambivalent, images of the woman's body in modernist art oscillated between fragmented horror and sexualised availability, between submissive domesticity and threatening defiance.

In addition, race and ethnicity (the former an often unsatisfactory method of defining certain groups based largely on biological differences or perceived differences, the latter a way of understanding the cultural characteristics of certain people groups) add another vital element to our study of the body. Like the female body, the body of the colonised or postcolonised individual is inscribed with an intrinsic sense of 'Otherness'. As the postcolonial critic Frantz Fanon put it, 'in the white world the man of color encounters difficulties in the development of his bodily schema. Consciousness of the body is solely a negating activity' (Ashcroft et al. 2006: 291). Fanon suggests here that post/colonial people are defined as 'Other' because, in a Western, Caucasian-centred world, they simply look different. It is their bodies that demarcate their Otherness and therefore these bodies necessarily become important political interventions.

Many historical grand narratives suggest a profound distinction between the body and the mind/soul/inner being. Much religion and philosophy have followed this route, 'the body as a sort of envelope for those aspects of the self that are specific or unique to the individual and cannot be touched' (Conroy 2010: 19). The modernist avant-garde responded to established understandings of the body in myriad ways, from inscribing it with political hierarchies to emancipating it through symbolist spiritualism, from blowing it to bits to reconnecting it firmly with the mind. Consequently, at all stages in this chapter we will find many moments of inspiration for contemporary performance, moments which will cause us to experiment, physically explore concepts and reassess the presence of the body on the stage.

THE POLITICAL BODY

When Meyerhold and Popova devised the constructivist stage for *The Magnanimous Cuckold* (1922), its innovative collection of ramps, stairs, plat-forms and wheels posed a potential performance problem. How should an actor act on this stage? Meyerhold's solution, biomechanics, came directly from the scientific advancements of the nineteenth and twentieth centuries, taking influences from both psychological research and modern industrial work patterns such as Taylorism (named after Frederick Winslow Taylor who, like Ford, searched for a means of production in which each worker would perform a repetitive task as if part of a machine). From the former he reimagined the idea of the reflex, the sense that our body reacts before we have fully formulated the reason. Psychologist William James described this process as 'I saw a bear, I ran, I was scared'; we might consider it as catching that teacup before it smashes to the floor or the involuntary movement of the leg when the doctor hits your knee with a surgical hammer. Neither action has anything to do with reason or logical thought; your body simply moves. With a degree of irony, new capitalist means of production also inspired the biomechanical system. As the industrial revolution progressed, owners of industry sought new ways of increasing profit. In doing so, factories adopted new methods whereby workers would simply perform single movements on a production line. Although this meant that the workers could not own the even-tual object in the same way as they had when they were farmers or weavers or blacksmiths, it did mean that they did not perform unnecessary movements, creating a more efficient process. While it might seem rather odd that a com-munist practitioner intent on mirroring the emancipation of the proletariat on his stage would turn to a system that repressed the workers' bodies, this sense of efficiency was key to Meyerhold's biomechanics: 'the human body was per-ceived as a machine' (Rudnitsky 2000: 93).

All this focus on the physical body and its unreasoned reflexes has led to misunderstandings about Meyerhold's intentions. Indeed, if one focuses solely on Meyerhold's interest in reflex and bodily efficiency, it can be easy to

Figure 7 William Rousey and Oksana Petrova demonstrate biomechanics, Moscow © 2014
        Performance Prompt

presume that he was uninterested in the mind. Certainly his theories rebelled against the Stanislavskian notion that actors had to use 'emotion memory' in order to perform even while both Russian practitioners advocated new freeing ways of using the body. Actually, as a practitioner of the Revolution, Meyerhold also wanted his audience and actors to realise the intellectual and emotional implications of the new Bolshevik state:

> Training! Training! Training! But if it's the kind of training which exercises only the body and not the mind, then No, thank you! I have no use for actors who know how to move but cannot think.
>
> (Gladkov 1997: 104)

Consequently, he (like his collaborator Popova in her manifesto *On Organizing Anew*) designed an equation – $N = A_1 + A_2$ – where 'the actor (N) was able to understand what he had to do (A_1) and had the physical capacity to do it (A_2)' (Leach 2004: 81). Rather than embodying and empathising with the character, Meyerhold compelled his actors to consider the political implications of their art and ideas, and then present them on the stage rather than merely mimicking pre-ordained moves.

He realised his equation through intense training using gymnastics and acrobatics and a selection of individual movements that required balance, fitness and control. These movements could be put together to produce the dactyl, a set exercise that began or ended a movement sequence, and the étude, a small theatrical scene. Some of the most famous études include Shooting the Bow and Throwing the Stone. Some are solo but many involve working closely with a partner, an important aspect of a biomechanical system that encouraged solidarity and community rather than individuality – that much vilified characteristic of bourgeois society. These études are as much about rhythm and flow as they are about the poses, and performers attempting these movements have much to consider that photographs and drawings cannot illustrate. Jonathan Pitches not only provides one of the best descriptions of the études but also a useful list of the basic skills required in order to successfully execute them: precision (performing with accuracy), balance, coordination (with all the muscles working at the same time), efficiency, rhythm, expressiveness (a 'heightened theatricality'), responsiveness (between a pair of performers), playfulness and discipline (Pitches 2003: 142–4).

The final two ideas may appear contradictory but, although Meyerhold's methods were based on scientific and industrial models, they also connected back to what James Symons refers to as 'man's primordial joie de vivre' (1971: 200). Meyerhold's historical perspective chimed with the projects of many modernist practitioners whose 'new' theatre looked suspiciously like reworkings of 'old' theatre. For Meyerhold, this meant looking back to performance conventions that revelled in the exuberance of movement and comedic performance, traditions such as *commedia dell'arte* and the fairground. Once again, this differentiated his productions from those at the Moscow Art Theatre; neither *commedia dell'arte* with its stock characters and *lazzi* (stage tricks) or the fairground with its clowning bear any resemblance to Stanislavsky's sense of character creation. Meyerhold infused his movements with an innate sense of joy and opportunities to explore the abilities of the newly emancipated body in post-Revolutionary Russia. He maintained 'it's essential that the actor find pleasure for himself in executing a given movement or action pattern. If you find pleasure, then everything will work out. Victory awaits you' (Gladkov 1997: 103). 'Victory' here may well be artistic but it surely also reflects the political triumph of the Bolsheviks.

Understanding these biomechanical movements in performance is tricky, so let us return to *The Magnanimous Cuckold* and examine the way Meyerhold's actors worked in Popova's set. Bruno, the jealous anti-hero, enacted his overblown monologues with grand, almost ridiculous gesture. However, his fellow actors performed acrobatic feats, combining them with burping when Bruno's speeches became particularly grandiloquent (Braun 1998: 183). The dextrous, comedic performers made Bruno (and his jealousy) seem ridiculous in comparison. Before they ran away, Bruno's wife Stella leapt spectacularly on to the cowherd's shoulders (Leach 2004: 90). The actors responded to the innate energy of the set, simultaneously transforming the structure into a kinetic space: 'in performance, action and construction were inseparable' (Baer 1992: 145). The centrality of movement in *The Magnanimous Cuckold* was exemplified in Popova's costumes of a shirt and jodhpurs for the men and three-quarter-length skirts for the women, 'intended to enhance the human form' rather than provide any sense of individual characterisation (Leach 1993: 108). Not only did the costumes resemble factory clothes and provide a sense of communality, they also resembled many of the designs for the futurist or dadaist stage.

Meyerhold's system of disciplined movements represented one way of responding to the modern body, using the machine as a model. However, practitioners and choreographers took a range of different courses in order to explore the corporeal. Indeed Meyerhold was certainly aware of these other methods: 'In creating Biomechanics, I tried to shield the young actor from a passion for the saccharine barefoot dancing à la Duncan' (Gladkov 1997: 194). Who was Duncan, the figure so vilified by Meyerhold? She was Isadora Duncan, an American dancer whose choreographic style, as you might guess from Meyerhold's comment, focused on bodily freedom and flow rather than discipline. She represented the other side of modernist physical expression.

THE FREE BODY

Duncan's description of her choreographic practice is striking in its difference from Meyerhold's. True, both expressed an interest in rhythm and balance, but whereas Meyerhold advocated movement as connected to the factory, sport and reflex, Duncan promoted dance as 'an expression of serenity' counteracting much modern dance in the process (Drain 1995: 248). She lamented, 'we do not know how to get down to the depths, to lose ourselves in an inner self' (Drain 1995: 248). One cannot imagine Meyerhold making any such proclamations. Duncan's dances reflected these assertions. As with many artists we have looked at, Duncan's ideas were less modern than they were harking back to ancient emblems and ideas. She was often pictured dressed in flowing robes and barefoot in typical Grecian style. In a recent book Carrie Preston describes such modelling as 'mythic posing [which] was part of a search for a reunified body and soul that modernity seemed to have severed' (2011: 239). So it was not merely an aping of ancient Greek culture or a romanticisation of a particular cultural period or set of theatrical conventions. Rather, the mythic posing responded directly to modernity just like futurist valorisation of the machine or expressionist screaming. It represented a quest to reconnect the body and the soul, a relationship shattered by war, science, urban growth and economics.

But Duncan was not alone in advocating what we will term 'free dance'. Indeed many practitioners created their own imagining of the free body. Loie Fuller, for example, another American dancer, used both modern movement techniques and innovative lighting methods. While using some of the key motifs of ballet, Fuller promoted a modernist rendering of the established and somewhat authoritarian dance tradition. Rhonda Garelick reflects 'effectively, she pared ballet down to a deeply aestheticized meditation on the human body's relationship to gravity, mechanicity, and light' (2007: 150). While Fuller's free dancing seemed far away from Meyerhold's biomechanics, in focusing on gravity, mechanicity and light, the two can be read as coming out of a similar impulse, even if the consequences of their enquiries stood in marked contrast. Fuller reconnected the body's movements with music and rhythm. She contended:

> Music, however, ought to indicate a form of harmony or an idea with instinctive passion, and this instinct ought to incite the dancer to follow the harmony without special preparation. This is the true dance.
>
> (Drain 1995: 246)

There is the sense here that the body is moving almost without active thought, instead responding in freedom to outer (and inner) catalysts.

Another American committed to revolutionising dance was Martha Graham. In *The Work of Dance*, Mark Franko describes Graham alongside many other choreographers and dancers who used dance to uncover the politics and social inequalities of the 1930s. While we do not have space to describe them in any detail here, Franko focuses on a range of examples which brought 'laboring bodies into visibility as historical agents' (2002: 2). So far, so like Meyerhold. Using terms we have already uncovered in the course of this book, in a later book Franko describes Graham's project as 'psychoanalytic modernism', looking to the connection between mind and body (2012: 6). One of Graham's most famous solo performances, *Lamentation* (1930), saw her dressed in a purple woollen tube which covered her moving body almost entirely. Beneath the purple wool, her movements made her seem peculiarly unbalanced at times and certainly had none of the beauty of, say, those in a traditional tutu-ed *Swan Lake*. Here is a prime example of a modernist take on the body, making the body seem strange and incomprehensible; Marcia Siegel even refers to Graham's body in *Lamentation* as a 'nearly inhuman shape' (1979: 40). The dehumanisation of the body seems to reflect the 1930s context. There is a tragic sadness in this piece and a grief that perhaps reflects the spread of the cityscape which seemed to engulf humanity with noise and dirt. Or perhaps it warns of the pervasive dictatorial political systems that were appearing across the world or perhaps the profound sense of isolation many felt as communities and societies began to splinter. One of the most wonderful and exciting aspects of Graham's dances, and particularly *Lamentation*, is that it forces us as audience members to ask questions about the world and humanity and not simply about artistic form.

Duncan, Fuller and Graham rejected the balletic tradition, where bodies were incarcerated into tight costumes and movements were often as painful as they were impressively beautiful. However, ballet itself was experiencing a tremendous shift; indeed, in this canon of work lies one of the most controversial and stimulating performances of the early twentieth century: *The Rite of Spring* (*Le Sacre du Printemps*, 1913). Later Martha Graham would

Figure 8 Martha Graham, *Lamentation*, 1935 (Oblique) © Library of Congress

dance in Léonide Massine's 1930s adaptation and, in 1984, she created her own version (Horosko 2002: 15). The original brought together some of the most prominent figures of the modernist avant-garde: the leader of the Ballets Russes Sergei Diaghilev, choreographer Vaslav Nijinsky and composer Igor Stravinsky. Again we are obliged to look back when we approach this highly innovative piece, for it was influenced by folk melodies and ritualised movement. Instead of prima ballerinas and a supporting *corps de ballet*, Nijinsky's dancers performed with twisted bodies and wild running. Lynn Garafola helps us to understand both the aesthetic challenge here and the way it connects to our comprehension of modernism:

> *Sacre* was a harbinger of modernity: of its assembly lines and masses, its war machines and cities of slain innocents. Stripped of their costumes, Nijinsky's masses were both the agents and victims of twentieth-century barbarism.
>
> (1989: 70)

The Rite of Spring, then, with its strikingly dissonant reinterpretations of folk song and its total overhaul of ballet, reflected some of the central concerns of the early twentieth century and is regarded as one of the most important, influential and shocking moments in modern music and dance.

Nijinsky's angular masses provided a dystopian view of the modernist period while Meyerhold's biomechanics represented a joyous celebration of communist revolution. In both cases the body is inscribed with the modern world. What, then, of the body in a place like Nazi Germany? Were moving bodies there also marked by conditions outside the theatre building? How did the prevailing political order affect the artistic movement of the body? In order to answer these questions and simultaneously offer a different political take on the body, we will turn to two German choreographers: Mary Wigman and Rudolf Laban. Wigman trained under Émiles Jaques Dalcroze, another important figure in free dance. Dalcroze created the concept of eurhythmics and advocated a 'condition of joy [which] is brought about in us by the feeling of freedom and responsibility, by the clear perception of the creative power in us, by the balance of our natural powers, by the harmonious rhythm between intention and deed' (Dalcroze 1917: 33). Wigman later trained under Laban.

Connecting a range of divergent practitioners, both Wigman and Laban associated with the dadaists, Wigman apparently hosting parties for the dada artists at her house (Melzer 1994: 98). One can only imagine what these parties might have looked like! Later both turned to a type of expressionism, though again the connection was not straightforward. Susan Manning helpfully suggests that the 'dances bore a family resemblance to expressionism' (2006a: 5). In Wigman's use of the term *Ausdruckstantz* (expressive dance) and Laban's choreography of darkly ecstatic pieces like the 1927 *Die Nacht* (*The Night*) one could certainly claim a parallel if not a direct link with an expressionist sensibility. Both also had ambiguous relationships with the Nazi Party, being employed by the regime to create dances or events. In 1936 the Nazi Minister for Propaganda Joseph Goebbels asked Laban to choreograph the spectacular ceremony for the Olympic Games, but was horrified by Laban's expressionistic take on the brief. Laban was sacked and Wigman took over, creating *Lament for the Dead* with music by Carl Orff (Newhall 2009: 53). Laban emigrated to England, breaking his connection with the Nazis. Wigman remained in Germany, although as the Nazi Party strengthened its control over the country and prompted a world war, she was increasingly ostracised as a decadent avant-gardist. Following our discussions in the previous chapter, the relationship between the modernist avant-garde and politics proves again to be complex and varied.

Although often read as conducting similar experiments in dance and movement, Laban and Wigman maintained slightly different approaches. Reflecting on the arguments of the 1928 Second Dancers' Congress in Essen, Mary Anne Santos Newhall describes the difference well: 'Did the future of dance lie with the *Ausdruckstanz*, which repudiated classical ballet altogether, or with dance-drama which incorporated aspects of ballet?' (2009: 35). Wigman advocated the former, Laban (along with his pupil Kurt Jooss whose 1933 *The Green Table* would provide a stimulating challenge for any contemporary performer interested in the body) plumped for the latter.

Wigman's primary experiments centred on using dance as a language and the creation of 'kinetic empathy', that is, the way a body moves effectively and the way that body communicates to other performers and the audience. This led to an intense mutual experience for both performer and audience member, hence her strong association with the expressionists. In creating this experience, Wigman looked not only to time, space and rhythm but also the way the body's muscles function. She created a continuous flow of bodily energy by focusing on *Spannung* (tension) and *Entspannung* (release) (Newhall 2009: 82). Clench your muscles and then let go and you will begin to see what Wigman meant. Clearly these two ways of holding the body, and the way one moves between these two states, creates an experience for both performer and audience member alike.

Despite the differences, Laban's methods have some similarities with Wigman's ideas, also centring on the body moving in space. Laban imagined a kinaesphere, an area around the body that the actor/dancer could explore. His aim was 'to become aware of, to feel and enjoy the free-standing body relating to the surrounding space, and the feeling of changing qualities of time and dynamics' (Preston-Dunlop 1998: 101). The kinaesphere has multiple dimensions: up–down, left–right and forward–backward (Newlove 1993: 25–6). This becomes fairly obvious when you start moving about, as I suggest you do now, unless you are in a public library. Stand on one spot and imagine you are surrounded by a great sphere, the dimensions of which are created simply by how far you can comfortably stretch without losing balance. Envisaging a kinaesphere is actually a marvellous way of uncovering your use of space on the stage and becoming aware of other actors as their kinaespheres overlap with your own.

Like Meyerhold (though clearly in a different way), Laban was fascinated by the way efficient, effective movement could transform society. For while not everyone could be a prima ballerina, everyone could learn to move more successfully. As part of his system, Laban created a collection of movement types ('efforts') which included 'pressing', 'flicking' and 'gliding'. One of Laban's most abiding legacies was the development of a code to tabulate these movements, similar to that a composer might use. This code became known as Labanotation. These efforts should be understood as intricately connected to notions of space (direct, for example in a straight line, and flexible, for example 'wavy, multi-directional movement'), time (sudden/quick and sustained/slow) and weight (strong and light). Direct space, sudden time and strong weight resist or fight against, whereas flexible space, sustained time and light weight yield or indulge (Newlove and Dalby 2004: 130).

Laban's ideas also exhibited a return to pre-civilised or primeval movements. Questioning the way our lives and movements are timed (by the trappings of mass industry and consumerism), Laban sought to reconnect with natural rhythms, leaving space for slowing down or speeding up depending on our body's preference. Laban's British pupil Jean Newlove (who devised the choreography for Theatre Workshop) suggests 'the speed with which we move to accomplish a purpose will tend to accelerate and decelerate depending on circumstance, making for a freer, irregular rhythm guided by our kinaesthetic sense' (1993: 58). All this might suggest that Laban's dances constantly flowed in beautiful unrelenting lines. While there is some truth to this, he also created pieces like *The Green Clowns* (1926) which critiqued the gaudy Berlin cabarets and the threat of fascism through the grotesque: movement five (*Firlefanz*), for example, contains 'silliness, frivolous stuff – junk, fluffiness, frippery, clowning around' (Bradley 2009: 81).

The free human body appeared many times across the modernist avant-garde. In many cases it fought against the repressive nature of modernity with its factories and production lines, and de-established the pre-eminence of restrictive balletic movement. But our reading of the free body in this section also points to another central issue: the body is always a political site, subjugated by hegemonic forces or acting as a release from those forces, able to fight for freedom or acquiesce with tyranny. 'Freedom' has a variety of different interpretations and for our final case study in this section I want to turn to New York in 1937 and to an evening of what was then termed 'Negro dance'. It responded to the Federal Theatre Project, a collective that certainly did a great deal to bridge racial divides which, in the American 1930s, were acute indeed. However, this evening moved beyond the FTP's valiant attempts to create a selection of dances that focused on leftist critique and racial identity. The evening contained dances from Africa and the West Indies as well as from America and included a piece entitled 'Scottsboro' about the unjust accusations of rape levelled at nine black men in 1931. In her analysis of this production Susan Manning concludes 'the male dancers in "Scottsboro" performed social protest with an Africanist accent' (2006b: 98). Certainly the surviving photograph showing the dancers' bodies displaying 'the separation of torso and pelvis characteristic of West African dance' would suggest as much (Manning 2006b: 98). Inscribed on the body here, then, were contemporary racial politics in America, the older racial politics of slavery and the idea of origins and history. This piece really did represent a call to freedom in every sense.

THE DISAPPEARING BODY: DEATH AND AFTER DEATH

In the Czech playwright Karel Čapek's 1920 play *R.U.R.*, the boss Mr Domin proudly shows Miss Helena Glory round his robot manufacturing plant. She is initially horrified by the seemingly inhuman way in which such creatures are put together and treated. While she naturally anthropomorphises the humanoid robots, Domin attempts to convince her that they are simply machines designed to perform the repetitive tasks of Taylorism or Fordism, thereby giving humans the leisure time to simply enjoy life. Rather inexplicably, Helena stays with Domin and his friends. However, gradually the utopian vision of a world without work is destroyed by the robots who rise up en masse, killing everyone except the insightful Alquist whose warnings about the dangers of making robots have gone unheeded and whose commitment to physical labour (he enjoys making walls) has been regarded as rather eccentric by his forward-thinking friends. In the final scene, Radius, the leader of the robots, visits Alquist to demand the secret of making robots. Having murdered all the humans, the robots are unable to create new life: 'the machines produce nothing but pieces of bloody meat. The skin does not adhere to the flesh and the flesh does not adhere to the bones. Formless lumps flood out from the machines' (Čapek 2012; act three). Despite experimenting on live robots in a scene akin to a modern day horror film, Alquist is not able to discover the secret and, in a rather curious finale, it falls to the robots Primus and Helena to fall in love and recreate a new humanity. There are many ways one could read this play: as a warning about the extreme industrialisation of the world, as a pre-emptive picture of the subjugated working class rising up and challenging the owners of industry, as an apocalyptic response to the First World War. Whichever way you choose to understand it, at its centre is not a human body but a robot body, a simulated reproduction of humanity. Indeed this play introduced the word 'robot' into the English language.

While we have made a strong case for the importance of the body in modernist avant-garde theatre, we must also explore the converse narrative: the disappearance of the human body altogether. Indeed the surviving photographs of the Theatre Guild's 1922 performance of *R.U.R.* in New York focus on the human body vanishing from view beneath the onslaught of the robots (Čapek

Figure 9 Robot rebellion scene from Karel Čapek's *R.U.R. (Rossum's Universal Robots)*, 1928–29 © Billy Rose Theatre Division, The New York Public Library for the Performing Arts, Astor, Lenox and Tilden Foundations

1929–30). Moreover the robots seem to change from mimetic representations, so similar to humans that Helena is unable to tell the difference, to more mechanical, metallic objects as they take over. Kara Reilly makes the case for the importance of automata in theatre history, returning to René Descartes (of 'I think therefore I am' fame). Čapek's play founds her claim that 'automata are central to debates about mimesis or the representation of reality in the historical period in which they exist' (Reilly 2011: 1). The primary concern of *R.U.R.* seems to rest precisely on this issue, whether exemplified by Domin's disconnected treatment of his robots as machines or Helena's ongoing concern for robot welfare. In 1922 the frightening mechanisation of society and worker welfare were hot topics and *R.U.R.*, a science fiction play after all, reflects this most acutely.

The most obvious and yet most unperformable disappearing body is, of course, the corpse. Staging death has always been a complicated endeavour. The modernist period forced practitioners to again confront dead bodies as, in Lisa Perdigao's terms, 'materialized representations of absence and difference' (2010: 5); corpses are like us but are not us, they lack something intangible while retaining the familiar material elements, even if the limbs and organs are gradually decomposing as soon as life has gone. Given the context, it is no wonder that corpses became a recurring presence; this was a period of war, famine and new science that forced people to confront the troubling thought that we might just be animals made of carbon. Let us take a look at two examples: Maurice Maeterlinck's *The Intruder* (1890) and Elmer Rice's *The Adding Machine* (1923).

Maeterlinck's play confronts death at every corner without, in typical symbolist style, ever being explicit. The body is described as 'dead' even when it is not: the grandfather refers to his blindness as 'dead eyes' and his family as 'pale as the dead' (Maeterlinck 1914: 46). Even when the wife dies in the final scene, it is signified only by the Sister of Charity, dressed in black, making the sign of the cross (1914: 55). However, more cryptically, throughout there remains the suggestion of someone/something else close at hand: who is in the garden? whose steps can be heard? Ultimately one concludes that the personification or presence of death is padding around the house.

Distinct from the German expressionist tradition, Rice's expressionism rests on his presentation of issues in 'visually and aurally imaginative ways' (Walker 2005: 187). *The Adding Machine* narrates the story of Mr Zero; bored by his mundane job and loveless marriage, he murders his boss and is sentenced to death. However, his execution occurs only midway through the play. In the second half he finds himself buried in a graveyard and journeying to a heaven-like place which he rejects as too permissive, filled with 'loafers an' bums' (Rice 1965: 54). Rejecting this tolerant, open-minded space, Zero accepts a position operating an adding machine in an undefined post-death place before eventually being reincarnated as a production line worker. The essence of the play is described by Charles, the shadowy presider over the post-death office:

> You're a failure Zero . . . A slave to a contraption of steel and iron . . .
> True, you move and eat and digest and excrete and reproduce. But any microscopic organism can do as much.
>
> (1965: 61)

Breaking away from any sense of naturalist realism, Zero's body is supposedly destroyed by the executioner and yet he reappears in the next scene, dead but apparently relatively unchanged physically. The bodily relaxation of the Elysian Fields (he even takes his shoes off!) is a temporary interruption until Zero once again places himself under the physically repressive capitalist work ethic. Charles's pity for Zero centres primarily on the latter's bodily functions, detached from any sense of what really makes a human, human. Zero's reanimated body enables Rice to make broader comments on economic systems and physical incarceration.

The acclaimed American designer Lee Simonson created the sets for Theatre Guild's performance of *The Adding Machine*. In surviving photographs the graveyard is a creepily backlit collection of headstones with an irregular iron railing cutting through it. Two figures (presumably Mr Zero and his dead compatriot Shrdlu) occupy the scene, one sitting upright in his grave, the other peering through the railings. Neither resemble dead bodies in any way, the suggestion of death given only through the set and atmospheric lighting (Rice 1923). One of the most profoundly liberating aspects of avant-garde experimentation remains its disdain for illusory logic. This becomes particularly useful when one needs to represent death.

Dead people have a distinctive perspective on life. Forever separated from life and the living, they are uniquely placed to comment on earthly matters. The American playwright Thornton Wilder knew this only too well when he created Emily, a figure we follow through her life, death and beyond in his analysis of smalltown America, *Our Town* (1938). After death Emily visits her family before realising that the dead have no place among the living. However, her reflections illustrate her newly discovered awareness: 'Oh earth, you're too wonderful for anybody to realize you. Do any human beings ever realize life while they live it? – every, every minute?' (Wilder 2000: 89). Emily poses a challenge, one that continues to have resonance for contemporary audiences.

THE DISAPPEARING BODY: MASKING AND PUPPETRY

If these images of death made the audience reconsider notions of presence and absence then many other techniques and innovations also played with these ideas, causing spectators to rethink their understanding of the human body or else reimagine bodies made strange by theatrical conventions. The re-emergence of the mask, a central motif on the ancient Greek stage, provided one such convention, making the face appear oddly unknowable. The mask remained vital in many theatrical traditions across the world and now modernist avant-garde innovators were rediscovering its power. In all cases, the mask was primarily used to make emotion obvious and suggest certain character traits; historically some were tragic (the Japanese Noh mask) and some were comic (from the Greek Old Comedies). Defining the worth and usefulness of the mask, the theatre scholar John Emigh confirms 'for the actor, the otherness of the mask becomes both the obstacle and the goal. He or she must redefine the sense of self in order to wear the other's face' (1996: xviii). It is just such an obstacle and goal for the audience member, separated from the actual face of the actor and yet potentially better able to see the character.

In *At the Hawk's Well* (1916), W.B. Yeats used masks for his central characters. Yeats praised the masks, designed by Edmund Dulac, as 'the face of the speaker should be as much a work of art as the lines that he speaks or the costume that he wears, that all may be artificial as possible' (1921: preface). Yeats made his intentions clearer in his preface for Ezra Pound's *Certain Noble Plays of Japan* (1916) in which he maintains

a mask will enable me to substitute for the face of some common-place
player, or for that face repainted to suit his own vulgar fancy, the fine
invention of a sculptor . . . in poetical painting & in sculpture the face
seems the nobler for lacking curiosity . . . it is even possible that being is
only possessed completely by the dead.

(Pound 2005: preface)

Yeats's ideas were realised by Dulac in the latter's feathered headdress for the
Hawk (played by Japanese actor Michio Ito) with a long coloured plume cover-
ing the head, the actor's eyes peering out from beneath a black mask.

While one of Europe's most celebrated poets explored the mask as a theatrical mode, those purveyors of anti-art, the dadaists, also employed the mask.
Indeed dadaist performers used masks frequently in their Cabaret Voltaire
performances. The Romanian Marcel Janco created many masks for the dada
performers, combining ancient Greek and Japanese traditions with a nod to
contemporary art. Using the masks, the performers created dances such as
Nightmare:

The dancing figure starts from a crouching position, gets straight up,
and moves forward. The mouth of the mask is wide open, the nose
is broad and in the wrong place. The performer's arms, menacingly
raised, are elongated by special tubes.

(Melzer 1994: 32)

The description of *Nightmare* recalls many modernist masks in paintings such
as Pablo Picasso's *Les Demoiselles D'Avignon* (1907) or, earlier, the Belgian
James Ensor's *Masks Confronting Death* (1888), which brings a sense of cohe-
sion to our argument here by presenting a skeleton Death at its centre, surrounded by various oddly masked figures with large noses and striking red
lips. The overtly theatrical figures in Ensor's painting seem to be challenging
Death, confronting him through their grotesque masks with their comedic
liveness.

We find another useful perspective on the mask in the work of the
American playwright Eugene O'Neill whose expressionist-inflected plays
about race (*All God's Chillun Got Wings*, 1924, *The Emperor Jones*, 1920),
adultery (*Desire Under the Elms*, 1924), working-class identity (*The Hairy
Ape*, 1922) and his retelling of ancient Greek stories (*Mourning Becomes
Electra*, 1931) mark some of the most interesting contributions to modernist
theatre, both in terms of theme and form. O'Neill advocated the use of masks
in many of his plays, suggesting that masks enable the inner workings of the
human mind to be presented in a clearer way. In order to understand quite
what he meant, let us turn to his 1932 recommendations for *The Hairy Ape*,

a play that follows the central character Yank, a ship's stoker, as he gradually realises that he is part of a capitalist machine that makes him little better than the eponymous ape:

> In *The Hairy Ape*, a much more extensive use of masks would be of the greatest value in emphasizing the theme of the play. From the opening of the fourth scene where Yank begins to think, he enters into a masked world; even the familiar faces of his mates in the forecastle have become strange and alien. They should be masked, and the faces of everyone he encounters thereafter, including the symbolic gorilla's.
>
> (Krasner 2008: 188)

As Yank's perceptions are challenged, he becomes disorientated by the world around him and confused by the way others reject him. His bewilderment is reflected in the masks, simultaneously making the situation and characters as peculiar for the audience as for Yank.

In Chapter 2 I claimed a distinct if fractured genealogy of dada and surrealism starting with Alfred Jarry's *Ubu Roi* of 1896. Famous for its opening line, Jarry actually based *Ubu Roi* on many years of experimenting with the story in puppet form. His puppet drawing for Pa Ubu with its conical hat and grotesque obese body is well known, representing a horrific, terrifying yet satirically comical view of the bourgeoisie and their obsession with power. While faces were covered with masks, actors' bodies started to disappear too, with many practitioners replacing the human body with the puppet or marionette. As Christopher Innes suggests, these puppets 'stood in the same relationship to human individuals as a national flag does to a nation', that is, puppets symbolise humanity, just as the mask symbolises the face (1998: 186). The puppet can also stand in for the human rather as a crash test dummy stands in for the driver as its car ploughs into a wall. This is why the robots in Domin's factories look like humans; there is no innate need to make the robots look human but, given that they are doing human jobs and need to interact in human society, it seems best to make them symbolise humans. As Domin says, the inventor Old Rossum 'could have produced a Medusa with the brain of a Socrates or a worm fifty yards long. But being without a grain of humor, he took it into his head to make a vertebrate or perhaps a man' (Čapek 2012).

Puppets were in no way a new theatrical idea. Back in the nineteenth century, the German dramatist Heinrich von Kleist wrote a short dialogue that helps us to understand the modernist experiments (Kleist 1810). After seeing a marionette theatre, the dialogue's protagonist questions its potential for high art. Reminding us of the robots in *R.U.R.*, the responder replies, 'such a figure would never be affected'; one could simply present character on the stage without the errors or distractions that haunt human actors. In fact the responder ends up suggesting that 'it appears to best advantage in that human bodily structure has no consciousness at all – or has infinite consciousness – that is, in the mechanical puppet, or in the God'. It seems that idiotically flawed human beings are a liability both on the stage and off it! While we cannot be entirely sure whether Kleist was serious in his claims or whether he was merely throwing ideas around, this essay helps us to understand some of the intentions of the modernist puppet. And here we return to Edward Gordon Craig.

Craig's propositions on the marionette provide a conundrum for the contemporary artist. In one sense, they are remarkably rich in ideas and inspiration; in another, it remains difficult to understand quite what Craig had in mind. His seminal 'The Actor and the Übermarionette' (1908) sheds some light on his concepts while persistently avoiding explicit claims. The actor, Craig decided, has little to do with art at all. Irritatingly, the human actor has individuality and character that interrupt artistic performance even if she or he does their best to suppress them. For this reason 'as *material* for the theatre he is useless' (Krasner 2008: 89). We are therefore left with a dilemma. For many years, the actor had been foremost in the theatrical experience; what could possibly replace this vital component of the live performance? Craig contended that the marionette might provide an alternative. Like the mask (another motif that delighted Craig, who actually named his theatre magazine *The Mask*), the marionette smashed through all those annoying human habits and customs, enabling Craig to produce art. In Olga Taxidou's terms, Craig desired 'an actor minus "personality"' (1998: 168). The following dense description of his so-called Übermarionette ('super puppet') exemplifies both Craig's intense idealist vision and his seeming inability to fully explain what this figure might look like:

> The über-marionette will not compete with life – but will rather go beyond it. Its ideal will not be the flesh and blood but rather the body in Trance – it will aim to clothe itself with a death-like beauty while exhaling a living spirit.
>
> (Krasner 2008: 97)

In response to applause, acclamation or rejection from the audience, the marionette's face and body do not change: there is no heart to beat faster, no sweat to dampen their armpits, no ego to be stroked. This marionette figure could be an integral, though not domineering, factor in the general *mise en scène* which might include lighting, set, music etc. Craig never fully realised his idea in performance so it became a prophetic model rather than a practical experiment. Nevertheless, whether advocating the disposal of actors altogether in favour of marionettes or encouraging actors to ape marionette-like movements and gestures, Craig's conclusions provide an interesting catalyst for contemporary performers seeking to explore new ways of creating theatrical scenarios.

Others were more explicit in their use of the puppet. New York in particular became a prominent site of puppetry experimentation and in this burgeoning community arose a vital yet under-researched company called Modicut. A Jewish puppet theatre set up by Zuni Maud and Yosi Cutler in 1925, Modicut's shows, according to Edward Portnoy, merged 'Yiddish with avantgarde art and popular culture to produce humor as well as political and cultural criticism' (Bell 2001: 106). The puppets they created were caricatures of New York Jewish life, often resembling their creators. They were extraordinarily intricate, with strings attached to the back of the puppet allowing the puppeteers to lift the puppet's eyebrows or perform other delicate movements (Bell 2001: 117). My favourite of their designs is a puppet of Hitler: as the puppet raised his arm in salute, its mouth would open to reveal fangs and a lock of his hair would stand straight up (Bell 2001: 117). Modicut stood as an example of innovative theatrical performance from a minority group seeking to create entertaining, artistically innovative theatre that addressed contemporary political issues.

In 1936 puppetry reappeared again on the American stage, this time in Detroit with the premier of Gertrude Stein's spectacularly titled *Identity or I Am Because My Little Dog Knows Me*. Stein, whom we mentioned as an awkward contributor to an American dadaist and surrealist tradition, began a correspondence with puppeteer Donald Vestal in 1934 and, with dramaturgical help from fellow playwright Thornton Wilder, created a visually arresting collection of odd exaggerated characters. Resembling Evreinov's *Theatre of the Soul*, *Identity* features two main characters: Human Mind and Human Nature. Vestal created two metallic marionettes for these characters, faintly reminiscent of some of the figures of the futurist or dadaist stages of Europe some years previously. In his article discussing Stein's use of puppets, the theatre scholar John Bell describes the appearance of these two protagonists:

> The two puppets are quite similar, but Human Nature features a skeleton with a rib cage, and has no facial features, while, in contrast, Human Mind has eyes, nose, mouth, and a full body, no doubt a reflection of the earth-bound mortality of Stein's Human Nature versus the completeness of the Human Mind.
>
> (2006: 94)

While Christopher Innes claims that modernist puppets are representational, standing in for the human (a claim certainly substantiated by Craig's ideas), for Stein and Vestal it was the puppets' ability to disrupt our understanding of the human that made them useful. Vestal even maintained that marionettes 'must

never be representational . . . [but instead] exaggerated to the point of caricature in expression and over-size' (Bell 2006: 91). So the worth of the marionettes in Stein and Vestal's case was not that they represented the human but
that they simply represented themselves; they were devices on the stage just
like other props or objects. In this way Craig and Vestal represent two similar
yet unequivocally divergent versions of the modernist puppet.

One of the most interesting and unusual examples of modernist puppetry came in a collaborative project between the playwright Aleksandr Blok
and Vsevolod Meyerhold. Years before Meyerhold developed his system of
biomechanics, he experimented with a kind of symbolist *commedia dell'arte*,
producing Blok's lyric play known as *The Puppet Show* or *The Fairground
Booth* (in Russian *Balaganchik*) at Vera Komissarzhevskaya's Theatre in St
Petersburg (1906). In this ancient tradition of *commedia dell'arte*, actors performed in companies, each one taking a particular stock role. Many of these
are still recognisable to us today: Harlequin, Pantalone, Pierrot. Meyerhold's
version of *The Puppet Show* used many of the techniques described in this
chapter; some characters wore masks and Death, dressed in white robes with
a scythe in her hand, wandered around the stage as a threatening presence.
So why, then, is Blok's play called *The Puppet Show*? The answer to this
question can be found in Pierrot's final speech when he laments the death of
Columbine. Pierrot refers to her as a 'cardboard bride', made out of inexpres-
sive material, just like a puppet (Blok 2003: 33). Yet there is a profound irony
here. The characters may be puppetlike and malleable, but the author seems
to have entirely lost power. Pre-empting Pirandello's metatheatrical *Six
Characters in Search of an Author*, the author of Blok's play constantly tries to
intervene, assuring the audience that this is a real drama not a puppet theatre:
'I wrote a most realistic play' (Blok 2003: 26). But the author is unable to
retake control; it is, if you like, a puppet show without an effective puppeteer.
Meyerhold's staging played on this metatheatricality with the flies, ropes and
wires visible to the audience and the prompter lighting a candle in his box
rather than pretending he was not there at all as in most theatrical productions (Braun 1998: 63).

The use of marionettes and puppets points us to another ongoing modernist
debate. The audience, say, for a performance of the British seaside tradition
Punch and Judy is more likely to be sand-caked children eating ice-creams
and their harassed parents than trained middle-class theatregoers. The title
of Blok's play, *The Fairground Booth*, suggests a similar celebratory, holiday
setting. Puppetry crosses any perceived divide between so-called high and
low, between popular and elite. Actually its appeal to modernist avant-garde
practitioners was not simply aesthetic but also, as Harold Segal suggests, 'the
world of the child became newly attractive to artists as a source of opposition, and an antidote, to the conservatism and traditionalism of bourgeois

culture' (1995: 37). Segal's comment perhaps helps us to understand a great deal of the modernist avant-garde experiment we have been exploring in this book. So much of the experimental work we have examined so far exhibits the wild behaviour of a child, engaging in actions with little expectation other than to have fun. In this sense childhood becomes the perfect antidote to the dull monotony of industrialised life or the painfully remembered horrors of war.

As Taxidou recognises, studying the body is a vital undertaking as we explore modernist avant-garde theatre, primarily because it takes us beyond a simple study of written texts towards a more fluid concept of performance as 'an emergent aesthetic notion' (2007: 213). Focusing on the body, we cannot simply think in terms of playscripts and manifestos but are obliged to reconstruct these events and ideas in a visual and audible way. The modernist body exemplified the contradictions and complexities of the period, oscillating between liberation and incarceration, freedom and subjugation, fragmentation and unity, isolation and community. In exploring all these different facets of twentieth-century experience, the body became a central focus of contention and power, what Martin Puchner refers to as 'the troubling presence of the human actor on the stage' (2002: 5). Alongside this 'troubling presence', performances used the conventions of many different genres, producing challenging, multi-dimensional, cross-disciplinary work. But the way practitioners engaged with dance, music, poetry, visual art and cinema differed considerably. The next chapter will look at these varied models and hopefully provide more ideas for contemporary performance.

PRACTICAL EXPLORATION

While we cannot possibly hope to emulate true practitioners of biomechanics, it is interesting to try out Meyerhold's methods, not least to catch just a small glimpse into the discipline of body and mind required in order to truly become proficient. Follow the patterns laid out by Jonathan Pitches in *Vsevolod Meyerhold*, part of the Routledge Performance Practitioners series. Attempt to perfect a dactyl and one of the études. Shooting the Bow provides a good starting point.

Students can also simply attempt to follow Laban's methods even if they have no dancing background. Consult Jean Newlove and John Dalby's book *Laban for All* which includes a section entitled 'For Those Who Act' (209–23). The instructions are straightforward and the connection with *commedia dell'arte* is particularly interesting.

Read Edward Gordon Craig's 'The Actor and the Übermarionette' in Michael Huxley and Noel Witts' *The Twentieth Century Performance Reader* (chapter 20). Discuss how these ideas might be used on the stage.

The mask became a vital tool for the modernist avant-garde. What are the strengths and weaknesses of the mask? Likewise, why should the puppet have taken on such a prominent role?

Take the final part of scene 5 from Eugene O'Neill's *The Hairy Ape* (from where the crowd come out of church). O'Neill suggested that this play would benefit from a greater use of masks. Create your own masks for this scene, taking your lead from O'Neill's stage directions, and perform it in small groups.

CHAPTER 5

Total Theatre and Interdisciplinarity

TOTAL THEATRE

In 1909 the Russian artist Wassily Kandinsky composed *The Yellow Sound*, publishing it in the 1911 *Blaue Reiter Almanac*, which he co-edited with the German painter Franz Marc. It is an odd theatrical scenario reflecting the proclamations of his essay *On Stage Composition* by realising his concept of total theatre. In the introduction to the *Blaue Reiter Almanac*, Kandinsky and Marc predicted a 'spiritual awakening' where art reflected inner relationships knowing 'no borders or nations, only humanity' (Danchev 2011: 37). In contrast to many more materialist theatrical concepts we have looked at in this volume, Kandinsky's total theatre came directly out of this search for spiritual connectivity. *The Yellow Sound* begins with orchestra chords, an intense dark blue colour and choral singing. The words/lyrics are poetic, punctuated by pauses. When the material world appears it is always through subjective, almost anthropomorphic, imagery: 'clods of earth pregnant with puzzling questions' and 'speaking rocks' (Cardullo and Knopf 2001: 174). The rest of the play contains virtually no dialogue, only sounds, colours, dances, music and odd characters. All these different art forms unite in the minds of the audience members so that (reflecting the conclusions of *On Stage Composition*) 'ultimately, drama consists here of the complex of inner experiences (spiritual vibrations) of the spectator' (Cardullo and Knopf 2001: 185).

Throughout this book, I have used the word 'performance' rather than 'theatre' or 'drama', not because these two concepts are redundant (far from it), but because of their script/language-based connotations. 'Performance' potentially enables a more nuanced, interdisciplinary reading than 'theatre' or 'drama' might allow. We have already looked at dance as part of a reinterpretation of the body and now it is time to look at other genres. Combining different art forms was certainly nothing new; much of the verse of ancient Greek theatre was performed to music. However, in the nineteenth and twentieth centuries, practitioners theorised these interdisciplinary performances in new (often contradictory) ways.

In *On Stage Composition* Kandinsky mentioned (not altogether favourably) one of the most prominent and important contributors to this move towards interdisciplinary performance: 'Wagner here remains entirely in the old traditions of the external' (Cardullo and Knopf 2001: 184). The German opera composer Richard Wagner devised the concept of *Gesamtkunstwerk* or 'total work of art'. He defined this central idea in his 1849 'The Art-Work of the Future', identifying three artistic faculties – dance, tone (music) and poetry – 'three primeval sisters . . . mutually bound up in each other's life, of body and of spirit: that each of the three partners, unlinked from the united chain and bereft thus of her own life and motion, can only carry on an artificially inbreathed and borrowed life' (1895: 95). Wagner personifies these arts, his description resembling a dance. In fact the human body occupies a unique position in Wagner's concept; as Arthur Symons suggests in his study of the composer's ideas, for Wagner 'the ground of all human art is bodily motion' (Bentley 1979: 288). So, in one sense, *Gesamtkunstwerk* starts with the moving human body but, importantly, Wagner could not envisage the three performance elements as disconnected from one another. He not only contended that all three should appear in any work of art but that they should be intertwined, laced together with such force that the whole effect would be irreparably damaged if they were ripped apart. Wagner's politics have been heavily critiqued, particularly his anti-semitism which was later so attractive to the Nazis. But his theories continue to resonate, even in contemporary theatre, and provided a starting point for many modernist thinkers whether they built on or rejected the German's ideas. Martin Puchner even suggests that Wagner invented 'what subsequently became avant-garde theatricalism' (2002: 8).

Many others devised equivalent models of 'total theatre'. The Ballets Russes, under the guidance of Sergei Diaghilev and choreographer Michel Fokine, certainly created a *Gesamtkunstwerk* model, with dance influenced by painting, music and drama (Garafola 1989: 45). The founder of the Paris-based Théâtre du Vieux-Colombier, Jacques Copeau, developed a similar style, merging lighting, movement and text (Levitz 2012: 183). This 'total theatre' style could be applied to a range of plays and performances, from the very old to the contemporary. The German director Max Reinhardt, for example, demanded that even ancient Greek plays be performed in cross-disciplinary ways, although, in many ways, this marked a return to the original performance conditions of Athens. Reinhardt maintained that:

New life will arise out of the classics on the stage: colour and music and greatness and splendour and merriment. The theatre will return to being a festive place which was its original meaning.

(Fischer-Lichte 2005: 46)

Reinhardt's 'festival plays', as he termed them, required 'a fusion of all the arts in the best symbolist tradition' (Styan 1982: 87). Reinhardt, like so many others, merged a return to vibrant historical theatre practice with a contemporary avant-garde approach.

One might initially look at Brecht's performed works and claim that he too presented a 'total work of art', clearly using music and movement (gestus) as part of his aesthetic. However, here we have stumbled across the other potential way of combining genres: that is, not combining them at all. Whereas Wagner's mixed genre concept represented a delicate arrangement, connecting art forms seamlessly in order to have the maximum empathetic effect on the audience, Brecht's multi-disciplined theatre rejected unity in favour of fragmentation. In Brecht's plays, music interrupts the dialogue, making comment on the scene. He even threw in comedic songs after a particularly distressing scene or a poignant ballad after raucous slapstick. In 'On the Use of Music in an Epic Theatre' Brecht cites his reworking of John Gay's eighteenth-century classic *The Beggar's Opera* as *The Threepenny Opera* (1928) as an example of epic theatre music: 'Its most striking innovation lay in the strict separation of the music from all the other elements of entertainment offered' (Brecht 2001: 85). Composed by Brecht's long-time collaborator Kurt Weill, the songs of *The Threepenny Opera*, therefore, do not create atmosphere or mood but make specific political comments. This use of music exemplifies Brecht's rejection of Wagner's *Gesamtkunstwerk*: *The Threepenny Opera* is not an integrated total work of art but a fragmented performance of independent artistic genres. Opposing Wagner, Brecht's type of fragmented cross-disciplinary theatre oscillated between innovation and tradition; while his plays still feel new, contemporary and relevant (both aesthetically and politically), his style has a precursor in the variety theatre tradition discussed in Chapter 1.

Brecht's intention, in fact, amounts to the exact opposite of Wagner's, challenging (what he understood as) the techniques of Wagnerian opera: 'We see entire rows of human beings transported into a peculiar doped state, wholly passive, sunk without trace, seemingly in the grip of a severe poisoning attack' (Brecht 2001: 89). Brecht's episodic style, interspersed with songs existing entirely independently of the main narrative, challenged this audience response. Indeed, he wrote *The Rise and Fall of Mahagonny* (1930) in response to the errors of Wagner's ideas. In his notes to the play (referred to as an 'opera'), Brecht wrote 'so long as the expression "Gesamtkunstwerk" (or "integrated work of art") means that the integration is a muddle, so long as the arts are supposed to be "fused" together, the various elements will all be equally degraded' (2001: 37). 'Words, music and setting must become more independent of one another', Brecht suggested (2001: 38). This stands at the opposite end of the spectrum from Wagner's wholly integrated model.

Cross-disciplinary, multi-generic performances dominated the modernist avant-garde, whether exhibiting the flowing integration of Wagner or the disjointed fragmentation of Brecht. As with many of the artistic traditions we have explored, these ideas crossed typical national, political, chronological and aesthetic boundaries, reappearing in various guises in the work of many practitioners. The theatre scholar David Roberts makes a strong case for the pre-eminence of the total work of art, even suggesting it as the defining factor of modernism. He maintains that 'the modern idea of the total work of art both intends a critique of existing society and anticipates a redemptive or utopian alternative' (2011: 3). Despite the profound differences between the various models posited above, perhaps Roberts's conclusion might bring some sense of initial dialogue. Behind the total work of art lies a desire to find a utopia where art forms (and perhaps even human beings) might reside together. This utopia remains highly ambivalent, of course; exemplified by regimes such as Nazi Germany and Stalin's Russia, utopias are as often defined by repression as by freedom. But a search for a better world often provides a catalyst for inter-disciplinary art. Once again we return to an ongoing claim that the modernist avant-garde, even in its most metaphysically symbolist manifestations, always represented a response to contemporary society.

NON-WESTERN MODES

As modernist practitioners in the US and Europe sought vibrant performance models that challenged established bourgeois methods, many turned to traditions and techniques from across the world. In this chapter it seems worthwhile to discuss this connection between the European and American avant-gardes and (what I will somewhat problematically refer to as) non-Western theatre, particularly as many practitioners used overseas conventions in order to create more cross-disciplinary work. It must be acknowledged that some of the examples are rather problematic as colonial misappropriations, but many provide potentially vibrant archetypes.

Brecht's interest in the Chinese actor Mei Lan-Fang, for example, origi-nated in his profound admiration for the way the Chinese performer seemed to pre-empt the German's notion of *Verfremdungs-Effekt*, the method used to distance the audience from the action so that spectators might address themes with a critical eye. According to Brecht, Mei Lan-Fang 'limits himself from the start to simply quoting the character played' (2001: 94). His style marked a counterpoint to Stanislavsky's emotion memory where actors were compelled to identify with and embody the character. Brecht goes on, 'he acts in such a way that nearly every sentence could be followed by a verdict of the audience' (2001: 95). In this way Mei Lan-Fang's acting style must have appealed to Brecht, whose whole aesthetic relied on this sort of distancing effect. Meyerhold admired Mei Lan-Fang too, even hosting the Chinese actor in Moscow in 1935, at an event which, in a remarkable moment of connection, Brecht also attended (Leach 1993: 55).

A number of practitioners looked to Asia for inspiration. Comparing Japanese Noh acting to the Western stage, Yeats concluded that the former 'separate from the world and us a group of figures, images, symbols, enable us to pass for a few moments into a deep of the mind that had hitherto been too subtle for our habitation' (Pound 2005: preface). One can see Yeats's symbolist perspective in his description of Japanese theatre. While there would initially appear to be little common ground between Yeats's folkloric symbolism and Meyerhold's communistic constructivism, actually the Russian admired Noh theatre too, mainly because of the Japanese way of combining gymnastics and acting to create action rather than relying too heavily on language, text and script (Leach 1993: 56).

Many other modernists looked to non-Western traditions; the dada-ists, for example, were interested in African art, both in terms of language and dance. Most noticeably, Tristan Tzara's 1916 play *The First Celestial Adventure of M. Antipyrine* problematically used a pseudo-African language which he used to 'shock the sensibilities of Zurich bourgeoisie' (Melzer 1994: 70). The expressionists, too, looked to the 'primitive tribes in Africa or Oceania' (Berghaus 2005a: 58). Even Stanislavsky, seeking a realist onstage vision, used elements of yoga to encourage relaxation and effective breathing.

Antonin Artaud, too, applied non-Western theatre models to his aesthetic, pointing particularly to Balinese theatre as a pertinent model. He suggested that work influenced by the gestures, movements and sounds of Balinese theatre challenged the typical characteristics of the European stage, particu-larly psychological naturalism. This is not to say, however, that it disposed of realism or of the desire to explore the real on the stage; actually, Artaud reflected, 'Orientals are more than a match for us in matters of realism' (2010: 39). Overlooking Artaud's problematic language use here, he made an interest-ing point. It is clear that Artaud's admiration for Balinese theatre sprang from his incessant desire to escape logical language:

> In fact the strange thing about all these gestures, these angular, sudden, jerky postures, these syncopated inflections, formed at the back of the throat, these musical phrases cut short, the sharded flights, rustling

branches, hollow drum sounds, robot creaking, animated puppets
dancing, is the feeling of a new bodily language no longer based on
words but on signs which emerges through the maze of gestures,
postures, airborne cries, through their gyrations and turns, leaving not
even the smallest area of stage space unused.

(Artaud 2010: 38)

Here is an extremely vivid interpretation of Balinese theatre, detailing the way
it might re-energise the moribund European stage.

Why did all these practitioners turn so resolutely towards alternative geographical spaces? Certainly non-Western theatres were seen as more exciting
and connected, somewhat problematically, with a primeval sensibility. Figures
such as Artaud regarded non-Western traditions as untainted by bourgeois
techniques and expectations. But, and here it provides another way of reading
the material on movement in the previous chapter, these traditions were also
imagined as more visceral, less rational, less text-based. All these facets led to
the influx of Eastern methods into the Western theatres, a perceived 'return to
man's "roots", whether in the psyche or prehistory' (Innes 1993: 3).

But is this simply a case of colonial imperialism, of a Western appropria-
tion of culturally specific traditions and conventions? While dadaist Richard
Huelsenbeck's Negro poems (as he termed them) might sound hugely problematic to our twenty-first-century ears, his interest in African drumming
traditions was engendered by an admiration rather than any sense of contempt.
Should we reject his art outright as an imperialist project? Urmila Seshagiri
unpacks this accusation in *Race and the Modernist Imagination*, a book she begins
with an analysis of the Ballets Russes' 1911 *Schéhérazade*, thereby embedding
what is a fairly literary text in issues of performance. She challenges the idea
that 'artistic treatments of race in early twentieth-century England were predominantly or univocally imperialist, demonstrating instead that modernism
conceived of race as shifting rather than set, disordered rather than hierarchical'
(Seshagiri 2010: 6). Seshagiri's comment provides a useful, pithy answer to our
question. Of course, there remained elements of imperial smugness but, by and
large, practitioners such as Brecht and Artaud admired non-Western methods,
learning from them rather than simply appropriating them.

HEARING THE AVANT-GARDE

In an ancient forest a collection of blind people and a Priest sit silently. 'I hear
nothing coming,' says the Second Blind Man; 'He told us to wait for him in
silence,' voices the very Old Blind Woman; 'I can no longer understand any
of the noises,' worries the Sixth Blind Man (Maeterlinck 1914: 62, 66, 76).

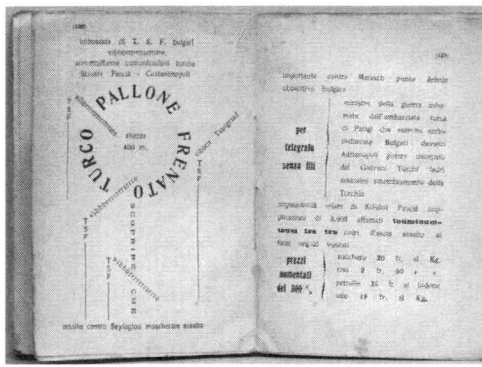

Figure 10 Concrete poetry from Filippo Tommaso Marinetti, *Zang Tumb Tumb*, 1914
© 2013 Filippo Tommaso Marinetti / Artists Rights Society (ARS), New York /
SIAE, Rome

Gradually the characters start to panic; unable to see the terrors of the forest, they imagine them through their other senses, particularly hearing. Through all this the Priest does not stir and one can only conclude that he has died and the blind people are left alone, enable to return to their home. Maeterlinck's *The Blind*, for which this description provides a brief synopsis, is a terrifying symbolist vision. While the audience can see the stage and the silent Priest, the other characters remain figuratively and literally in the dark. The absence of sight leads to far more acute hearing, every sound regarded as potentially dangerous. If the total work of art defined the modernist avant-garde, then hearing remained a primary sensual experience. Clearly in works such as Ibsen's *Ghosts* or Shaw's *Mrs Warren's Profession*, the audience pays close attention to the language, following the storyline primarily through the dialogue. However, as language gradually exploded, modernist avant-garde practitioners found new ways of encouraging audience members to hear. Maeterlinck's Third Blind Man exclaims 'I hear on my left a sound I do not understand' (1914: 109). We might be tempted to make a similar proclamation.

Although the symbolists largely resided in quiet, soporific atmospheres, much modernist avant-garde experimentation featured audio chaos, multiple voices and sounds overlapping and squabbling with one another. We will focus on three examples: Marinetti's sound poems, Ball's *Gadji Beri Bimba* and Edith Sitwell's *Façade*. And so to the first: Marinetti's *Zang Tumb Tumb* (1914), a concrete poem (that is, a poem that looks rather like a picture because of the arrangement of the words on the page) imbued with noise. The futurist composer Luigi Russolo quoted from early drafts in his 1913 *The Art of Noises: A Futurist Manifesto*. Rejecting bourgeois conceptions of music or pleasant sounds, Russolo turned to the tempi, rhythms and voices of the modern age: 'we must break out of this restricted circle of pure sounds and conquer the infinite variety of noise-sounds' (Rainey et al. 2009: 134). Russolo's concept of sound emanated from the grinding machines, the noisy city crowds and the jolting clangs of the tram. But, in keeping with the ideas of the futurists, war also influenced the sounds. Indeed, the origins of *Zang Tumb Tumb* as cited by Russolo may initially appear to be a nonsensical mass of noises:

> krooook-kraaak shout of officers to bang like brass plates pan over here pack over there chinck BOOOM.
>
> (Rainey et al. 2009: 136)

However, when one understands that Marinetti penned these words while a journalist at the 1912–13 Battle of Adrianople between Bulgaria and Serbia and the weakening Ottoman Empire, it becomes far easier to understand and follow. It morphs into a war report. The eventual full-length piece became one of Marinetti's most performed works. He described his performance method in his 1916 *Dynamic and Synoptic Declamation*, citing a particular 1914 performance at the Doré Gallery in London. Marinetti used hammers to imitate gunfire, set up blackboards in order to provide sketches and used the drumming talents of painter Christopher Nevinson as cannon. Reflecting on the audience reaction, Marinetti stated 'they were participating, their entire bodies inflamed with emotion, in the violent effects of the battle described by my words-in-freedom' (Rainey et al. 2009: 224). Martin Puchner describes Marinetti's notion of words-in-freedom as 'freeing words, or rather letters, from the constraints of the lexicon and grammar' (2005: 90). While connecting his work with specific landscapes and events (thereby adding another confusing contribution to our already complex understandings of realism), Marinetti also questioned the solidity of language. Therefore aesthetic experiment (language) and realist representation (the warscape) merged. This Italian innovation can be read alongside its Russian futurist counterpart *zaum*, a term created by the poets Velimir Khlebnikov and Aleksei Kruchenykh to describe their version of non-linear, non-grammatical language poems.

Our second example of noisy modernism returns to the dadaists, namely the work of Hugo Ball who was influenced by Kruchenykh and Khlebnikov's ideas. His *Verse Ohne Worte* ('poems without words') or *Lautgedichte* ('sound poems') became staples at the Cabaret Voltaire as part of the dadaists' peculiar variety theatre evenings. Interestingly, and providing a linear through narrative for this chapter, Ball was also influenced by Kandinsky's sounds (Melzer 1994: 41). In his poetry, Ball, like Marinetti, rejected language's conventional structures. In 1916 he set out his ideas: 'spit out words: the dreary, lame, empty language of men in society . . . reach an incomprehensible unconquerable sphere' (Melzer 1994: 41). Using drums, rattles and bells, Ball performed these incantations as a shaman might. James Harding describes Ball's performance of the 1916 *Gadji Beri Bimba* as 'packed with sounds of incantation and magic: *abracadabra* sounds' (2013: 5). When you listen to this poem (as you can on the open access website Ubuweb) you may well oscillate between perplexity and hysteria, incredulity and a strange sense of panic as the language you thought you knew disintegrates. However, as with all dadaist performance, it would be wholly untrue to suggest that there is no meaning here. Rather, Ball's poem can be read as a particular response to a particular issue. Remember, in 1916 war raged across Europe, a war Ball rejected as imperialist posturing. If language is a tool of the powerful, what action could be more subversive than totally repudiating its communicative abilities? The state has appropriated logical language; to fight against it, one need only question language's ability to tell the truth (Harding 2013: 6). No politician could appropriate the words of *Gadji Beri Bimba* for his or her unscrupulous purposes.

Our last example of modernist poetic performance takes us to Britain and to the work of Edith Sitwell. Marinetti, Ball and Sitwell represent a strikingly unusual (and perhaps unworkable) triumvirate, but they all explored ideas about language that challenged conventional thought and played with notions of interdisciplinarity, refusing to separate poetry (generally regarded as the domain of muses, quiet contemplation and babbling brooks) from other art forms or from contemporary events. Sitwell's *Façade* (1923) consisted of numerous poems set to music by the famed British composer William Walton. While the first performance took place in 1923, *Façade* has a fascinating history; by 1942 a new performance saw the artist John Piper design the curtains. Sitwell (and others) performed the poems through a Sengerphone, a large megaphone. If you listen to this work (readily available on YouTube) you will find a collection of odd poems which Sitwell reads rhythmically but without any particular tonal changes. Despite the music in the background, she does not sing the words but neither are the words entirely absent of musical feel. In fact *Façade* can be read alongside dadaist experiments, although the parallel is not wholly straightforward, particularly as Sitwell seemed to take the whole performance rather seriously. If Marinetti celebrated the sounds of war and Ball critiqued the politicians' use of language, what was the contemporary relevance of *Façade*? Alan Young suggests that *Façade* attacked a 'self-satisfied and Philistine middle-class establishment', challenging audiences to rethink their conceptions of art (1983: 51).

The uniting factor here is that in all three cases the audience was forced to reimagine the notion of poetry. The poem was no longer purely a romantic, contemplative mode to be read but a more performative mode to be heard and seen, even if this process remained rather perplexing. This transformed poetry from introspective narratives to be enjoyed in silence to noisy, complex responses to contemporary society. The difference between poetry and performance grew increasingly difficult to discern. In fact, reflecting the central ideas of this chapter, Taxidou suggests that 'in many ways, the whole epic tradition from Wagner to Brecht presents such an attempt to poeticise the stage' (2007: 100).

In his introduction to *The Cambridge Introduction to Modernist Poetry*, Peter Howarth makes a useful connection; he parallels the multiplicity of voices and discordant layering with technological innovations, namely the gramophone and the radio (2012: 25). The ability to record and replay voices significantly transformed the way auditors heard art, being able to listen in an entirely different context from that of the original artwork; today one can listen to a war correspondent reporting back from Afghanistan while eating dinner in Finchley, or to the headline act at Glastonbury without navigating the muddy fields.

Many modernist playwrights worked in radio, using this modern invention to ensure that theatre reached a mass audience. This use of radio became particularly prevalent in Britain where writers such as W.H. Auden and Louis MacNeice wrote particularly innovative radio plays that reached many more people than a typical theatre-based performance might have done. The BBC (British Broadcasting Corporation) remained at the forefront of this new trend. As Christina Baade writes in *Victory through Harmony*, the BBC became synonymous with British (or perceived British) values of culture, challenging the empty consumerist popular American cultural scene with a more educational, uplifting programming engendering a 'common culture' that transcended class borders and enabled everyone to access the best music, documentaries and plays (2012: 16). This became ever more important as the Second World War took hold, with the BBC becoming as much a tool of propaganda as a source of entertainment for a population contending with blitzes and blackouts.

There are many examples of the radio play but we will focus on Louis MacNeice's *Christopher Columbus* (1942). At first listen this might seem like a fairly straightforward piece of historical poetic drama about the adventures of the fifteenth-century Spanish explorer. However, context is useful here. MacNeice wrote his play just as the US entered the war and the piece is about the initial discovery of Britain's new ally. Using conventions from Greek epic, MacNeice created two antagonistic choruses: the Doubt Chorus and the Faith Chorus. This dialogue between doubt and faith audibly exemplified the debates of war where armies could be victorious or defeated, could stand in solidarity or else battle against each other. MacNeice's poetry – 'West of Europe lies a world/ Never heard of, never seen,/ But the sails that still are furled/ Soon shall reach a new demesne./ All the things that might have been – / When we cross the Western Sea,/ All those things shall be, shall be' (Faith Chorus) (1942: 21) – illustrates the inner debate of Columbus while also reflecting some of the contemporaneous issues of the mid twentieth century. The Faith Chorus's positive approach repudiates the Doubt Chorus's discouragement, leaving the audience with the impression that this world 'West of Europe' (that is, America, of course) could come to the Allies' aid. Even now, reworking these plays would be an excellent test for any performer, relying far more on the inflection of the voice, recorded sounds and music than physical gesture. We can become so used to sight as the primary sense in the theatre that radio plays, forcing us to use other senses, prove a challenging test.

If radio became a medium for transporting words, it became an even more popular conduit of music. During the twentieth century, music, and the way people accessed music, changed considerably. Our three poetry examples all explored music in different ways; Marinetti used drumming, Ball turned to bells and tapped rhythms, and Sitwell collaborated with Walton to provide the musical accompaniment needed. Music remained a key part of Brecht's and Wagner's contrasting concepts of total theatre, interrupting the action for the former and supplying atmosphere and unity for the latter. Many musicians adopted a similarly experimental attitude as their theatrical cousins: composers such as Igor Stravinsky, Arnold Schoenberg, Béla Bartók and Erik Satie among many others. I would recommend exploring the work of these musicians even if their works may pose a challenge to our ears. Indeed, Daniel Albright suggests that more than any other artistic genre, music embodies and promotes a sense of the modern. This is largely, he contends, because one can study a Roman statue or read Petrarch's sonnets but cannot really be sure what ancient Greek music, for example, sounded like. Before the advent of recording techniques (such as the radio), music 'has always been the most temporally immediate of the arts' (Albright 2004: 1). Perhaps the same could be said in the technological age where music continued to reside at the cusp of the vanguard and search for newness.

Even old established musical forms such as opera underwent a profoundly disturbing transformation. Whereas Wagner's concept of opera as an integrated form continued to hold influence over many modernists, others seemed to actively challenge this understanding of the opera mode. One clear example is from the Russian futurist canon: *Victory Over the Sun* (1913). Described as the world's first futurist opera (and presented in a rather unusual double bill with *Vladimir Mayakovsky: a tragedy*, performed the day before), *Victory Over the Sun* brought together Kruchenykh and Khlebnikov's *zaum* language with Mikhail Matiushin's anti-music and Kazimir Malevich's abstract sets. The performance was predictably noisy, with the sound of propellers, odd songs and recitation of *zaum* words which seemed little more than a collection of vowels and consonants (Bartlett and Dadswell 2012: 42–4). A contemporary reviewer focused on the peculiar sounds he heard:

> At the beginning there was a Borodin-like indulgence of seconds,
> then whole-tone scales, later still muddle and more muddle,

Surprisingly, in the middle of the latter flashed hints of the melodies of Puccini's *Bohème*.

(Bartlett and Dadswell 2012: 92)

This reflection is insightful; the reviewer acknowledged both the music's potential intertextual relationships (rather surprisingly, with works by stalwarts of the romantic traditions in Russia and Italy) while also admitting its completely incomprehensible originality. A later comment from one of the student performers of *Victory Over the Sun* confirms the perplexingly innovative characteristics of the music: 'these arias, as in all the music of Matiushin, sounded like Verdi played wrongly' (Bartlett and Dadswell 2012: 199).

Later in the century Theodor Adorno promoted modernist music as a direct provocation to years of predictable rhythms and dreamy melodies. In his 1948 *Philosophy of Modern Music*, Adorno made some remarkable and contentious claims, opposing the history of music since Beethoven with the twelve-tone music of Schoenberg. The latter, Adorno suggested, creates 'music, compressed into a moment . . . valid as an eruptive revelation of negative experience' (Albright 2004: 273). For Adorno the world of the Holocaust, famine and total war could not be expressed in melodic tunes but, rather, in the disquieting, disconnected notes of Schoenberg's vision. Once again, the modernist world and modernist art reflected each other. Despite the disturbing combination of notes, Schoenberg celebrated the connections between art forms, thereby contributing another facet to our growing understanding of cross-disciplinary art. Indeed, these connections became particularly clear in 1911/12 correspondence between Schoenberg and the artist who began our chapter: Kandinsky. Responding to *The Yellow Sound*, Schoenberg expressed some concern over terminology but clearly admired the piece, suggesting particular parallels between the two artists' work:

We must become conscious that there are puzzles around us. And we must find the courage to look these puzzles in the eye without timidly asking about 'the solution'.

(Albright 2004: 171)

Irritatingly obtuse as this may seem, Schoenberg's comments about *The Yellow Sound* remain startlingly liberating and freeing. His description equally chimes with the intentions and ideas of some of the key avant-garde movements; expressionism in particular, with its focus on the unconscious intangible, seemed to connect with modernist music, which sought to break through recognisable systems and tones to find some latent unusual sounds lying underneath.

In many of the movements we have examined during the course of this book, music proved a central concern, even if that music can seem rather alien to our ears. In the *Manifesto of Futurist Musicians* (1911), Francesco Balilla Pratella concluded that musicians must 'free one's own musical sensibility from all influence or imitation of the past' and to this end 'desert musical lyceums, conservatories, and academies, and . . . consider free study as the only means of regeneration' (Rainey et al. 2009: 79). Just as many choreographers freed dance from the confines of ballet shoes and repressive training institutions, so Pratella encouraged musicians likewise to shun tradition in favour of experimental innovation. In fact Émile Jaques Dalcroze (choreographer, inventor of eurhythmics and Mary Wigman's teacher) suggested new ways of understanding the relationship between music and dance where, challenging the Wagnerian model, each art form remained autonomous. Rather than art forms slavishly following the demands of each other, each could find its own path, respectfully complementing one another rather than dictating conventions. Then 'moving plastic' (Dalcroze's term for modern dance) 'will live its own life, vibrate with its own rhythms, assert itself according to its own ordering' (Albright 2004: 89).

Whether understood as an independent art form or as accompaniment, music became a defining characteristic of modernist performance. Emmy Hennings, for example, contributed much of the music for the dadaist soirées. As a professional cabaret performer, fellow dadaist Richard Huelsenbeck reflected, 'she sang Hugo Ball's aggressive songs with an anger we had to credit her with although we scarcely thought her capable of it' (1969: 16). Ignoring Huelsenbeck's irritating condescension, his comment points to Hennings's style of performance. She traversed the boundary between cabaret singer and modernist musician, between the popular tradition and the innovatively avant-garde. As with many female avant-garde artists, all too often commentators refer to Hennings as a peripheral figure in the dada project, more famous for being Hugo Ball's wife than as an artist in her own right. When she is mentioned, by and large it is her colourful life (as drug addict, prostitute and later Catholic convert) rather than her career which takes centre stage. However, Ball and others regarded her influence over the burgeoning dada movement as far more important; in fact, in her important reassessment of 'dada's women', Ruth Hemus convincingly claims that, as an initial instigator and artist (both as a cabaret singer and performance poet), Hennings should be regarded as the 'mother' of dada just as Ball is regarded as the 'father' (2009: 18).

Jean Cocteau, too, having provided the scenario for the Ballets Russes' 1917 *Parade* (a highly influential work, particularly for the surrealists), placed music at the centre of his aesthetic project. Just a year after, he published the rather wonderfully titled *Cock and Harlequin*, a collection of ideas and deliberations about music, performance and art. The document resembles a surrealist manifesto with disconnected, dreamlike statements jostling within a largely unstructured narrative. *Cock and Harlequin* provides a new way of looking at music, detached from typical concepts of harmony, melody and natural rhythm. Music should not simply transport the audience to another world, it should in some way reflect the everyday. Cocteau likened it to a chair, a useful, everyday object (Albright 2004: 325). This might appear a remarkable comment from a surrealist thinker, but remember surrealism is as much about everyday life (and seeing through the façades of the everyday) as it is about dreamscapes and the fantastical. An artwork is surreal only when it focuses on making the ordinary extraordinary or the familiar unfamiliar.

In Spain, Gabriel García Lorca constructed very different theatrical work. In 1934 Lorca contended that contemporary theatre lacked vibrancy and intention, and 'has no right to call itself theatre, but an amusement hall, or a place for doing that dreadful thing known as "killing time"' (Krasner 2008: 204). In order to confront this perceived dullness, music took a central place in his aesthetic. In a 1930 talk Lorca discussed the importance of the *duende* to his work. '*Duende*' proves a difficult word to translate, for it may refer to either a soul or a sensibility, or a figure from folklore often associated with flamenco dancing. In Lorca's talk I like to imagine he means a little of both. The *duende* rises up from music and, according to Lorca, causes creativity and pain almost simultaneously. Art from all geographical areas potentially exhibits the *duende*, despite its relationship with flamenco. Understandably, the *duende* works on the body, causing it to move with a profound sense of magic. Finally the *duende* 'does not repeat himself, any more than do the forms of the sea during a squall' (Drain 1995: 264). While the *duende* remains rather difficult to grasp, two things become clear; firstly, the *duende* (and subsequently Lorca's project) is imbued with a spiritual, almost mystical element, something we cannot quite define while we are yet convinced of its presence. Secondly, music provides the catalyst.

Lorca both incorporated music into his plays but also constructed each play like a musical score. Take his best-known play, *Blood Wedding* (1934). The play is punctuated by songs: the mother-in-law's lullaby for the baby in act 1, scene 2, the bridal song in act 2, scene 2, the Moon's lyrical poetry in act 3, scene 1. But the entire piece seems to be suffused with musical motifs and sounds; as Herbert Blau and the San Francisco Actors' Workshop discovered in 1952, its lyricism is like a dithyrambic chant, its language influenced by *cante jondo* or gypsy songs, the whole effect pulsing with an 'incantatory power' (Blau 2013: 23). It is impossible to perform *Blood Wedding* without a ready awareness of its musicality.

Arguably the startlingly way these performances sounded – their words and music – marks the greatest change in the theatrical spaces of the modernist avant-garde. In my first-year Modern European Drama class, nothing causes more consternation than Ball's *Gadji Beri Bimba*! Before we move on, however, I should make the case for the unparalleled influence of musical rhythm over modernist avant-garde performance, and particularly in the way performances were structured. We have already claimed that the fragmented narratives of the expressionists or the variety theatre-influenced evenings of the dadaists reflected the importance of musical forms, but I want to end this section by focusing on a case study that exemplifies the power and importance of music to the modernist dramatic form. August Strindberg, the Swedish playwright who worked with symbolist, expressionist and naturalist methods during the course of his career, wrote *The Ghost Sonata* in 1907 as part of a series of chamber plays, a dramatic form structured in three parts using a small cast. As well as nodding to a range of other conventions we have already explored (the metatheatrical mention of attending the theatre, the influence of fairy tales and the oral tradition, and a focus on the spiritual unseen), *The Ghost Sonata* suggests the importance of music simply through its title. Like the chamber play, the sonata is often structured in three parts and often the three exhibit little overt resemblance to each other, express-ing different moods, speeds and atmospheres. That said, a sonata might well contain musical phrases that reappear throughout the piece; in the Old Man's terms 'the same theme, the leitmotif, returns again and again, like clockwork' (Cardullo and Knopf 2001: 138). With its three contrasting parts, *The Ghost Sonata* certainly resembles a musical sonata. It opens with a quickly paced scene between the Student and the Old Man; the middle scene takes us into the creepy Round Room, slowing the action yet interspersing it with strik-ing moments of revelation. The final scene quietly concludes the piece and stresses the central themes of living in deceit and dying to attain freedom. Bringing us full circle, the theatrical work the Old Man encourages the student to attend is Wagner's *The Valkyrie*, part of his *Ring Cycle*. Music provides a vital structural method here; in fact Evert Sprinchorn goes so far as to say that unless the viewer understands *The Ghost Sonata* as a sonata 'it is impossible to appreciate its artistic wholeness and the way in which all the pieces fit together' (Cardullo and Knopf 2001: 132).

SEEING THE AVANT-GARDE

If the modernist avant-garde transformed the way we hear performance, it also changed the way we see it. There developed an innate connection between visual art and set design; Lyubov Popova and Vsevolod Meyerhold, as we have seen, shared a remarkably fruitful artistic relationship. But we can identify many other striking examples. The collaboration of John Piper (who created the curtains for the later version of Sitwell's *Façade*) and Stephen Spender on the latter's expressionistic 1938 *Trial of a Judge* stands as a useful (and, it must be said, rare) British example. Detailing the rise of fascism and its rejection of judicial law, the original version employed Piper's terrifying backdrop of geometrical shapes and shadowy corners (Sidnell 1984: 231). The stage visually embodied the central theme: the ascendancy of repressive fascist dictatorship. When, towards the end, the Chorus of Red Prisoners affirmed they will 'be free' and will 'find peace', the walls dividing the prison cells collapsed so the prisoners could join hands (Spender 1938: 112). The set reflected the hopeful change in perspective with walls (literal and metaphorical) collapsing in the face of optimistic solidarity.

In 1919 the German architect Walter Gropius established a school called the Bauhaus. At this juncture, I should add that a number of architects experimented with modernist techniques during the early decades of the twentieth century. While I have no intention of venturing down this path, it would certainly be worth wandering through the magnificent photographs of buildings by Le Corbusier and Mies van der Rohe, particularly if you are a theatre set designer. Set design and architecture reflected similar (typically modernist) concerns: space, functionality and the disposal of superfluous features. Refusing to be restricted by disciplinary borders, Gropius transformed himself from architect to theatre designer, advocating a united approach to building a new world in his 1919 *What is Architecture?*:

> Painters and sculptors, break through the barriers to architecture and become fellow builders, fellow strugglers for the final goal of art: the creative conception of the cathedral of the future.
>
> (Danchev 2011: 161)

Examining images, buildings and designs created by the Bauhaus, certain traits stand out. Objects were functional, with unnecessary decoration discarded in favour of utility. Posters presented geometrical shapes (not unlike the constructivists), using clear fonts far removed from the traditional German *Fraktur* script yet retaining an element of aesthetic beauty. Buildings became functional boxes, with tactile curves and large white surfaces. Compare them to the fussy Gothic revival style of the nineteenth century and you will get a clear sense of the modernist transformation of architecture. While the Bauhaus focused on architecture and visual art, theatre remained a primary concern, particularly in Gropius's collaboration with fellow German Erwin Piscator.

Piscator propagated an epic theatre model not far removed from Brecht's. In fact the two admired each other, working together on a range of projects. Brecht described Piscator's innovations in glowing terms:

> Piscator's experiments broke nearly all conventions. They intervened to transform the playwright's creative methods, the actor's style of

representation, and the work of the stage designer. They were striving towards an entirely new social function for the theatre.

(Brecht 2001: 131)

Like Brecht, then, Piscator aimed for a theatre that would not merely entertain but also tell the audience about the world outside the theatre walls, educating spectators by smashing through illusion, deceit and political hegemony. In doing so Piscator turned to the design of his stage. For hundreds of years, Piscator maintained, the stage imagined 'there were no spectators in the house' (Drain 1995: 104), creating an insurmountable separation between stage and auditorium. This is not, of course, wholly fair or accurate; clearly without an audience present even the most naturalistic of actors would not bother to take to the stage. However, Piscator advocated a newly democratised arena for spectators, imagining a different way of designing sets, one that used the latest technological developments and provided new functional spaces for actors. In fact John Willett suggests that Piscator's grasp of stage design 'far excelled that of any other director of his time' (1978: 184).

Piscator remained evangelical in his desire to transform the stage: 'the way ahead seemed clearer, a way which would lead to political drama and to the hotly disputed technical revolution in the theater' (Piscator 1980: 77). He described the central aims of his project thus:

What I had in mind was a theater machine, technically as perfectly functional as a typewriter, an apparatus that would incorporate the latest lighting, the latest sliding and revolving scenery, both vertical and horizontal, numerous projection boxes, loudspeakers everywhere, etc.

(1980: 179)

In seeking ways of dramatically transforming the stage, Piscator turned to some of the leading artists of the day, including Gropius. In 1921 Piscator demanded a theatre building that would enable him to present politically engaged work. Gropius responded to this call. He designed a theatre based on the principles of the Bauhaus. Unrelentingly flexible, Gropius's performance space centred on a circular stage which could provide a theatre-in-the-round, an arena stage or a thrust stage. Piscator could even change between these types of stages mid performance. Twelve pillars would act as film projection screens, surrounding the audience with images (Patterson 1981: 118). Gropius described his designs as 'total theatre', though clearly his intention remained quite different from Wagner's:

The aim of this theater is no longer to accumulate a collection of fanciful technical apparatus and gimmickry; everything is a means to an end: the end is to draw the spectator into the middle of the scenic events, to make him part of the space in which events are taking place and prevent him from escaping from them under cover of the curtain.

(Piscator 1980: 183)

Sadly the designs never made it to the stage and, due to financial constraints, Piscator reined in his ambition, although the collaborative designs remain some of the most revolutionary of the modernist period.

Piscator continued to work with a range of visual artists including the Hungarian Lázló Moholy-Nagy and the German George Grosz. The designs of the latter transformed Piscator's 1928 version of *The Good Soldier Schweik*. Based on a 1923 novel by the Czech Jaroslav Hašek, the story follows the bumbling soldier Schweik through numerous ridiculous adventures during the First World War. For Piscator, the appeal of Hašek's tale lay in its focus on an ordinary soldier rather than the machinations of war *per se*. Instead we see these machinations through the eyes of Schweik, who witnesses the snobbery of the generals, the class-ridden hierarchies of the army and the wholly unnecessary deaths of millions at the whims of rich, powerful men sitting far away from the Front. In response to these themes, Grosz created filmed cartoon sequences and grotesque cut-out marionettes. Scene 4, for example, saw Schweik waving his crutch in the air pushed in a wheelchair by his landlady while, in the other direction, the cut-out figures travelled past them on a moving treadmill (Willett 1978: 91). The effect must have been extraordinary and paved the way for many future developments in set design.

In addition, many painters turned to performance as another artistic method. Oskar Kokoschka and Jean Cocteau would be two examples. Indeed, one can identify the interdependent relationship between the stage and the gallery (their dramatic art and their visual art) in their plays. *Murderer Hope of Womankind*, for example, contains a selection of graphic tableaux, resembling paintings rather than fully narrated dramatic scenes. Cocteau's *The Eiffel Tower Wedding Party* (1921) is equally visual. The vista of Paris from the top of the Eiffel Tower provides the backdrop and the characters are seen through the camera of the Photographer who attempts to get them into coherent groups. The arrival of the wedding party is announced by two actors dressed as Phonographs, forcing us again to reimagine the human body (and voice) in mechanical terms. The listing of wedding party guests enables small tableaux to form (Cocteau 1967: 164). But the mechanical and the orchestrated framed pictures are interrupted by the arrival of a Cyclist who Phonograph 1 calls a 'mirage . . . that bicycle girl is actually pedalling along the Chatou road' (1967: 166). As one would expect in an ostensibly surrealist play (envisioned as a ballet), incongruous characters and images can burst through settled tableaux, transforming the way we, as audience members, see the stage.

THE CINEMATIC AVANT-GARDE

In 1925 Piscator mounted a new production entitled *In Spite of Everything*, a documentary play narrating the recent history of Germany through the First World War and on to the deaths of the communist agitators Karl Liebknecht and Rosa Luxemburg in 1919. Piscator described the set as a selection of platforms and terraces standing on a revolving stage. On this stage Piscator searched for a 'means of showing how human-superhuman factors interact with classes or individuals' (Drain 1995: 105). As Piscator identified, film provided the answer:

> These shots brutally demonstrated the horror of war: flame thrower
> attacks, piles of mutilated bodies, burning cities; war films had not
> yet come into 'fashion', so these pictures were bound to have a more
> striking impact on the masses of the proletariat than a hundred lectures.
>
> (Drain 1995: 105)

Today images from around the world are constantly beamed into our living rooms and can even be accessed on our phones. Imagine the profound shock such graphic images of war would have caused to 1920s audiences unused to such realism on the screen.

Interest in cinema grew exponentially in the modernist period, prompting a range of responses to this new dominant medium. Chiming with the central contentions of modernism, cinema 'in its early years [was] inseparable from the cultural and conceptual fascination with questions of motion and movement' (Marcus 2007: 18). Yet the brash new form met with a mixed response. Some rejected cinema as empty mass entertainment, bombarding its viewers with images yet giving little scope for real intellectual or artistic engagement. Others celebrated its potential as a form or its democratising effect. Certainly many of the movements and practitioners mentioned here were also involved in film. Some of the most interesting examples came from the surrealists. Indeed, the very early experiments in the cinematic form pre-emptively exhibit a strange, otherworldly sense of the surreal: check out George Méliès's wonderful 1902 *The Trip to the Moon*, featuring the iconic image of the space capsule landing in the Moon's eye. The surrealists' interest in cinema is no surprise, for perhaps more than any other art form, film can juxtapose the real and the dreamlike in fascinating ways. The Mexican film director Luis Buñuel's *Cinema, Instrument of Poetry* (written in 1958) provides an insightful interpretation of the value of cinema for surrealist artists. The article begins with a damning critique of contemporaneous cinema which hypnotises the spectator and neglects any sense of poetry or mystery. However, he refused to reject cinema as a form, proposing it as a 'magnificent and perilous weapon when wielded by a free spirit' (Hammond 1991: 119). Indeed, cinema 'seems to have been invented to express the subconscious life', able to combine the real and the fantastical to 'open up to me the marvellous world of the unknown, of all that which I find neither in the newspaper nor in the street' (Hammond 1991: 120–1). Films such as Buñuel's *Un Chien Andalou* (*An Andalusian Dog*, 1929, produced in collaboration with artist Salvador Dalí), René Clair and Francis Picabia's *Entr'acte* (another collaboration between film-maker and artist, 1924) and *The Seashell and the Clergyman* (directed by Germaine Dulac in 1928 from a screenplay by Antonin Artaud) all reflect the surrealist preoccupation with making the everyday fantastical and the real peculiarly unreal. All three also supply particularly vibrant catalysts for contemporary stage performance, particularly if you are looking to experiment with surrealist imagery in a devised piece or new script.

While we have only really mentioned this influential art form in passing, it is important to grasp cinema's significance, not least because of its tremendous influence over live theatrical performance. Piscator's experiments for *In Spite of Everything* can be read as part of an ongoing modernist project to integrate the arts, using film as a key component of theatre. While not many practitioners used film directly on the stage during this period, the influence of the cinematic can be felt everywhere. Charlie Chaplin, in particular, seemed to be a figure admired by many modernist theatre figures. Brecht, for example (whose own foray into film can be seen in his 1932 socialist movie *Kuhle Wampe – Who Owns the World?*), described Chaplin as an epic actor (2001: 56) while Meyerhold concluded that his techniques closely resembled those of biomechanics (Pitches 2003: 74–5). The Marx Brothers also interested modernist artists, with Artaud (the figure, do not forget, who created the Theatre of Cruelty) claiming that the events of *Animal Crackers* (the Marx Brothers' comical 1930 film) should be applauded for the 'kind of powerful disturbance that their effect ultimately produces in the mind' (1976: 242). Modernist admiration for mainstream comedy once again deconstructs typical divides between high and low art.

One of the most influential thinkers about cinema came from the Russia of Meyerhold and the constructivists: Sergei Eisenstein. Eisenstein's films remain widely known and widely available, still highly influential over contemporary film-makers. Many of his scenes are iconic, including the baby's pram falling down the steps from his 1925 *Battleship Potemkin*, mirrored as late as 1987 in the gangster film *The Untouchables*. His films retain a strong political bent, reanimating actual events (*October*, 1928) or critiquing pre-communist Russia (*Strike*, 1925). While he remains best known as a revolutionary film-maker, Eisenstein also worked in the theatre, attempting to create dramatic performances that furthered the advances of the new Bolshevik party and celebrated working-class experience. His most influential idea confronted the issue of narrative structure and united his theatre with his film work. He termed this innovation the 'montage of attractions'. I will leave it to Eisenstein to describe what he meant:

> I regard the attraction as being in normal condition an independent and primary element in structuring the show, a molecular (i.e. compound) unity of the *effectiveness* of theatre and of *theatre as a whole*.
>
> (Drain 1995: 89)

Perhaps we are, as yet, none the wiser. For Eisenstein the 'attraction' was a moment, a specific instance of shock, surprise, aggression. If one structures a theatre event in this manner, any sense of unitary flow disappears, replaced by a fragmented collection of images, a 'montage' to use Eisenstein's terminology. This means that film-makers can 'shift the focus of attention to the essential'; spectators are drawn into a specific image/moment/event which, though part of a larger context, suddenly becomes the primary focus (Drain 1995: 90). The pram image in *Battleship Potemkin* provides a visual rendering of what Eisenstein meant here. Actually the famous image is simply one moment in a far larger tsarist massacre on the Odessa Steps, Ukraine. The baby in the pram bumping its way precariously down the enormous stone staircase memorably interrupts the massacre with a moment of extreme individual peril.

So what difference might this make to the theatre? Well, as with many of the traditions and conventions we have explored during the course of this book, the montage of attractions disrupts narrative flow, creating a selection of fragments. In this sense Eisenstein's ideas resemble the living newspapers of the Federal Theatre Project, the *Verfremdungs-Effekt* of Brecht, the jagged movements of Martha Graham, or the *Stationendrama* of the expressionists. Eisenstein's ideas can be read in parallel to (or even directly influenced) all these innovations. One of the most fruitful direct collaborations was between Eisenstein and the constructivist playwright Sergei Tretyakov. In 1923 Tretyakov wrote *Earth Rampant*, a play about a troop mutiny. He focused on specific events ('attractions' in Eisenstein's terms), separating them into individual images. Produced at the Meyerhold Theatre, *Earth Rampant* took the idea of theatrical montage to new levels, focusing on the way actors should respond to such fragmented narratives. Using Tretyakov's own words, Robert Leach gives some sense of the Russian's methods:

> He [Tretyakov] himself defined the problem as being 'to teach the actor-worker not to converse and not to declaim, but to speak'. This he attempted to do by shifting the emphasis away from the melodic elements in speech, the vowels, on to the 'articulatoryonomatopoeic (the consonants)', and away from 'conversational intonation (usually unreal

anyway, since real conversation accumulates verbal rubbish as well as all sorts of drawings in of breath, hiccoughs, clearings of the throat and other messy noises)'.

(Christie and Taylor 1993: 117)

So not only was the play structured as an Eisensteinian montage, the very way the actors spoke reflected the film-maker's conclusions. Cinematic methods not only affected the structure of the theatre but also the behaviour of its actors. In the same year, Eisenstein and Tretyakov collaborated on another production entitled *Gas Masks* which they actually staged in a factory, pushing the constructivist vision of a factory stage to new limits.

TRAVERSING ARTISTIC BORDERS

All the figures mentioned in this chapter searched for methods that would enable them to create cross-disciplinary theatrical models, whether resembling the integrated ideas of Wagner or the more fragmented methods of Brecht. Indeed, as I have suggested, many of the performances discussed in previous chapters complement the argument here, from the variety theatres of the dadaists and futurists, to the pageants of Soviet Russia or Nazi Germany. Despite significant differences, it would not be remiss to read the work of Chekhov or Shaw in this cross-disciplinary way. In concluding, I simply encourage you to view each performance you encounter as stretching the very notion of theatre, questioning the primacy of the written script and creating works that, to borrow Eisenstein's term, 'attract' in some way. This approach remained a central premise as the century progressed and the twenty-first century dawned. As an example, in 1960 Guy Debord, the founder of the situationists (a group that built on modernist avant-garde innovations by critiquing late capitalism and its reliance on spectacle and consumption), promoted a new art 'against particularized art, it will be a global practice with a bearing, each moment, on all the usable elements' (Danchev 2011: 350). In our Conclusion we follow Debord's proclamation and discover a community of artists continuing the modernist avant-garde project.

PRACTICAL EXPLORATION

In order to understand modernist avant-garde performance it seems increasingly vital to situate it within broader narratives of modernism. Take the time to explore paintings, music, sculpture and film. It is worth consulting some of the excellent introductions to modernism mentioned in

Chapter 1. But it is equally worth simply taking yourself on a fascinating journey through the art of the twentieth century. If you need some prompts then turn to some of the more well-known: Edvard Munch's *The Scream*, Pablo Picasso's *Les Demoiselles D'Avignon*, Pierre Mondrian's *Composition A*, Igor Stravinsky's *The Rite of Spring*, Arnold Schoenberg's *Erwartung*, Marcel Duchamp's readymades, Jacob Epstein's *Rock Drill Bronze*, Bertolt Brecht's *Kuhle Wampe*, Sergei Eisenstein's *Battleship Potemkin* and René Clair and Francis Picabia's *Entr'acte*. What makes these artworks modernist and how might they help us to understand modernist performance better?

Consider the use of senses in the theatre. Using an extract from *Christopher Columbus* or another of the BBC radio plays, perform it before a small audience who have their eyes closed. Then perform it again for the audience with their eyes open. What problems did the audience discover?

Playing with the senses was an ongoing preoccupation of the modernist avant-garde. Using either the short futurist play or the living newspaper piece you wrote earlier, consider the way you might create a multi-sensory experience. How might you work this out on the stage?

Try performing one of Marinetti's sound poems or Ball's *Verse Ohne Worte*. What are some of the challenges/joys involved?

Ensure you have a full understanding of the differences between the Wagnerian and Brechtian models. What are the differing intentions and effects?

Watch the Odessa Steps scene from Eisenstein's *Battleship Potemkin* (you can access this easily on YouTube). Can you identify the key elements of his montage of attractions from this scene? How might you relate this method to the theatre?

Before we go on to the Conclusion, revisit your 'shifts of accent' table created in Chapter 1. How might you add to it or change it?

In the Conclusion we briefly examine a range of contemporary practitioners who use or parallel modernist avant-garde techniques. Before we discuss these, can you think of any late twentieth-century or even current playwrights/directors/actors/companies who build (consciously or otherwise) on these modernist foundations?

Conclusion

In the opening paragraphs of this book, I suggested multiple ways of under-standing 'modernist' and 'avant-garde'. They might denote a specific period of time from the late nineteenth to the mid twentieth centuries, but also might describe ways of creating oppositional new artworks by pushing boundaries and responding (often antagonistically) to art history. In our everyday parlance we continue to use both words, with 'avant-garde' in particular transcending chronological partitions and even appearing in contemporary arts reviews sections of mainstream newspapers.

Scholars and practitioners continue to question these troublesome terms, sometimes claiming any artwork exhibiting unusual aesthetic characteristics as 'modernist' or 'avant-garde'. This creates potential problems, for terminology can become virtually meaningless in the face of such myriad definitions. But such an open-ended approach also engenders potential new dialogues and parallels. As mentioned in the introduction, from a scholarly perspective Douglas Mao and Rebecca L. Walkowitz sum up the change in modernist studies in one word: 'expansion' (2008: 737). This 'expansion' can be read artistically (modernist scholarship now focuses on everything from pottery to ship design), geographically (the US and Britain are not necessarily regarded as the dominant centre points) and in terms of identity politics, with welcome new examinations of artistic work by women and people of colour.

Having refused to be drawn on issues of terminology throughout this book, I have no intention of becoming embroiled in them now. However, I do think it is perfectly possible to identify persisting elements of modernist avant-garde theatrical experimentation in late twentieth-century theatre and even in contemporary performance. I use as my guarantor here the German scholar Hans-Thies Lehmann, whose book *Postdramatic Theatre* (first published in

1999 on the cusp of the new century) continues to influence a wide range of contemporary performance scholars and practitioners. Lehmann suggests that postdramatic theatre (a troublesome term indeed) builds on the innovations of the modernist avant-garde, for 'here the conventional dramaturgy of unity was first disrupted' (2010: 57). It is an approach similarly taken by Bruce McConachie in chapter 9 of his co-edited introductory textbook *Theatre Histories* (Zarrilli et al. 2010). He entitles the chapter 'Modernism in drama and performance, 1880–1970', smashing through the genealogical boundary lines we tentatively drew up in the Introduction to this book. McConachie concludes that three generations of modernist theatre succeeded each other: 1880–1910, 1910–40 and 1940–70. It is a bold claim and yet his evidence from Chekhov to Beckett gives a strong (if multi-directional) sense of genealogy. McConachie also presents ideas and aesthetics now familiar to us, such as 'theatres for reform and revolution', as transcending any typical modernist dates, instead becoming pre-eminent traditions of the whole twentieth century. Positing a 'postmodern avant-garde', Günter Berghaus argues that mainstream culture appropriated avant-garde techniques in the second half of the twentieth century, ridding them of their antagonistic intensity. And yet, he suggests, there remain 'artists and artistic trends who represented a last flourish of the avant-garde' (2005b: 78). In fact, he concludes *Avant-Garde Performance* with the hopeful proclamation that the turn of the last millennium marked a 'threshold of a Second Modernity that ushered in a new age of avant-garde experimentation' (2005b: 259).

So, in what ways do the sensibilities of the modernist avant-garde remain and how have they influenced later performances? In this final section I propose to give only a brief overview of practitioners, performers and happenings that seem to build on the techniques of the modernist avant-garde, even if they are more commonly referred to as 'postmodern' or 'neo-avant-garde' or, indeed, ignore problematic terminology altogether. Some of these figures nod to their historical modernist precursors and some seem keen to present their work as entirely new. Either way, these later performative moments can nevertheless be read as part of a distinct modernist avant-garde genealogy.

The Polish artist, designer and director Tadeusz Kantor, for example, used mannequins as central figures in his theatrical productions. Although different in intention, Kantor's work can be read as part of the project to bring the non-human to the stage as exemplified in the work of Edward Gordon Craig some years earlier. The British director Peter Brook remains open about his modernist roots, citing Artaud as a major influence. Brook's 1964 version of Peter Weiss's *Marat/Sade* remains a seminal moment in the history of avant-garde theatre, a working out of Artaud's ideas on the Royal Shakespeare Company stage. Brook's theatre is also indebted to the work of the Polish director and thinker Jerzy Grotowski, whose concept of 'poor theatre' reflects one of the central modernist concerns to strip theatre back to its essential elements rather than competing with new technologies like film and television. Like the dadaists and futurists before him, Grotowski also viewed applause with suspicion, preferring instead 'special silence' (1981: 44). Similar to Meyerhold's or Laban's methodologies, his actors received rigorous physical training and, as with all the modernists in their unique ways, dug underneath the everyday with its assumptions and set beliefs to find 'what is hidden behind our everyday mask' (Grotowski 1981: 37). One of Grotowski's pupils, Eugenio Barba, an Italian living in Denmark, advocates a cross-cultural theatre, admiring the Indian *Kathakali* form and Japanese *Kabuki* just as Brecht revered Mei Lang-Fan. The founder of the Odin Teatret in Oslo in 1964, Barba's actor training employs a range of approaches from Meyerhold, Stanislavsky, Craig and Copeau (Turner 2004: 13). Another figure who adopts a distinctly cross-cultural perspective is the American Richard Schechner. Schechner's focus on the performer and his/her training challenges reliance on dramatic text or dull prescriptive templates in a similar way to his modernist precursors. Indeed, he states that his central ideas have 'been implicit in western theater since the end of the nineteenth century' (2003: 239). His groundbreaking *Dionysus in '69* (The Performance Group, New York, 1969) took the ancient Greek story of *The Bacchae* by Euripides and reinterpreted it for a modern audience. Performing the piece with minimal costume (and later naked), actors invited audience members to view the show from wherever they wanted and to join in with certain scenes. The piece resembled a ritualistic ceremony rather than theatre *per se*. It caused enormous controversy, not least because of the perceived exploitation of the actors, compelled to perform naked among groping strangers. Also, as Christopher Innes suggests, when you invite audience members to participate without particularly defined roles, the performance moves away from inclusive ritual and towards an 'alien rite' where only certain people get it and the rest simply imitate (1981: 184). Nevertheless it remains one of the most compelling and influential moments of post-war twentieth-century performance.

While Innes's reflection is correct, it is not universally accurate. The Briton Tim Crouch, for example, explores the dynamics of the auditorium, beginning with his 2003 *The Arm* in which, perhaps mirroring Duchamp's readymades, he invited audience members to lend their personal belongings which he transformed into characters in the story. Audience participation remains a vital part of his theatre making, illustrated by his 2013 *What Happens to the Hope at the End of the Evening* in which two characters adopt markedly different roles, one addressing the audience directly from a lectern and one creating a naturalistic rendering of his story. Stephen Bottoms writes that Crouch's work is less about authorial presence than about exploring 'ways to *authorize* the spectator's participation in the performance process' (2009: 67). In doing so, Bottoms rightly suggests, Crouch's work insists 'upon the creative potentialities of "ordinary" audience members, on their ability to transform the mundane' and on the importance of literary drama and art performance 'existing *for* an audience rather than remaining self-sufficiently aloof' (2009: 76). All these reflections on Crouch's work are reminiscent of comments from the dadaists or futurists, from Laban or Brecht.

Like Schechner's *Dionysus in '69*, many other pieces have imbibed a sense of ritualism. In 1968 the US-based Living Theatre caused enormous controversy with its *Paradise Now!*, inviting audience members to writhe around on stage with almost naked performers in a 'love pile' (Freshwater 2009: 63). The US artist Ron Athey provoked a similar storm with his 1994 *Four Scenes in a Harsh Life* when he cut his fellow performer and hoisted bloodstained cloths in the air, leading to unwarranted panic about the potential spread of HIV. The violence of futurism, the shamanistic incantations of the dadaist Ball and the surrealist exploration of the body all act as intertextual precursors to these two events.

The 1960s Happenings movement (to which *Dionysus in '69* could be regarded as a contributor) exhibited a range of responses to the modernist avant-garde, some accepting it as a useful predecessor and others suggesting they were moving away from past traditions, however revolutionary. Allan Kaprow, one of the most prominent voices in the movement, contended that the first New York Happenings groups added to a 'direct line of historical stimulation (usually conscious) . . . [from] the Futurist manifestoes and noise concerts, Dada's chance experiments and occasional cabaret performances, Surrealism's interest in automatic drawing and poetry' (Sandford 1995: 219). Certainly many of the Happenings events (licking jam from cars etc.) resembled those of earlier in the century: experiential performance combining the mechanics of modernity with the visceral human body. The freedom of the Happenings was embodied in the ideas of Fluxus, a group that included the Lithuanian George Maciunas and the German Joseph Beuys. Advocating a quasi-dadaist notion of anti-art, the Fluxus group played with ideas of visual art and performance. Just like their predecessors, Fluxus artists (in the words of Maciunas's 1963 manifesto) wanted to 'purge the world of bourgeois sickness, "intellectual", professional & commercialised culture' (Danchev 2011: 365).

Reconsideration of the body remained a central concern for post-Second World War artists. Pina Bausch and her Tanztheater Wuppertal (established in 1973) based their movement techniques on emotion rather than learned technique. Bausch's training with Laban's pupil Kurt Jooss at the Folkwang School in Essen provided a clear expressionist foundation for her work (Climenhaga 2009: 4). In 1975 she produced a contentious version of that pinnacle of modernist performance, Stravinsky's *The Rite of Spring*, the dancers writhing on a red dirt floor. Like so many of the modernists, actor and innovator Jacques Lecoq worked with masks, enabling the actor to rid him or herself of artificial gesture. The resultant 'neutral mask, in the end, unmasks', that is, it unveils some deep inner truth (Lecoq 2002: 39). Escaping pretence and discovering truth was at the heart of much modernist mask work too. Recent performance artists have again questioned the limitations of the body, with the Cypriot artist Stelarc even surgically attaching an ear to his left arm (2007). Work like this not only challenges conceptions of the body but also disturbs the generic distinctions between performance and visual art.

In the so-called post-human age, the body has been intertwined with technology to create what Jennifer Parker-Starbuck describes as 'cyborg theatre', that is, theatre that fragments the human body (specifically the *female* human body) with technologies. Examples include the work of La Fura dels Baus (a Spanish company founded in 1979) and British director Katie Mitchell. Interestingly Parker-Starbuck suggests that twenty-first-century cyborg theatre, while associated with contemporary post-humanism, actually has a long history right back to ancient Greece. But she chooses to focus particularly on modernist figures such as Appia, Craig, the futurists, the constructivists, Piscator and the Federal Theatre Project (Parker-Starbuck 2011: 4–5). Certainly the term 'cyborg theatre' reminds us of the robots in *R.U.R.* Even the companies and practitioners Parker-Starbuck mentions acknowledge the persistent influence of modernism, with La Fura dels Baus producing *Ombra* (1998), constructing a performance from the fragmented texts of Lorca, and Katie Mitchell directing a version of Virginia Woolf's *The Waves* (2008).

The growth in new writing also points to the innovations of the modernist avant-garde. Often these new plays have caused enormous controversy. Edward Bond's *Saved* (1968), with its infamous baby-stoning scene, divided audiences and was instrumental in the eventual abolition of censorship in Britain. In 1980 Howard Brenton's *The Romans in Britain* led to a well-documented court case with its depiction of attempted homosexual rape. Both in part resemble their modernist predecessors, *The Romans in Britain* with its nod to antiquity (reminiscent of plays by Yeats and Eliot) and *Saved* in its naturalistic depiction of violence and social malaise. More recent playwrights such as Sarah Kane and Mark Ravenhill indicate the influence of modernist aesthetics on their work. In his critical study of so-called (and perhaps problematically called) 'in-yer-face theatre', Aleks Sierz connects the work of these playwrights with a strong legacy of agitational theatre or 'history of provocation' as he terms it (2001: 10). Artaud, Jarry, Strindberg, Wedekind and others, he suggests, pre-empted and influenced the work of late twentieth-century playwrights (2001: 14). Recent new writing builds on the legacy of the innovative realism of the naturalists and/or the poetic voice of the symbolists.

Many plays are also defined by a non-linearity, using fragmented, episodic structures in a similar manner to the expressionists; Martin Crimp's 1997 *Attempts on Her Life* springs immediately to mind. Since the publication of Sierz's book, new writing has continued to dominate the contemporary theatre scene, particularly in Britain, with innovative plays by Simon Stephens, Anthony Neilson and debbie tucker green among others. Gregory Burke's *Black Watch* (National Theatre Scotland, 2006) with its war theme, flexible playing space, use of projection and multiple avant-garde moments (such as the soldiers emerging foetus-like from the pub pool table) certainly chimes with the work of modernist figures such as Toller and Piscator. Its remarkable popularity, playing in Glasgow's SECC arena venue before touring internationally to sell-out crowds, confirms that such aesthetically and thematically challenging work can find an audience in the twenty-first century. This burgeoning new writing scene is not restricted to Britain. The Russian Presnyakov Brothers' (Oleg and Vladimir) 2002 *Terrorism*, for example, is structured in an episodic style with little to unite the separate scenes, combining realism with a lingering sense of surrealism. The Frenchman Michel Vinaver takes a similar attitude to structure in his plays. David Bradby even suggests that Vinaver 'produces a polyvalent drama well characterized by a comparison with the cubist art of Braque or Picasso' and that in Jarry's play *Ubu Roi* 'Vinaver identified the principal elements of what was to become his own play-writing practice' (Bradby 1993: 5–6). German Marius von Mayenburg's plays *Fireface* (1998) and *Parasites* (2000) focus on violent protagonists. But he also performed the role of dramaturg for a 2006 Berlin version of Ibsen's *Hedda Gabler*, pre-empting the claims of this volume when he said that Ibsen is rather dull and conventional on the page but 'his plays can work really well on the stage. They contain fascinating worlds' (Gallagher-Ross 2007: 91). All these playwrights push the boundaries of dramatic scripting, bombarding audiences with difficult, disturbing, upsetting or politically challenging images.

Other companies and playwrights have focused on reinterpretations of classic texts in new ways, most notably the Wooster Group whose versions of canonical American plays (such as Eugene O'Neill's *The Emperor Jones*) and works by Shakespeare (most recently *Hamlet*) remain strikingly revolutionary. As well as dance, this group utilises technology (particularly splicing film and live performance), a central characteristic of modernist practitioners from Piscator's use of cinema and treadmills to Meyerhold's collaborative stages with their turning windmills to Appia's remarkable kinetic light scenes. As technology has advanced during recent decades, so theatre practitioners have exploited these new methods. Bruce Nauman's 1969 *Performance Corridor* presents a series of films of the artist simply walking down a corridor, a performance, he suggests, that is not simply acted once but numerous times, with each showing (and each audience response) representing a new enactment (Kaye 2007: 66). Heinrich Müller's 1990 *Hamlet/Maschine: Shakespeare/Müller* performed at the Deutsches Theater reimagines Shakespeare's play using loudspeakers and televisions. More recently, the UK company Forced Entertainment's *The Last Adventures* (2013) combines computers and recordings with homemade props and costumes, creating a piece that seems to parallel earlier modernist performance renderings in both its technological experimentation and its almost childlike onstage objects. The dadaist Cabaret Voltaire could perhaps be read as a precursor.

As McConachie suggests, political theatre, endemic on the modernist cultural scene, continued to dominate the rest of the twentieth century: 'theatre performances become one public arena for the staging of conflict' (Zarrilli et al. 2010: 443). Groups such as the San Francisco Mime Troupe and the Bread and Puppet Theatre adopt distinctly agitational political positions, both reinterpreting ancient forms for contemporary aims (the former influenced by *commedia dell'arte*, the latter by the history of grotesque, satirical puppetry). Accordingly, these two groups reflect distinctly modernist aesthetic tropes and attitudes. The Italian Dario Fo likewise uses *commedia dell'arte* and the folk tradition of *giullari* to critique fascist politics. His 1970 *Accidental Death of an Anarchist* is one of the most hilarious and startlingly antagonistic plays of the past fifty years. Alongside his wife Franca Rame, Fo commits to bringing theatrical performance to the 'people', a project similarly undertaken by Augusto Boal. Boal's idea of the 'theatre of the oppressed' aims to transform spectators from passive observers to active participators: 'the theater is a weapon, and it is the people who should wield it' (2000: 122).

New groups have appeared with distinct agendas: feminist groups such as Monstrous Regiment and lesbian, gay, bisexual, transgender and queer groups such as Gay Sweatshop and Theatre Rhinoceros. Plays such as Caryl Churchill's *Cloud Nine* (1979) and Tony Kushner's *Angels in America* (1993) explored LGBTQ issues on the stage. Companies such as 7:84 challenged class hierarchies, creating plays such as the hugely influential *The Cheviot, the Stag and the Black, Black Oil* (1973) in order to tell local, specifically lower- or working-class stories to local, working-class audiences. While 7:84's founder, John McGrath, rejected some modernist traditions (the middle-class naturalism of Strindberg and Ibsen, and the theatrical avant-gardism of Pirandello), he simultaneously admired many of the traditions I have discussed in this book, namely the Russian Blue Blouse movement (McGrath 1996: 26–7). This example illustrates that, due to the profoundly diverse innovations of the modernist avant-garde, contemporary practitioners are likely to reject some precursors while eagerly praising others. Other collectives investigate issues of race, for example Tara Arts and Black Mime Theatre. In contemporary culture, theatre has become a mode of political subversion, an identifying trait of much modernist avant-garde experiment with groups such as the suffragette Actors' Franchise League, playwrights such as Brecht, pageant organiser Dubois and designer Piscator.

The twenty-first century is defined by a new trend in political theatre. Responding to issues such as the so-called War on Terror, the economic crisis, government spin or social unrest, performances in a documentary style have appeared across the world. None would look out of place in the canon of FTP's work. Many also imbibe the immediacy and vitality of early twentieth-century agitprop, such as Gillian Slovo's *The Riots*. Performed in November 2011 only three months after the violent demonstrations and lootings in London, Slovo constructed her play through a series of interviews with rioters and witnesses of the troubles. Rioting provided a similar catalyst for performance in Anna Deavere Smith's plays *Fires in the Mirror* (1992) and *Twilight* (1993), focusing on the racial unrest in New York and Los Angeles, respectively. Combining documentary theatre stylistics with typically avant-garde uses of fragmented speech patterns and technology, Alecky Blythe's Recorded Delivery project provides actors with an earpiece through which they hear the actual recorded words of the real life characters they are playing. Responding to complex world issues and a sense that journalism has rather lost its way (amid accusations of phonetapping, bias and underfunding of much 'serious' news reportage), documentary theatre has once more become a major art form.

Many of the productions and projects mentioned here reinterpret the position of the audience and the relationship between the audience and the actor. In her seminal book *Theatre Audiences*, Susan Bennett starts her analysis with 'naturalist theatre and reactions to it', providing an overview of the work of Meyerhold and Marinetti in particular (1990: 5–7). The shocking events of the Happenings movement, the challenging poetics or earthy dialects of new writing, the inclusive antagonism of political theatre and the disturbing imagery of performance art all contribute to a full re-evaluation of the audience. But, as Bennett contends, modernist avant-garde practitioners often conceived of the audience in similar ways.

In recent years a plethora of new performances have resonated with modernist avant-garde techniques and methods, from Robert Wilson's surrealist visions to Mabou Mines's puppetry. Marina Abramovic's 2010 installation *The Artist Is Present* at the Museum of Modern Art, New York, crossed boundaries between visual art and performance (as Kandinsky's *The Yellow Sound* did previously), questioning the relationship between actor and audience, and exploring issues of truthfulness that chime with Artaud's Theatre of Cruelty. Site-specific performance, that is, work that plays with space and the characteristics of that space, has become one of the defining forms of twenty-first century art. But the scholar Erika Suderburg situates it in a tremendously long and varied genealogy of performance, back to ancient sites such as

Stonehenge and the Great Sphinx. The modernist avant-garde becomes a key moment in Suderburg's lineage, which mentions work by Schwitters, Moholy-Nagy and Duchamp (2000: 10–12). The Milan-based Studio Azzurro's work using 'videoenvironments' to break down the division between performer and visitor responds directly to those quintessential objects of the dadaists: Duchamp's readymades. In fact Studio Azzurro invert Duchamp's project; whereas Duchamp took an everyday object and made it strange by placing it out of context in a gallery, Studio Azzurro create art that connects directly with people's everyday experience (Kaye 2007: 126–7). This example illustrates that new artists need not be simply responding with admiration and awe to their modernist avant-garde predecessors; in fact, in creating new avant-garde art, they may well be partly or wholly rejecting historical precursors just as the futurists or dadaists did before them. Site-specific and multimedia performances also cause us to question the very notion of performance: when is a happening a performance? when is an installation a performance? what is the difference between a performance and an intervention? Perhaps as we continue to probe these issues with all the inquisitive curiosity of our modernist avant-garde predecessors, such questions about the boundaries or definitions of performance become redundant.

All this is not to suggest that contemporary artists merely reproduce the innovations of their modernist predecessors. Neither am I claiming them as 'modernist' or even as 'avant-garde'. However, given these examples (and the many more I have, by necessity of space, excluded), one could make a strong case for the continuation of modernist avant-garde methods in the twenty-first century. Perhaps all we can really do is borrow the image of Jean-Michel Rabaté's reassessment of modernism and say that modernity (and its cultural equivalent, modernism) lingers as a 'ghost', haunting the artistic outputs of future generations (1996).

PRACTICAL EXPLORATION

Many of the companies and practitioners mentioned in the Conclusion have their own websites documenting their production history. Check out the websites for Forced Entertainment, Bread and Puppet Theatre Company and Alecky Blythe. From the information provided, how might you describe their projects? In what ways do these companies/practitioners reflect the aesthetic or thematic interests of the modernist avant-garde?

The next time you watch a piece of performance, ask yourself these two questions and write a short review detailing the ways the performance might be read through the innovations of the modernist avant-garde.

Now we have reached the end of our explorations, go back over the chapters and pick out:

a) areas of interest to you that you would like to research more
b) performances, happenings or events that you can imagine as influences for future work.

Create your own piece responding to all you have learned. The piece might be a dadaist variety show, a short futurist play, an agitprop street performance, a surrealist film, a practical exploration of the body, a set design or even a large-scale pageant. Feel the freedom to both take influences from the modernist avant-garde and reject anything that seems restrictive or unhelpful.

Glossaries

GLOSSARY OF TERMS

aesthetics: the artistic characteristics of an artwork

arbitrary: chosen almost at random

autonomous: independent

bourgeoisie: the middle class

capitalism: with exceptions, the prevailing world economic system where everything is interpolated into a system of buying and selling, supply and demand

commodification: understanding an object's value purely based on its economic worth

communism: a system designed by Karl Marx (although notions of communism appear throughout history from Plato's *Republic* to Gonzalo's utopian dream in Shakespeare's *The Tempest*) providing a critique of capitalism and suggesting that, through a series of class struggles, the world would move towards a classless society where the means of production are owned by all

egalitarianism: fairness and equality.

elitism: the sense that those at the top of the social hierarchy (due to education, wealth or birth) are better at governing countries, have more developed cultural tastes or are inherently worth more than those below

fascism: an authoritarian governing system prominent in Spain, Italy and Germany during the mid twentieth century advocating state ownership of the means of production, a rejuvenation of the nation and a violent rejection of certain groups deemed to be decadent, degenerate, weak or counteracting the prevailing ideology

feminism: the promotion of women's rights and gender equality

Frankfurt School: a group of philosophers and thinkers (Max Horkheimer,

Theodor Adorno, Walter Benjamin, Jürgen Habermas and others) flourishing in the 1920s and 30s, broadly along socialist lines

Gesamtkunstwerk: 'total work of art' as defined by composer Richard Wagner, with all artistic genres merging together to form one synthesised experience

hegemony: a term used particularly by Italian philosopher Antonio Gramsci to refer to those in charge who govern indirectly by presenting ideology as universally accepted common sense

heterogeneity: differences

homogeneity: similarities

montage: a way of constructing art from fragments

Other: a philosophical term particularly used by postcolonial philosophers whereby I understand who you are because you are not like me, i.e., you are Other

postcolonialism: a philosophical approach that studies the legacies of colonisation on national identity, language and culture

polemic: politically engaged

proletariat: the urban working class

satire: politics and humour combined to poke fun generally at those in positions of responsibility

secularisation: the move away from understanding the world in terms of religion or theism

transnational: across national borders

GLOSSARY OF MOVEMENTS

Naturalism: challenging contemporary themes, everyday dialogue/situations, linear structure, perfect illusion of reality, materialist

Symbolism: indistinct setting and characters, spirituality and otherworldliness, linguistic complexity, focus on effect rather than object, metaphorical images

Futurism: machines, the future, speed, war, total rejection of the past, violence, noise, cleansing a decadent and effeminate world

Dada: anti-art, anti-bourgeois, anti-taste, anti-war, anti-authority, illogical, nonsense, an egg

Surrealism: oddly juxtaposed images, dreams/reality, surprise, the unconscious, anti-reason, play

Expressionism: screams, heightened emotions, intensity, poetic voices, individualism, fragmented structures, nightmares

Constructivism: geometry, supportive of the Revolution, urban, materialist, machine, proletarian

Agitprop: declamatory, communistic, working-class, unorthodox performing spaces: outdoor, factories, workers' clubs, amateur, educative, disciplined

Living newspaper: fragmented, contemporary theme, polemic, multimedia agitprop, anti-hegemonic, educative

GLOSSARY OF PRACTITIONERS / COMPANIES TO LOOK AT FOR EACH MOVEMENT

As we approach these movements for the first time, it seems useful to include a list of the most prominent practitioners or thinkers for each movement. This proves a rather unsuccessful enterprise, particularly when one acknowledges the way different practitioners worked with the conventions of a range of different movements. We might have placed August Strindberg, for example, in naturalism, symbolism or expressionism. Sean O'Casey is included in the 'naturalism' category yet his later plays certainly exhibited a strong sense of expressionism. There are plenty of other figures associated with these movements, but this list of central figures provides a starting point. There are also plenty of others that don't seem to fit into any category particularly well and yet still warrant further investigation: Luigi Pirandello would certainly be one such figure.

Naturalism: Konstantin Stanislavsky, Elizabeth Robins, Henrik Ibsen, Anton Chekhov, August Strindberg, George Bernard Shaw, Gerhart Hauptmann, André Antoine and the Théâtre Libre, Sean O'Casey

Symbolism: Maurice Maeterlinck, W.B. Yeats, Adolphe Appia, Edward Gordon Craig

Dada: Hugo Ball, Emmy Hennings, Tristan Tzara, Richard Huelsenbeck, Francis Picabia

Surrealism: André Breton, Gertrude Stein, Antonin Artaud, Jean Cocteau

Expressionism: Frank Wedekind, Ernst Toller, Georg Kaiser, Sophie Treadwell, Ivan Goll, Elmer Rice, Eugene O'Neill, Rudolf Laban, Mary Wigman

Vorticism: Wyndham Lewis, Ezra Pound

Futurism: F.T. Marinetti, Vladimir Mayakovsky, Valentine Saint-Point, Enrico Prampolini

Constructivism: Vsevolod Meyerhold, Lyubov Popova, Evgeny Vakhtangov, Alexander Tairov, Alexei Gan

Agitprop: Workers' Theatre Movement, Blue Blouse

Living Newspaper: Federal Theatre Project, Hallie Flanagan, Unity Theatre

Epic theatre: Bertolt Brecht, Erwin Piscator

Further Reading

The full bibliography contains all the sources mentioned in this book, but if you are looking for introductory resources then here are some suggestions:

Bentley, Eric (1979), *The Theory of the Modern Stage*, Harmondsworth: Penguin.
This seminal collection contains manifestos, treatise and documents from some of the foremost modernist figures from Zola to Wagner, Artaud to Brecht.

Berghaus, Günter (2005), *Theatre, Performance and the Historical Avant-Garde*, Basingstoke: Palgrave Macmillan.
This comprehensive study focuses on historical avant-garde performance in context and includes a good deal of information about the non-theatrical influences (war, philosophy etc.) as well as detailed descriptions of the major movements.

Cardullo, Bert and Knopf, Robert (eds) (2001), *Theater of the Avant-Garde, 1890–1950: A Critical Anthology*, New Haven, CT: Yale University Press.
As well as containing a range of documents and sources, this book also includes some very comprehensive introductory discussions of the various movements.

Harding, James and Rouse, John (2006), *Not the Other Avant-Garde: The Transnational Foundations of Avant-garde Performance*, Ann Arbor: Michigan University Press.
Using distinctly performance-based analysis, this book aims to broaden our understanding of the avant-garde by focusing on a range of geographical spaces.

Innes, Christopher (1993), *Avant Garde Theatre 1892–1992*, London: Routledge.
This book provides a more historical perspective than others, using the idea of the primitive as its grounding concept.

Leach, Robert (2004), *Makers of Modern Theatre*, London: Routledge.
A concisely written introduction to the foremost figures of modernist theatre: Brecht, Stanislavsky, Artaud and Meyerhold.

Shepherd-Barr, Kirsten (2010), 'Staging Modernism: A New Drama', in Peter Brooker, Andrzej Gasiorek, Deborah Longworth and Andrew Thacker (eds), *The Oxford Handbook of Modernisms*, Oxford: Oxford University Press.
This chapter captures the revolutionary fervour and intent of the naturalists.

Taxidou, Olga (2007), *Modernism and Performance: From Jarry to Brecht*, Basingstoke: Palgrave.
Taxidou's book is a welcome study of modernism from a distinctly performance-based perspective, focusing on the body, the director, transnational collaboration, the influence of ancient Greek motifs and contemporary politics.

Warden, Claire (2015), 'Modernism in European Theatre/Drama', in Stephen Ross and Allana Lindgren (eds), *The Modernist World*, London: Routledge.
This chapter enables European modernist performance to be read alongside a range of other genres, innovations and contexts.

Bibliography

Abel, Lionel (1969), *Metatheatre: A New View of Dramatic Form*, New York: Hill and Wang.

Albright, Daniel (2004), *Modernism and Music: An Anthology of Sources*, Chicago: University of Chicago Press.

Appia, Adolphe (1962), *Music and the Art of the Theatre*, trans. Robert W. Corrigan and Mary Douglas Dirks, Miami: Miami University Press.

Arent, Arthur (1937), *Power*, http://newdeal.feri.org/power/pwr2-06.htm (accessed 18 July 2013).

Aronson, Arnold (2000), *American Avant-Garde Theatre*, London: Routledge.

Artaud, Antonin (1976), *Selected Writings*, ed. Susan Sontag, Berkeley: University of California Press.

— (2010), *The Theatre and its Double*, trans. Victor Corti, Richmond: Oneworld.

Ashcroft, Bill, Gareth Griffiths and Helen Tiffin (2003), *The Empire Writes Back*, London: Routledge.

— (2006), *The Postcolonial Reader*, London: Routledge.

Auslander, Philip (1997), *From Acting to Performance: Essays in Modernism and Postmodernism*, London: Routledge.

Baade, Christina (2012), *Victory through Harmony: The BBC and Popular Music in World War II*, Oxford: Oxford University Press.

Baer, Nancy van Norman (1992), *Theatre in Revolution 1913–1935*, London: Thames and Hudson.

Bartlett, Rosamund and Sarah Dadswell (2012), *Victory Over the Sun: The World's First Futurist Opera*, Chicago: University of Chicago Press.

Bay-Cheng, Sarah (2004), *Mama Dada: Gertrude Stein's Avant-Garde Theater*, New York: Routledge.

Bell, John (2006), 'Gertrude Stein's Identity: Puppet Modernism in the US', *TDR*, 50 (1), 87–99.

Bell, John (ed.) (2001), *Puppets, Masks and Performing Objects*, Cambridge, MA: MIT Press.

Benedikt, Michael and George Wellwarth (eds) (1964), *Modern French Theatre: The Avant-garde, Dada and Surrealism: An Anthology of Plays*, New York: Dutton.

Benjamin, Walter (2001 [1936]), 'The Work of Art in the Age of Mechanical Reproduction', in Vincent B. Leitch (ed.), *The Norton Anthology of Theory and Criticism*, New York: Norton, pp. 1166–85.

Bennett, Susan (1990), *Theatre Audiences*, London: Routledge.

Benstock, Shari (1987), *Women of the Left Bank 1900–1940*, Austin: Texas University Press.

Bentley, Eric (1979), *The Theory of the Modern Stage*, Harmondsworth: Penguin.

Berghaus, Günter (2005a), *Theatre, Performance and the Historical Avant-Garde*, Basingstoke: Palgrave.

— (2005b), *Avant-Garde Performance: Live Events and Electronic Technologies*, Basingstoke: Palgrave.

Berghaus, Günter (ed.) (2000), *International Futurism in Arts and Literature*, Berlin: Walter de Gruyter.

Blau, Herbert (2013), *Programming Theater History*, London: Routledge.

Blok, Aleksandr (2003), *Trilogy of Lyric Dramas*, London: Routledge.

Boal, Augusto (2000), *Theater of the Oppressed*, London: Pluto.

Bodek, Richard (1997), *Proletarian Performance in Weimar Berlin: Agitprop, Chorus and Brecht*, Columbia, SC: Camden House.

Bottoms, Stephen (2009), 'Authorizing the Audience: The Conceptual Drama of Tim Crouch', *Performance Research*, 14 (1), 65–76.

Bradby, David (1993), *The Theater of Michel Vinaver*, Ann Arbor: University of Michigan Press.

Bradby, David and John McCormick (1978), *People's Theatre*, Lanham, MD: Rowman and Littlefield.

Bradley, Karen (2009), *Rudolf Laban*, London: Routledge.

Bradshaw, David and Kevin J.H. Dettmar (eds) (2006), *A Companion to Modernist Literature and Culture*, Oxford: Blackwell.

Braun, Edward (1998), *Meyerhold: A Revolution in Theatre*, London: Methuen.

Brecht, Bertolt (1998), *Collected Plays: Six*, London: Methuen.

— (2000), *Mother Courage and Her Children*, London: Methuen.

— (2001), *Brecht on Theatre*, ed. John Willett, London: Methuen.

Brooker, Peter (1992), *Modernism/Postmodernism*, London: Longman.

Brooker, Peter and Andrew Thacker (eds) (2005), *Geographies of Modernism: Literatures, Cultures, Spaces*, Oxford: Routledge.

Brooker, Peter, Andrzej Gasiorek, Deborah Longworth and Andrew Thacker (eds) (2010), *The Oxford Handbook of Modernisms*, Oxford: Oxford University Press.

Bru, Sascha and Gunther Martens (2006), *The Invention of Politics in the European Avant-Garde 1906–1940*, New York: Rodopi.

Bürger, Peter (1984), *Theory of the Avant-Garde*, Minneapolis: Minnesota University Press.

Butler, Judith (2001 [1990]), 'Gender Trouble', in Vincent B. Leitch (ed.), *The Norton Anthology of Theory and Criticism*, New York: Norton, pp. 2488–501.

Butsch, Richard (2008), *Citizen Audience: Crowds, Publics and Individuals*, New York: Routledge.

Calinescu, Matei (1987), *Five Faces of Modernity*, Durham, NC: Duke University Press.

Čapek, Karel (2012), *R.U.R.*, http://ebooks.adelaide.edu.au/c/capek/karel/rur/index.html (accessed 17 June 2013).

— (1929–30), photograph of Act 3, *R.U.R.*, http://brbl-dl.library.yale.edu/vufind/Record/3748472 (accessed 12 August 2013).

Cardullo, Bert and Robert Knopf (eds) (2001), *Theater of the Avant-Garde, 1890–1950: A Critical Anthology*, New Haven, CT: Yale University Press.

Childs, Peter (2000), *Modernism*, London: Routledge.

Christie, Ian and Richard Taylor (1993), *Eisenstein Rediscovered*, London: Routledge.

Clark, Jon, Margot Heinemann, David Margolies and Carole Snee (eds) (1979), *Culture and Crisis in Britain in the Thirties*, London: Lawrence and Wishart.

Climenhaga, Royd (2009), *Pina Bausch*, London: Routledge.

Clurman, Harold (1967), *The Fervent Years: The Story of Group Theatre and the Thirties*, New York: Hill and Wang.

Cocteau, Jean (1967), *The Infernal Machine and Other Plays*, New York: New Directions.

Conroy, Colette (2010), *Theatre & the Body*, Basingstoke: Palgrave Macmillan.

cummings, e.e. (1968), *Three Plays and a Ballet*, London: Peter Owen.

Dalcroze, Émiles Jaques (1917), *The Eurythmics of Jaques-Dalcroze*, London: Constable.

Danchev, Alex (2011), *100 Artists' Manifestos: From the Futurists to the Stuckists*, Harmondsworth: Penguin.

Deak, Frantisek (1993), *Symbolist Theater: The Formation of an Avant-Garde*, Baltimore: Johns Hopkins University Press.

Dorn, Karen (1984), *Players and the Painted Stage*, Brighton: Harvester.

Dorra, Henri (ed.) (1994), *Symbolist Art Theories: A Critical Anthology*, Berkeley: University of California Press.

Drain, Richard (ed.) (1995), *Twentieth-Century Theatre: A Sourcebook*, London: Routledge.

Eliot, T.S. (1966), *Selected Essays*, London: Faber and Faber.

Elliott, Bridget and Jo-Ann Wallace (2004), *Women Artists and Writers: Modernist (Im)positionings*, London: Routledge.

Emigh, John (1996), *Masked Performance: The Play of the Self and Other in Ritual and the Theatre*, Philadelphia: Pennsylvania University Press.

Esslin, Martin (1968), *Theatre of the Absurd*, Harmondsworth: Penguin.

Evreinov, Nikolai (1915), *Theatre of the Soul*, http://www.archive.org/stream/theatreofsoulmon00evreuoft/theatreofsoulmon00evreuoft_djvu.txt (accessed 4 July 2013).

Eysteinsson, Ástrádur and Vivian Liska (2007), *Modernism*, Amsterdam: John Benjamins.

Farfan, Penny (2004), *Women, Modernism and Performance*, Cambridge: Cambridge University Press.

Federal Theatre Project (FTP) (1935), *Manual for the Federal Theatre Projects*, http://memory.loc.gov/cgi-bin/ampage?collId=ftscript&fileName=farbf/00010003/ftscript.db&recNum=0 (accessed 18 July 2013).

— (1937), photo of Supreme Court Scene in *Power*, http://newdeal.feri.org/library/d82a.htm (accessed 12 August 2013).

Fischer-Lichte, Erika (2005), *Theatre, Sacrifice, Ritual: Exploring Forms of Political Theatre*, London: Routledge.

Fischer-Lichte, Erika, Barbara Gronau and Christel Weiler (eds) (2011), *Global Ibsen: Performing Multiple Modernities*, London: Routledge.

Fischer-Lichte, Erika and Benjamin Wihstutz (eds) (2013), *Performance and the Politics of Space: Theatre and Topology*, London: Routledge.

Flanagan, Hallie (1936), *Brief before the Committee on Patents, House of Representatives*, http://memory.loc.gov/cgi-bin/ampage?collId=ftscript&fileName=farbf/00040002/ftscript.db&recNum=3 (accessed 18 July 2013).

Flannery, James W. (1976), *W.B. Yeats and the Idea of a Theatre*, New Haven, CT: Yale University Press.

Forsyth, Alison and Chris Megson (eds) (2009), *Get Real: Documentary Theatre Past and Present*, Basingstoke: Palgrave Macmillan.

Franko, Mark (2002), *The Work of Dance: Labor, Movement and Identity in the 1930s*, Middletown, CT: Wesleyan University Press.

— (2012), *Martha Graham in Love and War: The Life in the Work*, Oxford: Oxford University Press.

Freshwater, Helen (2009), *Theatre & Audience*, Basingstoke: Palgrave Macmillan.

Gale, Maggie B. and Gilli Bush-Bailey (2012), *Plays and Performance Texts by Women, 1880–1930*, Manchester: Manchester University Press.

Gallagher-Ross, Jacob (2007), 'Ibsen Our Contemporary: Contemporary Directors on the Playwright's Centenary', *Theater*, 37 (3), 86–115.

Garafola, Lynn (1989), *Diaghilev's Ballet Russes*, Oxford: Oxford University Press.

Garelick, Rhonda (2007), *Electric Salome: Loie Fuller's Performance of Modernism*, Princeton: Princeton University Press.

Gladkov, Aleksandr (1997), *Meyerhold Speaks, Meyerhold Rehearses*, ed. Alma Law, Amsterdam: Overseas Publishers Association.

Goldman, Jane (2004), *Modernism 1910–1945: Image to Apocalypse*, Basingstoke: Palgrave Macmillan.

Graham, Robert (2009), *A Documentary History of Libertarian Ideas*, Montreal: Black Rose.

Greenblatt, Stephen and M.H. Abrams (eds) (2006), *The Norton Anthology of English Literature: volume 2*, New York: Norton.

Grotowski, Jerzy (1981), *Towards a Poor Theatre*, London: Eyre Methuen.

Groys, Boris (1992), *The Total Art of Stalinism: Avant-garde, Aesthetic, Dictatorship and Beyond*, Princeton: Princeton University Press.

Hammond, Paul (1991), *The Shadow and Its Shadow: Surrealist Writing on the Cinema*, Edinburgh: Polygon.

Harding, James (2013), *The Ghosts of the Avant-Garde(s): Exorcising Experimental Theater and Performance*, Ann Arbor: University of Michigan Press.

Harding, James and John Rouse (eds) (2006), *Not the Other Avant-Garde: The Transnational Foundations of Avant-garde Performance*, Ann Arbor: University of Michigan Press.

Hemus, Ruth (2009), *Dada's Women*, New Haven, CT: Yale University Press.

Hochman, Stanley (ed.) (1984), *McGraw-Hill Encyclopaedia of World Drama*, Maidenhead: McGraw-Hill.

Horosko, Marian (2002), *Martha Graham: The Evolution of her Dance Theory and Training*, Gainesville: Florida University Press.

Howarth, Peter (2012), *The Cambridge Introduction to Modernist Poetry*, Cambridge: Cambridge University Press.

Huelsenbeck, Richard (1969), *Memoirs of a Dada Drummer*, ed. Hans J Kleinschmidt and Joachim Neugroschel, New York: Viking Press.

Hughes, Robert (1991), *The Shock of the New*, London: Thames and Hudson.

Innes, Christopher (1981), *Holy Theatre: Ritual and the Avant-garde*, Cambridge: Cambridge University Press.

— (1993), *Avant Garde Theatre 1892–1992*, London: Routledge.

— (1998), *Edward Gordon Craig: A Vision of Theatre*, Amsterdam: Overseas Publishers Association.

— (2000), *A Sourcebook on Naturalist Theatre*, London: Routledge.

Jameson, Fredric (ed.) (2007), *Aesthetics and Politics*, London: Verso.

Jannarone, Kimberly (2010), *Artaud and his Doubles*, Ann Arbor: University of Michigan Press.

Jarry, Alfred (1980), *Selected Works of Alfred Jarry*, London: Eyre Methuen.

Jencks, Charles (1980), *Late-modern Architecture and Other Essays*, New York: Rizzoli.

Kaes, Anton, Martin Jay and Edward Dimendberg (1994), *The Weimar Republic Sourcebook*, Berkeley: University of California Press.

Kaye, Nick (2007), *Multimedia: Video, Installation, Performance*, Abingdon: Routledge.

Kleist, Heinrich von (1810), *On the Marionette Theatre*, http://www.english.emory.edu/DRAMA/KleistMarion.html (accessed 17 June 2013).

Kolocotroni, Vassiliki, Jane Goldman and Olga Taxidou (eds) (1998), *Modernism: An Anthology of Sources and Documents*, Edinburgh: Edinburgh University Press.

Krasner, David (ed.) (2008), *Theatre in Theory 1900–2000*, London: Wiley-Blackwell.

Kuhns, David (1997), *German Expressionist Theatre: The Actor and the Stage*, Cambridge: Cambridge University Press.

Leach, Robert (1993), *Vsevolod Meyerhold*, Cambridge: Cambridge University Press.

— (1994), *Revolutionary Theatre*, London: Routledge.

— (2004), *Makers of Modern Theatre*, London: Routledge.

Lecoq, Jacques (2002), *The Moving Body*, London: Methuen.

Lehmann, Hans-Thies (2010), *Postdramatic Theatre*, London: Routledge.

Levenson, Michael (1999), *The Cambridge Companion to Modernism*, Cambridge: Cambridge University Press.

Levitz, Tamara (2012), *Modernist Mysteries*, Oxford: Oxford University Press.

Lewis, Wyndham (1914), *BLAST*, http://dl.lib.brown.edu/pdfs/1143209 523824858.pdf (accessed 12 November 2012)

— (2003), *Collected Poems and Plays*, Manchester: Carcanet.

London, John (ed.) (2000), *Theatre under the Nazis*, Manchester: Manchester University Press.

Lorca, Federico García (1993), *Plays: One*, trans. Gwynne Edwards, London: Methuen.

Love, Lauren (2011), 'Performing Jewish Nationhood: "The Romance of a People" at the 1933 Chicago World's Fair', *TDR*, 55 (3), 57–67.

MacNeice, Louis (1942), *Christopher Columbus: A Radio Play*, London: Faber and Faber.

Maeterlinck, Maurice (1914), *The Intruder and Other Plays*, New York: Dodd, Mead and Co.

Manning, Susan (2006a), *Ecstasy and the Dances of Mary Wigman*, Minneapolis: Minnesota University Press.

— (2006b), *Modern Dance, Negro Dance: Race in Motion*, Minneapolis: Minnesota University Press.

Mao, Douglas and Rebecca L. Walkowitz (2008), 'The New Modernist Studies', *PMLA*, 123 (3), 737–48.

Marcus, Laura (2007), *The Tenth Muse: Writing about Cinema in the Modernist Period*, Oxford: Oxford University Press.

Marx, Karl (1852), *The Eighteenth Brumaire of Louis Bonaparte*, http://www.marxists.org/archive/marx/works/download/pdf/18th-Brumaire.pdf (accessed 6 June 2013).

Mayakovsky, Vladimir (1913), photographs from *A Tragedy*, http://max.mmlc.northwestern.edu/~mdenner/Drama/plays/atragedy/1tragedy.html (accessed 18 July 2013).

—(1995), *Mayakovsky: Plays*, trans. Guy Daniels, Evanston, IL: Northwestern University Press.

Mayakovsky, Vladimir, David Burliuk, Alexander Kruchenykh and Victor Khlebnikov (1917), *A Slap in the Face of Public Taste*, http://www.marxists.org/subject/art/literature/mayakovsky/1917/slap-in-face-public-taste.htm (accessed 12 November 2012).

McGrath, John (1996), *A Good Night Out: Popular Theatre: Audience, Class and Form*, London: Nick Hern.

McGuinness, Patrick (2000), *Maurice Maeterlinck and the Making of Modern Theatre*, Oxford: Oxford University Press.

Melzer, Annabelle (1994), *Dada and Surrealist Performance*, Baltimore: Johns Hopkins University Press.

Meyerhold, Vsevolod (2008), *Meyerhold on Theatre*, ed. Edward Braun, London: A&C Black.

Miller, Tyrus (1999), *Late Modernism: Politics, Fiction and the Arts between the World Wars*, Berkeley: University of California Press.

Mumford, Meg (2009), *Bertolt Brecht*, London: Routledge.

Murphy, Brenda (2005), *The Provincetown Players and the Culture of Modernity*, Cambridge: Cambridge University Press.

Murphy, Richard (1999), *Theorizing the Avant-Garde: Modernism, Expressionism and the Problem of Postmodernity*, Cambridge: Cambridge University Press.

Newhall, Mary Anne Santos (2009), *Mary Wigman*, London: Routledge.

Newlove, Jean (1993), *Laban for Actors and Dancers*, New York: Routledge.

Newlove, Jean and John Dalby (2004), *Laban for All*, London: Nick Hern.

Nicholls, Peter (1995), *Modernisms: A Literary Guide*, Basingstoke: Palgrave Macmillan.

Nochlin, Linda (2001), *The Body in Pieces: The Fragment as a Metaphor of Modernity*, London: Thames and Hudson.

O'Brien, Patrick and Roland Quinault (1993), *The Industrial Revolution and British Society*, Cambridge: Cambridge University Press.

Paget, Derek (1990), *True Stories: Documentary Drama on Radio, Screen and Stage*, Manchester: Manchester University Press.

Parker-Starbuck, Jennifer (2011), *Cyborg Theatre: Corporeal/ technological Intersections in Multimedia Performance*, Basingstoke: Palgrave Macmillan.

Patterson, Michael (1981), *The Revolution in German Theatre 1900–1933*, London: Routledge.

Perdigao, Lisa (2010), *From Modernist Entombment to Postmodernist Exhumation: Dead Bodies in Twentieth-century American Fiction*, Farnham: Ashgate.

Phelan, Peggy (1993), *Unmarked: The Politics of Performance*, London: Routledge.

Pirandello, Luigi (1922), *Six Characters in Search of an Author*, trans. Edward Stoner, New York: E.P. Dutton.

Piscator, Erwin (1980), *The Political Theatre*, London: Eyre Methuen.

Pitches, Jonathan (2003), *Vsevolod Meyerhold*, London: Routledge.

Poggioli, Renato (1968), *The Theory of the Avant-Garde*, Cambridge, MA: Harvard University Press.

Portnoy, Edward (1999), 'Modicut Puppet Theatre: Modernism, Satire and Yiddish Culture', *The Drama Review*, 43 (3), 115–34.

Postlewait, Thomas (2009), *The Cambridge Introduction to Theatre Historiography*, Cambridge: Cambridge University Press.

Pound, Ezra (2005), *Certain Noble Plays of Japan*, http://www.gutenberg. org/files/8094/8094-h/8094-h.htm#link2H_INTR (accessed 18 June 2013).

Preston, Carrie (2011), *Modernism's Mythic Pose*, Oxford: Oxford University Press.

Preston-Dunlop, Valerie (1998), *Rudolf Laban: An Extraordinary Life*, London: Dance Books.

Puchner, Martin (2002), *Stage Fright: Modernism, Anti-theatricality and Drama*, Baltimore: Johns Hopkins University Press.

— (2005), *Poetry of the Revolution: Marx, Manifestos and the Avant-gardes*, Princeton: Princeton University Press.

Rabaté, Jean-Michel (1996), *The Ghosts of Modernity*, Gainesville: Florida University Press.

Rainey Lawrence, Christine Poggi and Laura Whitman (eds) (2009), *Futurism: An Anthology*, New Haven, CT: Yale University Press.

Reilly, Kara (2011), *Automata and Mimesis on the Stage of Theatre History*, Basingstoke: Palgrave Macmillan.

Rice, Elmer (1965), *3 Plays*, New York: Farrar, Straus and Giroux.

— (1923), photograph of the Grave Yard from Theatre Guild's *The Adding Machine*, http://brbl-dl.library.yale.edu/vufind/Record/3764389 (accessed 12 August 2013).

Ritchie, J.M. and H.F. Garten (eds) (1980), *Seven Expressionist Plays*, London: John Calder.

Roberts, David (2011), *The Total Work of Art in European Modernism*, Ithaca, NY: Cornell University Press.

Robinson, Marc (1997), *The Other American Drama*, Baltimore: Johns Hopkins University Press.

Rudnitsky, Konstantin (2000), *Russian and Soviet Theatre: Tradition and the Avant-garde*, London: Thames and Hudson.

Saint-Simon, Henri Comte de (1952), *Selected Writings*, ed. and trans. F.M.H. Markham, Oxford: Blackwell.

Samuel, Raphael, Ewan MacColl and Stuart Cosgrove (1985), *Theatres of the Left 1880–1935: Workers' Theatre Movements in Britain and America*, London: Routledge and Kegan Paul.

Sandford, Mariellen R. (ed.) (1995), *Happenings and Other Acts*, London: Routledge.

Schechner, Richard (2003), *Performance Theory*, London: Routledge.

Schnapp, Jeffrey (1996), *18BL and the Theater of the Masses for the Masses*, Palo Alto: Stanford University Press.

Schneider, Rebecca (1997), *The Explicit Body in Performance*, London: Routledge.

Schumacher, Claude (ed.) (1996), *Naturalism and Symbolism in European Theatre 1850–1918*, Cambridge: Cambridge University Press.

Scott, Bonnie Kime (1990), *The Gender of Modernism*, Bloomington: Indiana University Press.

Segal, Harold B. (1995), *Pinocchio's Progeny: Puppets, Marionettes, Automatons and Robots in Modernist Avant-garde Drama*, Baltimore: Johns Hopkins University Press.

Sell, Mike (ed.) (2011), *Avant-Garde Performance and Material Exchange: Vectors of the Radical*, Basingstoke: Palgrave Macmillan.

Seshagiri, Urmila (2010), *Race and the Modernist Imagination*, Ithaca, NY: Cornell University Press.

Sidnell, Michael (1984), *Dances of Death: The Group Theatre of London in the Thirties*, London: Faber and Faber.

Siegel, Marcia (1979), *The Shapes of Change: Images of American Dance*, Berkeley: University of California Press.

Sierz, Aleks (2001), *In-Yer-Face Theatre: British Drama Today*, London: Faber and Faber.

Sokel, Walter (1963), *An Anthology of German Expressionist Drama: Prelude to the Absurd*, New York: Doubleday.

Somigli, Luca (2003), *Legitimizing the Artists: Manifesto Writing and European Modernism 1885–1915*, Toronto: University of Toronto Press.

Spender, Stephen (1938), *Trial of a Judge*, London: Faber and Faber.

Stanford Friedman, Susan (2006), 'Planetarity: Musing Modernist Studies', *Modernism/Modernity*, 17 (2), 471–99.

— (2010), 'Periodizing Modernism: Postcolonial Modernities and the Space/ Time Borders of Modernist Studies', *Modernism/Modernity*, 13 (3), 425–43.

Stanislavsky, Constantin (1967), *An Actor Prepares*, Harmondsworth: Penguin.

Stein, Gertrude (1922), *Geography and Plays*, Boston: Four Seasons.

Stourac, Richard and Kathleen McCreery (1986), *Theatre as a Weapon: Workers' Theatre in the Soviet Union, Germany and Britain, 1917–1934*, London: Routledge and Kegan Paul.

Strindberg, August (1992), *Miss Julie*, New York: Dover.

Styan, J.L. (1981a), *Modern Drama in Theory and Practice: Volume 1 Realism and Naturalism*, Cambridge: Cambridge University Press.

— (1981b), *Modern Drama in Theory and Practice: Volume 3 Expressionism and the Epic Theatre*, Cambridge: Cambridge University Press.

— (1982), *Max Reinhardt*, Cambridge: Cambridge University Press.

Suderburg, Erika (2000), *Space, Site, Intervention: Situating Installation Art*, Minneapolis: Minnesota University Press.

Symons, James M. (1971), *Meyerhold's Theatre of the Grotesque: The Post-Revolutionary Productions, 1920–1932*, Miami: Miami University Press.

Taxidou, Olga (1998), *The Mask: A Periodical Performance by Edward Gordon Craig*, London: Harwood.

— (2007), *Modernism and Performance: from Jarry to Brecht*, Basingstoke: Palgrave Macmillan.

Tiffany, Daniel (2009), *Infidel Poetics: Riddles, Nightlife, Substance*, Chicago: University of Chicago Press.

Timms, Edwards and Peter Collier (eds) (1988), *Visions and Blueprints: Avant-garde Culture and Radical Politics in Early Twentieth-century Europe*, Manchester: Manchester University Press.

Toller, Ernst (1936), *Letters from Prison*, trans. R. Ellis Robert, London: John Lane.

— (2000), *Plays One*, trans. Alan Pearlman, London: Oberon.

Treadwell, Sophie (2012), *Machinal*, London: Nick Hern.

Turner, Jane (2004), *Eugenio Barba*, London: Routledge.

Tzara, Tristan (1992), *Seven Dada Manifestos and Lampisteries*, Michigan: River Run.

Wagner, Richard (1895), *Richard Wagner's Prose Works*, London: Kegan Paul.

Walker, Julia (2005), *Expressionism and Modernism in the American Theatre*, Cambridge: Cambridge University Press.

Warden, Claire (2012), *British Avant-garde Theatre*, Basingstoke: Palgrave Macmillan.

Washton Long, Rose-Carol (1995), *German Expressionism: Documents from the End of the Wilhelmine Empire to the Rise of National Socialism*, Berkeley: University of California Press.

Wilder, Thornton (2000), *Our Town and Other Plays*, Harmondsworth: Penguin.

Willett, John (1978), *The Theatre of Erwin Piscator*, London: Eyre Methuen.

Williams, Raymond (1978), 'Realism, Naturalism and their Alternatives', *Ciné-Tracts*, 1 (3), 1–7.

— (1989), *The Politics of Modernism: Against the New Conformists*, London: Verso.

Winkiel, Laura (2007), *Modernism, Race and Manifestos*, Cambridge: Cambridge University Press.

Wood, Paul (1999), *The Challenge of the Avant-Garde*, New Haven, CT: Yale University Press.

Yeats, W.B. (1921), *Four Plays for Dancers*, London: Macmillan, http://archive.org/stream/fourplaysfordancooyeatuoft/fourplaysfordancooyeatuoft_djvu.txt (accessed 11 October 2013).

Young, Alan (1983), *Dada and After: Extremist Modernism and English Literature*, Manchester: Manchester University Press.

Zarrilli, Philip B., Bruce McConachie, Gary Jay Williams and Carol Fisher Sorgenfrei (eds) (2010), *Theatre Histories: An Introduction*, London: Routledge.

Index

18BL, 77
7:84, 145

Abbey Theatre, Dublin, 29
Abramovic, Marina, 146
Adorno, Theodor, 3, 10, 74, 90, 127
agitprop, 15, 37, 79–82, 86, 91, 146, 148
Antoine, André, 33–4
Apollinaire, Guillaume, 56
Appia, Adolpe, 41, 143, 144
Arent, Arthur, 84
Artaud, Antonin, 39, 57–8, 69–70, 120–1,
    135, 140, 143, 146
Athey, Ron, 142
Auden, W. H., 8, 35, 125

Ball, Hugo, 8, 24, 46, 54–5, 57, 122–4, 126,
    128, 129, 138, 142
Balla, Giacomo, 58
Ballets Russes, 14, 31, 101, 117
    Parade, 128
    Schéhérazade, 121
    The Rite of Spring, 100, 102, 138, 143
Balzac, Honoré de, 33, 71
Barba, Eugenio, 141
Barnes, Djuna, 14, 58
Bartók, Béla, 126
Baudelaire, Charles, 2
Bauhaus, 24, 131–2
Bausch, Pina, 142
BBC, 21, 125, 138
Beckett, Samuel, 60, 69, 93, 140
Benjamin, Walter, 21
Bergson, Henri, 2
Berlin, 12, 46, 67, 104, 144
Beuys, Joseph, 142

Biomechanics, 96–9, 102, 113, 135
Black Mime Theatre, 145
Bloch, Ernst, 71
Blok, Aleksandr, 86, 113
Bloomsbury, 4
Blue Blouse, 79–80, 145
Blythe, Alecky, 146, 147
Boal, Augusto, 145
Boccioni, Umberto, 51
Bolsheviks, 66, 97, 98, 135
Bond, Edward, 143
Bread and Puppet Theatre, 145, 147
Brecht, Bertolt, 3, 26, 32, 41, 74, 87–9, 95,
    119–21, 125–6, 131–2, 136, 137, 141,
    142, 146
    Baal, 87
    Kuhle Wampe, 135, 138
    Mother Courage and Her Children, 89
    The Resistible Rise of Arturo Ui, 90,
    91
    The Rise and Fall of Mahogonny, 118
    The Threepenny Opera, 118
Brenton, Howard, 143
Breton, André, 24, 46–7, 54–6, 67, 69
Bristol, 83
Brook, Peter, 140
Buñuel, Luis, 48, 134–5
Burke, Gregory, 144
Burliuk, David, 52

cabaret, 25, 26, 54, 86, 104, 128, 142
Cabaret Voltaire, 69, 109, 123, 145
Cangiullo, Francesco, 51
Čapek, Karel, *R.U.R.*, 105–6, 110
Chaplin, Charlie, 86, 135
Chartists, 2

Chekhov, Anton, 33, 83, 137, 140
  The Seagull, 34
Chicago, 83, 76, 90
Churchill, Caryl, 145
Churchill, Winston, 90
Clair, René, 135, 138
Cocteau, Jean, 128–9
  The Eiffel Tower Wedding Party, 133
commedia dell'arte, 15, 25, 86, 98, 113, 114,
  145
constructivism, 7, 8, 12, 24, 44, 77, 85–7, 91,
  96, 120, 131, 135, 136, 137
Copeau, Jacques, 117, 141
Corra, Bruno, 49–51
Craig, Edith, 76, 94, 95
Craig, Edward Gordon, 31, 41, 77, 111–13,
  115, 140, 141, 143
Crimp, Martin, 144
Crommelynk, Ferdnand, The Magnanimous
  Cuckold, 85, 86, 91, 96, 98
Crouch, Tim, 141–2
Cunard, Nancy, 58
Curie, Marie, 2
Cutler, Yosi, 112

dada, 8, 12, 14, 15, 24, 26, 44–8, 53–61, 67–9,
  74, 93, 98, 102, 109, 110, 112, 120–1,
  124–5, 128, 130, 137, 141, 142, 145, 147,
  148
Dalcroze, Émiles Jaques, 102, 128
Dalí, Salvador, 48, 135
Darwin, Charles, 2, 19
De Valois, Ninette, 31
Delaunay, Sonia, 55
Diaghilev, Sergei, 14, 31, 101, 117
Dubois, W. E. B., 19, 25, 146
  The Star of Ethiopia, 76
Duchamp, Marcel, 21, 48, 138, 141, 147
duende, 129
Dulac, Edmund, 108–9
Dulac, Germaine, 135
Duncan, Isadora, 14, 99, 100

Easter Rising, 29–30
Eiffel Tower, 22
Einstein, Albert, 2, 59
Eisenstein, Sergei, 137
  Battleship Potemkin, 135–6, 138
  Gas Masks, 137
Eliot, T. S., 8, 26, 56, 72, 143
Engels, Friedrich, 19, 24, 81
Ensor, James, 109
Epstein, Jacob, 48, 138
Essen, 103, 142

Evreinov, Nikolai
  The Storming of the Winter Palace, 77
  Theatre of the Soul, 93–4, 112
expressionism, 18, 24, 39, 47–8, 60–6, 67, 71,
  74, 87, 102, 107, 127

fascism, 7, 66, 67, 71, 72, 83, 104, 131
Federal Theatre Project (FTP), 83, 85, 86,
  91, 104, 136, 143, 146
  Power, 84
Filonov, Pavel, 53
First World War, 47, 61, 67, 72, 74, 105, 133,
  134
Fitzgerald, F. Scott, 74
Flanagan, Hallie, 83, 86, 87
Fluxus, 142
Fo, Dario, 145
Fokine, Michel, 117
Forced Entertainment, 145, 147
Ford, Henry, 94, 96
Fordism, 94, 105
Frankfurt School, 3, 21
Freud, Sigmund, 2, 19, 61, 93
Fry, Roger, 4
Fuller, Loie, 99–100
futurism, 8, 12, 23, 24, 26, 35, 44–6, 48,
  49–53, 55, 60, 66–7, 70, 74, 85, 98–9,
  112, 122–3, 126, 128, 137, 138, 141, 142,
  143, 147, 148

Gan, Alexei, 24
Gauguin, Paul, 4, 22
Gay Sweatshop, 145
Glasgow, 83, 144
Goebbels, Joseph, 67, 102
Gorky, Maxim, 34
Graham, Martha, 136
  Lamentation, 100–1
Greek theatre, 17, 25, 56, 90, 99, 108, 109,
  117, 125, 126, 141
green, debbie tucker, 144
Gropius, Walter, 24, 131–2
Grosz, George, 133
Grotowski, Jerzy, 140–1
Group Theatre, 81

Hamilton, Cicely, 76
Happenings, 12, 142, 146
Harlem Renaissance, 2
Hašek, Jaroslav, 133
Hasenclaver, Walter, 63
Hauptmann, Gerhart, 33
Hennings, Emmy, 46, 128
Hitler, Adolf, 75, 90, 112

Holocaust, 5, 10, 127
Hulsenbeck, Richard, 24, 46, 56, 121,
    128

Ibsen, Henrik, 33, 64, 83, 94, 145
    A Doll's House, 36, 38, 53
    Ghosts, 86, 122
    Hedda Gabler, 144
    Peer Gynt, 39
Ionesco, Eugene, 70
Isherwood, Christopher, 8
Ito, Michio, 109

James, William, 96
Janco, Marcel, 109
Jarry, Alfred, 54
    Ubu Roi, 53, 60, 110, 143, 144
Jooss, Kurt, 142
    The Green Table, 103
Jung, Carl, 61

Kaiser, Fritz, 47
Kaiser, Georg, 63, 70
Kandinsky, Wassily, 23, 117, 123
    The Yellow Sound, 116, 127, 146
Kane, Sarah, 143
Kantor, Tadeusz, 140
Khlebnikov, Velimir, 52, 123, 126
Kleist, Heinrich von, 110–11
Kokoschka, Oskar, 7, 133
    Murderer Hope of Womankind, 47, 63
Kornfeld, Paul, 61
Kruchenykh, Aleksei, 52, 123, 126
Kushner, Tony, 145

La Fura dels Baus, 143
Laban, Rudolf, 102–3, 114, 141, 142
    The Green Clowns, 104
Lan-Fang, Mei, 119–20, 141
Lautgedichte, 123
Le Corbusier, 131
Lenin, Vladimir, 72
Lewis, Wyndham, 7, 23, 45
    Enemy of the Stars, 70
Liebknecht, Karl, 134
Littlewood, Joan, 83
Liverpool, 83
living newspaper, 82–4, 88, 91, 136, 138
Living Theatre, 12, 142
Lorca, Gabriel García, 129, 143
Los Angeles, 83, 146
Loy, Mina, 24
Lukács, Georg, 71–2
Luxemburg, Rosa, 134

Mabou Mines, 146
MacColl, Ewan, 48, 83
McGrath, John, 145
Maciunas, George, 142
MacNeice, Louis, 125
Maeterlinck, Maurice, 27–8, 31, 54
    The Blind, 41, 121–2
    The Intruder, 107
Magritte, René, 7
Malevich, Kazimir, 126
Mann, Thomas, 71
Marc, Franz, 116
Marinetti, F. T., 8, 23, 24, 25, 44–5, 49–52,
    53–4, 57, 66, 124, 138, 146
    Feet, 93
    Zang Tumb Tumb, 122–3, 126
Marx Brothers, 135
Marx, Karl, 2, 19, 24, 76, 81
Marxism, 16, 67
Matiushin, Mikhail, 126–7
Maud, Zuni, 112
Mayakovsky, Vladimir, 7, 48, 66
    Vladimir Mayakovsky (the play), 52–3,
    126
Mayenburg, Marius von, 144
Méliès, George, 134
melodrama, 27, 33–5, 71
Meyerhold, Vsevolod, 8, 10, 26, 39, 67, 72,
    86–7, 90, 94, 95, 97–9, 100, 102, 103,
    114, 120, 130, 135, 141, 144, 146
    The Fairground Booth (The Puppet Show),
    113
    The Magnanimous Cuckold, 85, 91,
    96
Milan, 12, 147
Mitchell, Katie, 143
Modicut, 112
Moholy-Nagy, Lázló, 133, 147
Mondrian, Pierre, 138
Monstrous Regiment, 145
montage, 136–7
Moscow, 12, 120
Moscow Art Theatre, 34, 98
Müller, Heinrich, 145
Munch, Edvard, 48, 60, 138
Munich, 91
music hall, 25–6, 37
Mussolini, Benito, 66, 72
mystery plays, 17

naturalism, 10, 18, 27, 32–42, 53–4, 61–2, 71,
    79, 80, 85, 86, 88, 95, 107, 120, 130, 132,
    141, 143, 146
Nauman, Bruce, 144

Nazis, 47, 67, 72, 75, 79, 88, 90, 102–3, 117, 119, 137
Negro Theatre, 83, 104
Neilson, Anthony, 144
Nemirovich-Danchenko, Vladimir, 34
Nevinson, Christopher, 123
New Deal, 83–4
New York, 12, 76, 77, 80, 81, 83–4, 104, 105, 112, 141, 142, 146
Nietzsche, Friedrich, 2, 19, 39
Nijinsky, Vaslav, 101, 102
Noh theatre, 29, 108, 120

O'Casey, Sean, 48, 67, 70
O'Neill, Eugene, 48
    The Emperor Jones, 144
    The Hairy Ape, 70, 86, 109–10, 115
Odets, Clifford, Waiting for Lefty, 81
Olympics, 77–8, 91, 102

Paladini, Vinicio, 55
Pankhurst, Emmeline, 90
Pannaggi, Ivo, 55
Paris, 12, 33, 44, 46, 54, 58, 76, 117, 133
Paterson Strike Pageant, 77
Pergola, Mina Della, Fidelity, 52
Picabia, Francis, 24, 46, 135, 138
Picasso, Pablo, 22, 109, 138, 144
Pinter, Harold, 60
Pioneer Players, 94–5, 76
Piper, John, 7
    Façade, 124
    Trial of a Judge, 130–1
Pirandello, Luigi, 113, 143, 144, 145, 146
    Six Characters in Search of an Author, 39–40
Piscator, Erwin, 131–2
    In Spite of Everything, 134, 135
    The Good Soldier Schweik, 133
Popova, Lyubov, 7, 85, 97–8, 130
    The Magnanimous Cuckold, 96
Pound, Ezra, 22, 45, 108
Prampolini, Enrico, 49–50
Pratella, Francesco Balilla, 128
Presnyakov Brothers, 144
Priestley, J. B., 39
Prolet Buehne, 15-Minute Red Revue, 80–1

Raikh, Zinaida, 95
Rame, Franca, 145
Ravenhill, Mark, 143
realism, 32, 35, 39, 47, 71, 86, 88, 107, 120, 123, 134, 143–4

Reinhardt, Max, 26, 117–18
Rice, Elmer, 48
    The Adding Machine, 61, 63, 107–8
Riefenstahl, Leni, Triumph of the Will, 75
Rivera, Diego, 24
Robins, Elizabeth, 14, 94
    Votes for Women, 36–8
Rodchenko, Alexander, 24, 85, 86
Rohe, Mies van der, 131
Rolland, Roman, 78
Roosevelt, Franklin D., 83, 91
Russolo, Luigi, 122–3

Saint-Simon, Henri, 4, 5
St Petersburg (Petrograd), 53, 77, 113
Saint-Point, Valentine de, 23, 44–5
Salmon, André, 54
San Francisco Actors' Workshop, 129
San Francisco Mime Troupe, 145
Satie, Erik, 126
Schechner, Richard, 141–2
Schoenberg, Arnold, 126, 127, 138
Schwitters, Kurt, 55, 147
Scottsboro, 104–5
Seattle, 83, 84
Second World War, 10, 12, 68, 73, 83, 125, 142
Settimelli, Emilio, 49, 50, 51
Shakespeare, William, 17, 25, 38, 40, 76, 90, 144, 145
Shaw, George Bernard, 34, 39, 64, 122, 137
Shkolnik, Iosif, 53
Simonson, Lee, 107
Sitwell, Edith, Façade, 122, 124, 126, 130
Slovo, Gillian, 146
Smith, Ana Deavere, 146
Spender, Stephen, Trial of a Judge, 48, 63, 130–1
Stalin, Josef, 9, 32, 71, 88, 94, 119
Stalinism, 67, 72
Stanislavsky, Konstantin, 34–5, 85, 98, 120, 141
Stationendrama, 62, 136
Stein, Gertrude, 7, 14, 58
    Do Let Us Go Away, 59–60
    Identity or I Am Because My Little Dog Knows Me, 112–13
Stelarc, 143
Stephens, Simon, 144
Stravinsky, Igor, 101, 126, 138, 143
Strindberg, August, 33, 39, 47, 61, 94, 143, 145
    Miss Julie, 36–8
    The Ghost Sonata, 130

Strohbach, Hans, 66
Studio Azzurro, 147
suffragettes, 2, 33, 37, 73
surrealism, 7, 18, 24, 43–4, 46–8, 53–61, 67,
    69, 75, 95, 110, 112, 128–9, 133, 134–5,
    142, 144, 146, 148

Tairov, Alexander, 86
Tara Arts, 145
Tatlin, Vladimir, 7
Taylor, Frederick Winslow, 96
Taylorism, 96, 105
Terry, Ellen, 14
Théâtre du Vieux-Colombier, 117
Theatre Guild, 105–7
Théâtre Libre, 33
Theatre Rhinoceros, 145
Theatre Workshop, 83, 104
Thingspiele, 77
Toller, Ernst, 61, 63, 67, 104, 144
    Masses Man, 65–6
Treadwell, Sophie, 48, 63
    Machinal, 64–5
Tretyakov, Sergei, 137
    Earth Rampant, 136
Trotsky, Leon, 24
Turin, 12
Tzara, Tristan, 24, 46, 48, 54, 68–9, 120
    The Gas Heart, 55–6, 93

Vakhtangov, Evgeny, 86
Van Gogh, Vincent, 4

variety theatre, 8, 25–6, 33, 49, 54, 86, 118,
    123, 130, 137
Verse ohne Worte, 54–5, 57, 123, 138
Vestal, Donald, 112–13
Vinaver, Michael, 144

Wagner, Richard, 32, 117–19, 125, 126, 128,
    130, 132, 137, 138
Walton, William, 124, 126
Wedekind, Frank, 26, 47, 143
Weigel, Helene, 95
Weill, Kurt, 118
Weimar Republic, 47, 72, 82
Weiss, Peter, 140
Wigman, Mary, 102–3, 128
Wilder, Thornton, 112
    Our Town, 108
Wilson, Robert, 146
Wolf, Friedrich, 82
Woolf, Virginia, 4, 56, 143
Wooster Group, 12, 144
Workers' Theatre Movement (WTM), 37, 80,
    82, 86, 91
    Meerut, 81

Yeats, W. B., 26, 31, 120, 143
    At the Hawk's Well, 108–9
    The Dreaming of the Bones, 29–30, 41

zaum, 123, 126
Zola, Émile, 35–7, 41
Zurich, 12, 26, 46, 67, 120